Roots and L̶i̶a̶b̶e̶

Roots and Wings
A Handbook for Parents

Raksha Bharadia

Rupa . Co

Typeset in Baskerville by
Mindways Design
1410 Chiranjiv Tower,
43 Nehru Place
New Delhi 110 019

Printed in India by
Nutech Photolithographers
B-240, Okhla Industrial Area, Phase-I,
New Delhi 110020, India

There are two lasting bequests we can give our children: One is roots, the other is wings.

HODDING CARTER

Contents

....

Acknowledgements

···

To my husband, Sanjeev, who has been my constant support always!

To my mother-in-law who helped me with household duties so that I could devote time to writing.

To my girls, Aishwarya and Sanaya, who are (still) more patient with me than I am with them.

To my mummy, who in my lean moments not once said, 'I told you so!' even though I did things exactly opposite to what she had advised. Instead, she extended whatever help and support I needed.

To my papa, who introduced me to the exciting world of board games—Conquest, Stock market, Scrabble etc. and which I, in turn, introduced my children to. We share more of each other through the game sessions...

To my sisters, Suman and Priti who helped me with my interviews.

To my brother Manish and sister-in-law Adity and the close bond that I share with them.

Preface

··

You tell your kid, 'Do not watch so much T.V. it will affect your eyes and brain'. And, come 9 pm and you are glued to your T.V. set and not a team of wild horses could drag you away. Mommy, are your eyes and brain made of different material?

You tell your child, 'Do not lie'. And the moment the phone rings you instruct her, 'Say I'm not here'. Mommy, is lying permitted after eighteen years of age?

You tell your child, 'Respect your elders'. And your child looks at you confused when you are giving your fifty-year-old cook a verbal bashing for the last fifteen minutes. Mom, is respecting elders subjective?

You tell your child, 'Learn to say thank you'. And you lisp those magic words very readily for the smallest thing done by an outsider but never waste your energy using them for any house members. Mommy, do I have to say 'thank you' only to and in front of outsiders?

You tell your child, 'Why don't you read during your leisure hours?' All your free time is spent in discussing the latest of who-did-what to whom. Mommy, is chatting over the phone as enlightening as reading?

You tell your child, 'Be generous. Share your toys with your friends'. And you penny-pinch and lie so that neighbours do not develop the bad habit of always coming to your doorstep for whatever they run out of. Mommy, I think I saw potatoes in the potato basket?

You tell your child, 'Learn to let go'. And the child hears you discuss at length the mistake committed by a friend/husband with another friend. The defaulter is crucified! Mommy, why don't you let your friend alone?

You tell your child, 'Learn to control your temper'. But when you get angry and yell your volume is turned to max. Mommy, I can hear even a volume lower!

You tell your child, 'Do not dig your nose'. But the moment you think no one is watching you give in to the temptation yourself and fling the residue away (your kid just saw you do that). Mommy, I am not supposed to dig my nose when someone is watching, right?

You tell your child, 'Do not hit others'. And you spank, hit or slap your child as punishment. Mommy, like you I was teaching her a lesson so that she doesn't bother me again.

You tell your child, 'You are not living up to what you promised'. And you promise your child an ice cream treat and cancel the programme because of a headache.

You tell your kids, 'Own up to your mistakes and errors'. But when you make one you rationalise it with 'I was so stressed, life is not easy for me'. Can I disown my mistakes whenever I think life is hard on me?'

You throw your hands up in exasperation! 'My children never listen to what I say'. But my dear they are copying you to perfection!

Water it seems is wet!

Raksha Bharadia

Introduction

....

Wanting the 'best' and doing the utmost to facilitate that 'best' in our children comes naturally to most parents. We stretch beyond our available resources—time, energy, finances, efforts etc. to provide an environment which would enable optimal growth in them. Our dreams for them are noble—we want them to be responsible, confident, intelligent, independent, creative, ethical and good.

The right dreams, passion for realising those dreams, and sustained efforts commensurate to that passion is there in us parents, yet the results are not always in line. Despite all our industry we see our children struggling with low self-esteem, anxiety, burn-outs, stress, loneliness, boredom, obesity, and depression, to name a few. We often find ourselves lost, exhausted and uncertain on the righteousness and efficacy of our efforts. Our parenting style comes from what we value; what we see around us; what influences us; how we were raised ourselves; others' opinions. Often we struggle, as new parents, with our own values, comparing them with the values of others. Consciously or unconsciously we fall into the measurable achievement trap (grades, trophies, variety of extracurricular etc.) where the 'child' becomes a product that we are trying to develop rather than a thinking, intelligent, individual with his/her unique desires, talents and personality.

Our instincts tell us that something is not right, yet what is, we do not know. Kids do not come with a manual and the jargon of work on parenting is often conflicting and polarised. We have all felt and still feel this lack of proper understanding, knowledge and information on:

The child vis-à-vis himself/herself (child's native interests, strengths and level)

The child vis-à-vis us (our expectations of him/her)

The child vis-à-vis the world

This book essentially addresses these three issues.

Some questions which I struggled with during the course of writing this book are:

➤ The Child

Is parenting about my child or about ME?

Unconsciously, the way we bring up our children is so loaded with our expectations of what we want from our children and what we think is right for them, that we disregard their native endowments, interests and strengths. Our knowledge of the child is also clouded with the overwhelming anxiety of the child vis-à-vis the world. The omnipresent fear, 'Will my child carve a successful and happy life in this fast-paced over-competitive global world?' influences and shapes most of our parenting strategies.

We forget that each child is gifted with unique qualities and the fundamental need to discover his/her place in 'the world'. But before he discovers his place, he has to discover himself. Each child has the inner desire to learn, grow, and become independent. And most importantly he has the right to his own bent. We need to trust that our children are following their individual timetable for development. Can we trust in the bigger picture even when we don't see it?

➤ Growth and learning

Is learning the result of teaching, or the logical outcome of curiosity, observation, experiments, mistakes and understanding of the learner? We must provide a congenial environment for that learning to occur. Children are like sponges—absorbing all that surrounds them. We can provide them with the tools—materials, exposure, space, guidance, security and freedom in a loving, supportive and encouraging environment and hope that they reach their potential; we can't reach it for them. A certain sense of humility and faith is required—humility that I can provide him the tools for success but not the success itself and faith that my child has his unique endowments which he will actualise at his own pace. My focus should be to help my child transform his/her natural curiosity and interest into a strong inner discipline and motivation. A question that I have often asked myself in this context is, 'Am I going to let my child find his own level?' Winston Churchill said, 'Where my reason, imagination or interest were not engaged, I would not or I could not learn.'

As a conscious parent I must always strive to understand afresh how do I draw a line between:

- Freedom and guidance
- Discipline and permissiveness
- Space and control
- Structured time and unstructured time
- Independence and scrutiny
- Being a guide and being a friend
- Challenging and supporting

➤ Children as witnesses to our path

I am my child's living example. What am I modeling?

If we do not model what we teach, then we are teaching something else.

I want my child to be persevering; am I so?

I want my child to be a good human; am I so?

I want my child to grow; am I growing—as a parent, individual, human?

My children are watching me make my way. Not about what I do, but how I do it. Not about my parenting style, but my personal style.

Says Joyce Maynard, 'As much as we watch to see what our children do with their lives, they are watching us to see what we do with ours. I can't tell my children to reach for the sun. All I can do is reach for it, myself.'

This book is a compilation of:

> My experiences

I am a mother of two girls and we often have open discussions and debates; question/answer sessions; introspection sessions; experiments in handling issues such as anger, fear, failure, relationships, education, learning, absorbing, etc. My children struggle with me almost as much as I struggle with them.

> Research

Research from books, journals, magazines, universities, institutions, etc. dealing in child psychology, philosophy, behavioural sciences, pedagogy, strategies, and attitudes have played a seminal role in shaping this work.

> Interviews of childhoods which have worked

I interviewed people we look up to, from all walks of life. I went behind their passions and challenges, their everyday life experiences and influences which have shaped and chiseled them to what they are today. Some names are Kumar Mangalam Birla, Jaya Bachchan, Sachin Tendulkar, Jogen Chowdhary, Mrinal Sen, Hemant Trivedi, Kiran Bedi, Javed Akhtar, Shreya Ghoshal, Jonny Lever, Pandit Jasraj, Harsh Neotia, Anup Jalota, Jatin Das, Darshana Zhaveri, Tanuja Chandra and Sanjeev Kapoor.

I interviewed ordinary parents—neighbours, friends, colleagues for their experiences which made for insightful learning.

I also interviewed about 500 children aged between five and twelve to know what really goes on in their minds and their magical world.

This book deals with:
- Attitudes that we want to develop in our children
- Love of learning

- An open mind
- Optimism
- Diligence
- Perseverance
- Responsibility
- Courage
- Confidence
- Sensitivity
- Sense of humour

Ethical values that we want to inculcate in our children
- Honesty
- Empathy
- Humility
- Respectfulness
- Kindness
- Generousity

Gifts that we need to give them
- Freedom
- Imagination
- Creativity
- Personal expression
- Security
- Love

There is no one right way, but there is a right direction—which is to keep in tandem with the child's natural self. If we can do this in a loving and respectful manner, we will have done enough. As Osho said, 'Everybody is trying to make you somebody else, whom you cannot become. You can only become yourself, or you can miss becoming.'

Lastly, as parents the healthiest thing we can do both for ourselves and our children is to grant ourselves the freedom of a few mistakes which we will inevitably make along the way for a planned parenting strategy, however detailed, falls short in many real situations. Besides, children are resilient—we will not lose them through a few mistakes.

Children's top 100 books

....

This list was tabulated from an online survey that ran at this web site from 1 November 1999 through 1 February 2000. The results leave no doubt that America's kids **LOVE** to read. You might want to compare this with Teachers' Top 100 Books for Children.

1. Harry Potter (series) by J.K. Rowling
2. Goosebumps (series) by R.L. Stine
3. *Green Eggs and Ham* by Dr. Seuss
4. *The Cat in the Hat* by Dr. Seuss
5. Arthur (series) by Marc Brown
6. *Charlotte's Web* by E.B. White
7. Shiloh (trilogy) by Phyllis Reynolds Naylor
8. *Hatchet* by Gary Paulsen
9. *Holes* by Louis Sachar
10. *The Giver* by Lois Lowry
11. *The Chronicles of Narnia* by C.S. Lewis
12. Tales of a Fourth Grade Nothing (series) by Judy Blume
13. Sideways Stories from Wayside School (series) by Louis Sachar
14. *The BFG* by Roald Dahl
15. The Boxcar Children (series) by Gertrude Chandler Warner
16. *One Fish Two Fish Red Fish Blue Fish* by Dr. Seuss
17. Ramona Quimby, Age 8 (series) by Beverly Cleary

18. Pokemon (series) by Tracey West, Maria S. Barbo
19. The Babysitters Club (series) by Ann M. Martin
20. Ralph S. Mouse (series) by Beverly Cleary
21. Little House on the Prairie (series) by Laura Ingalls Wilder
22. *Where the Sidewalk Ends* by Shel Silverstein
23. Charlie and the Chocolate Factory by Roald Dahl
24. *The Giving Tree* by Shel Silverstein
25. Clifford the Big Red Dog (series) by Norman Bridwell
26. *Stuart Little* by E. B. White
27. *Where the Red Fern Grows* by Wilson Rawls
28. The Adventures of Captain Underpants (series) by Dav Pilkey
29. *The Polar Express* by Chris Van Allsburg
30. The Berenstain Bears (series) by Jan and Stan Berenstain
31. Animorphs (series) by K.A. Applegate
32. *The Witches* by Roald Dahl
33. Nancy Drew Mystery Stories by Carolyn Keene
34. The Hobbit (series) by J.R.R. Tolkien
35. American Girls (series) by Susan Adler, Valerie Tripp, Connie Porter, Janet Shaw, et al
36. *Matilda* by Roald Dahl
37. *The Call of the Wild* by Jack London
38. *The Foot Book* by Dr. Seuss
39. *How the Grinch Stole Christmas* by Dr. Seuss
40. *James and the Giant Peach* by Roald Dahl
41. Junie B. Jones (series) by Barbara Park
42. *Stone Fox* by John Reynolds Gardiner
43. *Falling Up* by Shel Silverstein
44. A Wrinkle in Time (series) by Madeleine L'Engle
45. *Brian's Winter* by Gary Paulsen
46. Amber Brown (series) by Paula Danziger
47. *The North Star* by Peter H. Reynolds
48. Have a Nice Day: A Tale of Blood and Sweatsocks by Mick Foley (Mankind)
49. *Number the Stars* by Lois Lowry
50. *The Outsiders* by S.E. Hinton

84. I Spy (series) by Walter Wick, Jean Marzollo, Diana Noonan, et al
85. *Love You Forever* by Robert N. Munsch
86. *My Side of the Mountain* by Jean Craighead George
87. *The Trumpet of the Swan* by E.B. White
88. Walk Two Moons by Sharon Creech
89. Draw 50 Airplanes, Aircraft and Spacecraft (series) by Lee J. Ames
90. *Goodnight Moon* by Margaret Wise Brown
91. *The Adventures of Tom Sawyer* by Mark Twain
92. *The Rock Says* by Dwayne Johnson (The Rock)
93. *Tikki Tikki Tembo* by Arlene Mosel
94. *To Kill a Mockingb*ird by Harper Lee
95. *All About Sam* by Lois Lowry
96. *Black Beauty* by Anna Sewell
97. *Ella Enchanted* by Gail Carson Levine
98. Hank the Cow Dog (series) by John R. Erickson
99. *Piggie Pie* by Margie Palatini
100. *Sarah, Plain and Tall* by Patricia MacLachlan

Creativity

....

Aishwarya was in the fourth year of kathak and her cousin Juhi was in the sixth year of ballet. Both were curious about the other's form. They exhibited their styles and compared notes. Aishwarya then came up with a suggestion. She told Juhi, 'Why don't we mix the two forms and come up with a fusion, which we will perform for the family in the evening?' Their passion thereafter was such that they did not remain dancers, but became the dance itself, exploring, blending, synchronising, giggling, and all the time bringing to shape their 'Bal-thak' (that is what they called it). Their costumes too were creatively designed using old newspapers. As for us, their audience, we spent the evening cheering and shouting 'once more'.

Ashish had to write down the numbers 1-100 and he found the task boring. He began dressing up the zeros in different emotions and the numbers sprang to life. The zero of ten adorned a smiling face while that of twenty was scowling. There was a thoughtful zero with a small arm scratching its bald head, and there was a dreamy zero with eyes closed. Interestingly, most of his zero's wore different expressions and he now wanted to write beyond hundred to see whether he could still give new faces to express still different moods.

Pragya's pug did not have a kennel. She threw in a hello-kitty bed sheet, the softest pillow and placed her doll house on top. She placed the pug's chew balls, some old socks and even a small bowl of water. Bingo! The pug went and nestled inside.

It was Seher's dad's fortieth birthday and the house was preparing itself for a grand party. Cleaners, cooks, bartenders, music men, florists were setting things up for the evening. Problems, however, arose with the stream of bouquets which kept piling in, as the minutes ticked by. By 12 am the number had reached beyond a hundred, with still more arriving. The house looked like a flower shop. The looming question was: what to do with so many flowers? Flicking them in the bin seemed too cold, besides, how could one throw away exquisite fresh flowers arranged in beautiful patterns? It was then that twelve-year-old Seher came up with a brilliant idea. She invited a few friends over and turned the problem into a blessing.

They took the forty most beautiful bouquets and requested the florist to sell them off for them. The proceeds would go to the old people's home, they told the florist, which gave him the zest to work towards their sale. The rest of the bouquets were taken apart and turned into 200 small posies, each with a small note which said, 'Have a good day'. Carrying the small bundles they went on to the road, just outside their compound and started distributing them to the passers-by at random. They saw tired, stressed, harassed, sweaty faces turn into bright and smiling ones. They particularly remembered the expression of the salesman who was really down after having seven-eight doors slammed on his face. The roses brought the colour back into his cheeks and he was ready to take on the world afresh. After this they visited an orphanage nearby. They gave the children a petal shower, made rangolies and small craft items and even played a flower quiz with them. On their way home they stopped by the florist, collected a whopping four thousand rupees for their merchandise, and decided to buy eatables for the old people and scheduled the visit for the following Sunday. Seher reached home by six, just in time to dress up for the evening ahead. The colour on her cheeks, the brightness in her smile and the pride on her parents' face made this birthday memorable in ways other than the ordinary.

1.1 Defining creativity

Creativity can be expressed in many ways—a dance sequence, a painting, finding new solutions to old problems, composing a simple song, dressing up, pretending or even thinking of unusual or extraordinary answers. There is no clear definition of creativity. It is referred to in terms of imagination, divergent thinking, fantasy, intuition, curiosity, problem solving, and in terms of different combinations of these factors. Creativity is the ability to see beyond what exists, and to combine thoughts and experiences into new ideas. Though we might not be able to define creativity, we can recognise it when we come face to face with it either in our own selves or in others around us.

In children creativity comes naturally. Questioning (from 'why are the leaves green?' to 'where do babies come from?'), playing (with mud, food, fabrics, paints), exploring (the beetle, the tree, fire, three pin socket) dressing up, playing fantasy games (where they become *The Last Samurai*, the astronaut, Miss India, Batman, Catwoman)—it is hard to curb creativity in children. They are not bothered with stereotypes and inconsistencies, and so can think in fresh and flexible ways. The world is their stage and there are endless roles to be played.

According to Howard Gardner, children's creative thought is bolstered by the fact that 'the young child is not bothered by inconsistencies, departures from convention, non-literalness ... which often results in unusual and appealing juxtapositions and associations'.

Studies of the brain activity of preadolescent children offer empirical evidence that children do indeed have active imaginations (Diamond & Hopson, 1999). Even wide awake children experience theta wave activity, which mature adults primarily experience when their minds hover between being awake and falling asleep. Theta wave brain activity is more relaxed, freewheeling, and receptive to fleeting mental images. Eminent creative individuals in various fields report trying a host of techniques to capture theta wave activity, including meditation, keeping a lighted ink pen at bedside, and so forth (Runco & Pritzker, 1999).

> Children are perhaps innately creative because they generally:
> - Follow their own rhythm in what interests them
> - Have an innate sense of curiosity and wonder
> - Pursue novelty by experimenting and testing new ideas which strike them
> - Do not accept ideas without questioning and verifying
> - Are spontaneous
> - Are day dreamers...and in all of these there is creativity untouched by adult apprehensions and prejudices.

When Pablo Picasso was asked why his work improved as he grew older, he observed that it had taken him a lifetime to learn to draw as a child, and that:

'Every child is an artist. The problem is how to remain an artist once he grows up'

1.2 Benefits

Why is creativity important?

Creativity is the freest form of self expression. Three-year-olds may not know how to say they are frustrated and depressed, but they can paint

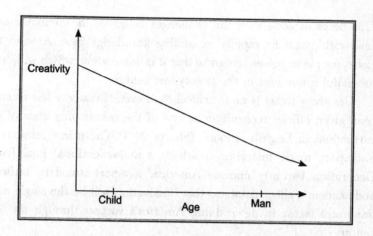

a picture using dark colours and bold, angry-looking strokes. They also learn and discover themselves through their creative activities.

Creativity provides for and nurtures intellectual growth. Children who mix red, yellow and blue to make brown are growing intellectually. They experiment with new ideas, try out new ways of thinking and problem solving and this in turn leads to their development and mental growth.

Creativity leads to problem solving. The peviously written flower episode is a point in case.

Creativity helps them understand, explore and experiment with the world around. When children engage in role play and become fire fighters, WWF wrestlers, teachers, they are not only trying to portray those characters but be that world themselves.

Creative children are eager learners!

Mental health practitioners have discovered that creative activities can serve to safeguard children from stress. (Honig, 2000) According to research (Sautter, 1994), 'Student involvement in creative activities (such as performing arts and group activities) has been found to reduce drop out rates and to improve student motivation.'

Creative activities help acknowledge and celebrate children's uniqueness and diversity. Whatever roles our children grow into, teachers, chefs, engineers, architects or musicians they will need to be in touch with the creative and the imaginative part of themselves.

This helps to cope with the challenges faced by the demands of a new world, with its rapidly expanding knowledge base. Around the globe, people in power recognise that it is 'innovation' which will drive successful economies in the twenty-first century.

Creativity today is more critical than ever. 'Creativity has recently been given official recognition as one of the overarching aims of the curriculum in English schools'. (Sharp, 2001) The prime minister of Singapore made fostering creativity a major national goal (Next Generation Forum) 'Innovate America,' a report issued by business and academic elite, maintains that 'innovation will be the single most important factor in determining America's success through the 21st century.'

Just a cute kid with a great imagination
or an aspiring engineer with talent that will shape our world?

What can we as parents do?

According to Cobb, 1977; Martindale, 2001, 'Despite growing evidence that childhood is the wellspring for later creative pursuits, adults frequently fail to develop those rich resources of imagination, creativity, curiosity, and playfulness'.

The problem has never been how to get young children to be creative. It is about how not to thwart their creativity in the name of education, socialisation process or a cultured upbringing. We encourage conformity, suppress their natural curiosity and emotions, train them to accommodate and in doing so, silence their voices and kill their awareness. We as parents have an obligation, first and foremost, to do no harm.

'When Alexander the Great visited Diogenes and asked whether he could do anything for the famed teacher, Diogenes replied: "Only stand out of my light".' Perhaps, some day we shall know how to heighten creativity. Until then, one of the best things we can do for our children is to stand out of their light.

1.3 Killers of creativity

Conformism–The nail that sticks out gets hammered. Fit in!

Seven-year-old Raaghav made a house with windows on the ground floor and the door on the first floor. He also placed a ladder which went up to the first floor, 'In case I am not in the mood to jump in through the window, I can simply climb up the ladder and walk into the house'. His mother, after giving him a customary hug, asked him to now draw a proper house with everything at the right levels.

Two examples of underground vegetables were onion and potato in Tina's science textbook. Her mother insisted that she write the names of these two vegetables if the question appeared in her examination sheet. 'She knows the two spellings by heart', beamed the mom.

When we insist that children reproduce similar work every time, be it in answering questions, making pictures, writing essays or doing projects, we discourage their creative exploration. Conformity is not the enemy. Our approach towards it can be. When we are learning something we need a place to start, a standard to refer to, hence the potato and the onion. The problem begins not in beginning as a conformist but in remaining one! Children are drilled to conform, accept and not question.

According to research (Moran et al., 1983), 'The percentage of original responses in ideational fluency tasks drops from about 50% among four-year-olds to 25% during elementary school, then returns to 50% among college students'.

We endorse 'knowing is better than questioning'. For us 'smart' equals 'knowing more' and so we heap our children with a vast base of knowledge and try and make them smart.

But how on earth do we get the time to stuff them with loads of information? By putting an end to time robbers some of which are:

'Whiling away time', but creativity above all requires leisure.
'Questioning and wondering time', but how will we encourage curiosity when we stifle questioning?
'Arguing time', but if they are taught not to debate, discuss and express their opinions they may very soon not bother racking their brains enough to have it, or when they do have it keep them to themselves.

In the process, the message that our children internalise is, 'why challenge the rules?', 'why run the risk of failing and looking foolish?', 'why think?' and thus 'why be creative'. They resign. The stubborn few who even after repeated instructions choose to defy and come up with fresh novel ideas and answers are reprimanded for wasting their time and dealt with labels like 'silly', 'wild', 'crazy', 'dreamer' and 'unrealistic' for as Mark Twain said, **'The man with a new idea is a crank until the idea succeeds.'**

When Edison tried to hatch a gosling

It is said about Edison that everything about nature fascinated him. He started doing research almost as soon as he could walk. One of his first experiments was in poultry incubation. When he was two he was visiting the farm of his older sister Mariané and disappeared. Mariané's husband finally found him in the barn sitting on a goose's nest. When asked what he was trying to do, Edison answered that he was trying to hatch goslings. Mariané's husband laughed at how silly a child can be, but Mariané was impressed. She told Edison that he did a very smart thing. 'If no one ever tried anything, even when some folks say it is impossible no one would ever learn anything. So he should keep on trying and maybe some day he will try something and it will work'. Edison took his sister's advice to heart.

Overemphasis on conformism and to 'fit in' has become the number one killer of imagination too. Einstein said, 'Imagination is greater than knowledge. For, while knowledge defines all we currently know and understand, imagination points to all we might yet discover and create.'.

Yes, knowledge is important. It is the stuff from which new ideas are made. But, knowledge alone cannot foster creativity. We need to use our imagination with knowledge. But for

> Bill Gates put it beautifully when he said, 'Microsoft is a company that manages imagination'.

most of us informed parents it is a choice of one at the expense of the other and our attraction towards knowledge is a national obsession.

☑ *Reality check*

What about you? How often do these lines make way into your conversation with your child?

> Let's make-believe.
> Give me something off the wall.
> For the fun of it.

Shock us!
Give me a wild scenario!
Loosen up.
Thanks for thinking.

SCRUTINISING, EVALUATING AND RIDICULING THEIR WORK

Kartikey and his four friends got together and decided to paint *diyas* for Diwali. They finished their artwork and went to Kartikey's mom and asked which one she thought was the best. On an impulse, Kartikey's mother pointed to the bright red coloured *diya* with the golden border. Prarit jumped with joy but for the others a beautiful *diya* was now only a red one with a golden border.

> 'The very essence of the creative is its novelty, and hence we have no standard by which to judge it.' – Carl R. Rogers, *On Becoming a Person.*

Judgement and evaluation kill creativity faster than anything else. If a child feels that his creations will inevitably be subject to judgments ('The bark of the tree should be green') or comparisons ('Put more colour in your drawings, like your brother does'), he will either stop producing altogether or will simply make what other people want him to make. Uniqueness will be replaced by clichés. Research states that people will tend to be less creative when they are focusing primarily on how their work is going to be evaluated. Both expected evaluation (Amabile, 1979; Amabile, Goldfarb, & Brackfield, 1990; Hennessey, 1989) and actual prior positive evaluation (Berglas, Amabile, & Handel, 1979) have detrimental effects on creativity.

At times even when we are in the appreciative mode we do so but with a 'but'.

> 'The model of the tiger is good, but a tail would have made it look complete'.
> 'The thoughts in your song are good but they do not rhyme'.

This gives the child a feeling of not being good enough. A picture, an essay, a dance composition doesn't have to be perfect; what is important is the child's involvement and expression. Creativity is not about doing something better than others; it is about thinking, exploring, discovering, and imagining.

Let us respect their efforts instead of trying to 'better' them.

'Be proud of my best,' Jessica told her mom.

Surveillance too kills creativity. According to research,

> 'If the child has enjoyed it and when he was painting he got absorbed in it, that's enough. He was in deep meditation, he moved with the painting utterly... he was lost in it! The painting is good because the painter was lost.'
>
> – OSHO

(Amabile, Goldfarb, & Brackfield, 1990), 'Surveillance is highly related to evaluation and probably operates because of evaluation. People will be less creative if they feel that there is someone watching them while they work'.

The overbooked child – No, 'nothing' time.

'I wish my parents had some hobby other than me,' one young patient told David Anderegg, a child psychologist in Lenox, Massachusetts, and professor of psychology at Bennington College. Anderegg finds

that anxious parents are hyper-attentive to their kids, reactive to every blip of their child's day, eager to solve every problem for their child, and believe that's good parenting. Meanwhile, more and more of these over-programmed kids are suffering from burnout—too much homework, too many extracurricular activities, no time to play, no time to be bored, no time just to 'be'.

Anahita hits home at 2 pm from school. She gets exactly fifteen minutes to push the lunch down before the art tutor arrives. After her art class she sits down to finish in succession one homework after the other, given by her school, special mathematics coaching class, GK class and the tuition teacher. It is milk time when she puts her three bags away and she rushes for her tennis (thrice a week, the other three days she goes for her dance class) only to return at 7.30 pm. She plops right in front of the television as she screams, 'I need some time for me too'. On weekends she has her French tuitions and piano classes. Dinner is usually in front of the T.V. and then she is ready for bed. In her spare time she...well, she doesn't really have any spare time.

Anahita's mother feels:

- Anahita enjoys every class that she goes to.
- That it is her duty to make sure that Anahita has an edge in whichever field she opts for later, as a career.
- Besides, if not for these classes, Anahita would be surely cooped up in front of the tube or just while away her time in doing nothing.

Anahita's mother is time-smart bringing up a time-smart child.

Why do we as parents do it?

Most of us have good intentions. We enroll our children in activities thinking we are laying the foundation for their successful and happy life. We even sacrifice our own time to make sure that our children are at practices and competitions.

Some parents fan their egos through their children, 'MY CHILD has NOT lost a single race in three years.' Some use children to relive their own childhood dreams, 'I did not have the support necessary to be a doctor, but I will make sure that you become one.' Some are motivated by social pressure, 'Since all the kids in my neighbourhood are into four-five activities, it seems only reasonable that my child also joins a couple of them.'

For one reason or the other we are a society of educated parents adept at the art of multi tasking in raising our superkids!

Kids aren't allowed to have fun anymore, unless it's organised fun. Kids today are over-regimented, overprotected, overscheduled and overcommitted. Says Alvin Rosenfeld, a child psychiatrist in New York and author of *The Over-Scheduled Child: Avoiding the Hyper-Parenting Trap*: 'I think it's the number one public health problem for families and kids in America'. Research of Teresa Amabile's at Harvard Business School, too shows that pressure and scrutiny diminish children's creativity. Creativity requires leisure.

Javed Akhtar said, 'Keeping a child totally occupied all the time is very dangerous. Because when a child has nothing to do, no toys to play, no games, the child starts fantasising. If everything is provided, you are keeping the child's attention on some toy or joy or other, all the time, then where is the time to fantasise? It is the fantasy which makes the child grow! You only fantasise when you are deprived. A certain degree of boredom, sense of deprivation is also necessary.'

Educationalists at the University of East Anglia call this 'boredom time' and argue that it is of enormous educational value. It's the one chance children have to reflect on the day's events, build castles in the air, daydream and make tentative plans for what they want to do with their lives—activities which are crucially important to their emotional and intellectual development.

The consequences of over-parenting

Our children will burn with all pushing and pressure even before they reach adulthood.

They will not have the time to discover motivation on their own—and motivation is often more important for success than talent.

They will never have the opportunity to discover who they are. Children need time to read, write, think, dream, draw, build, create, fantasise and explore special interests. Such activities promote self-awareness by helping children clarify who they are and what they are truly interested in. Children who are involved in too many programmed activities may have little time for these experiments in self-discovery.

They will not be able to handle time alone. Early-childhood-education specialist Peggy Patten, MA, agrees and notes that children today have many wonderful opportunities, but they need time to explore things in depth. When they are involved in too many different things, they sacrifice breadth for depth.

Studies have shown that the brains of stressed pre-schoolers now look remarkably like the brains of stressed adults, which have excessive levels of adrenaline and cortisol, the chemicals responsible for the body's fight-or-flight reaction.

Children will have no time or opportunity for family talks, discussions, game sessions or simple chill-out sessions where the family hangs around each other even when doing their own thing. This time is vital for warm and intimate relationships.

Andre Aelion Brooks, author and former *New York Times* journalist, was one of the first to call attention to the overscheduled child. For her book, *Children of Fast-Track Parents* she interviewed eighty mental health professionals and educators, in addition to sixty parents and some hundred children. Brooks concluded that exposing children to extracurricular activities too early is not necessarily a good idea. Some children are not able to function well with so many responsibilities and can develop stress disorders.

Rewards and praise as incentives

When we see creativity in our children we are at once motivated, 'I must help him be more creative'. And we intervene, praise and reward it. We believe that the motivation that stems from wanting to earn a good grade or receive a gold star or do better than the person sitting at the next desk is a positive force and we turn to an anode + trying to exude positive vibrations in every way that we can. But creativity is an intrinsic process and the reward we offer is extrinsic.

F. David Peat, a pioneer in this field distinguishes between two types of motivation—'Intrinsic motivation' which is defined as the motivation to do something for its own sake, for the sheer pleasure and enjoyment of the task itself; and 'Extrinsic motivation' which is the motivation to do something for some external goal. According to Amabile (1983, 1996), 'Intrinsic motivation is conducive to creativity and extrinsic motivation is almost always detrimental'. Research showed that as extrinsic motivation increases, intrinsic motivation must decrease, which in turn decreases creativity. Rewards and praise condition children to seek approval; they end up doing things to impress, instead of doing things for themselves. Pioneers in this research effort, Lepper, Greene and Nisbett investigated the effect of expected reward on young children's motivation and artistic performance in 1973. These researchers found that, 'For preschoolers who initially displayed a high level of intrinsic interest in drawing with magic markers, working for an expected "Good Player Award" significantly decreased their interest in enjoyment of the task.'

The over-civilised child: Pressures on cleanliness, right answer fixation, perfectionism, comparison

'Be proud of me even if I do not get all the answers right,' Sachi told her daddy.

'Tell me what I did right,' Anandi told her parents.

We have grandiose expectations from our children and unintentionally put pressure on them to measure up to our expectations. How many of us unwittingly pass comments like, '23 out of 25 is good but you have it in you to get a 25'. Anything short of perfect is simply not good enough for many parents. But the thought of 'not good enough' can put any child into a deep freeze.

When we insist on them being right every time, we become too critical, and discourage mistakes and risk taking. Risk-taking is necessary to generate fresh and original work. Children feel compelled to perform and this again deters experimentation, exploration, and innovation. In extreme cases this leads to stress and depression as they are unable to reach and maintain the unreasonable expectations set by their parents. The cartoonist Scott Adams captured this beautifully by saying, 'Creativity is allowing yourself to make mistakes. Art is knowing which ones to keep'.

Pressure is exerted even in the name of realism. Five-year-old Tanna was sure that 'Santa is real', 'she dances better than the *Nach balliye* stars' and 'she can fly planes'. She could not understand or believe that it can't be done. Her mother told her to stop being 'silly'. That only happens in fairy tales; life is not that simple. When we label a child's flights of fantasy as 'silly' or unattainable we bring the child down to earth with a crashing thud causing the inventive urge to curl up and die.

For some parents excessive insistence on cleanliness puts undue pressure on the child and he opts not to give credence to this creative desire rather than creating the mess for which he is likely to get screamed at. 'Why bother, let me watch T.V. instead'. Creating can't be much fun if 'be careful ... clean that up!' is the usual response. At times the energy spent in conforming to the rules of neatness and order is at the expense of the energy reserved for exploration and originality. Yes, children do need to help clean up but the over-civilised child is more likely to sacrifice originality for orderliness. Be comfortable with 'creative mess'.

Vinita Sirin on the cleanliness obsession

Here is how Vinita Sirin, a new-age mother, tackled her own cleanliness obsession. She says, 'Whenever I walked into the room of my two boys, it always looked hurricane struck. I remember getting into clearing up immediately and most of the times even lecturing them on their mess. But then I thought...is it not just a matter of perspective? I see their room in a mess. It is my obsession, my problem. They don't see it like that. To them it is lovely, comfortable...it is home. This is the space where they can do what they want. But if I see it as a problem I can clear it up...for my satisfaction. Where does right or wrong come into this picture?'

By saying this am I implying that they should be left with their mess and not even told about the virtues of tidy and neater space?

No, I am not. I just want parents to take a moment and think whether their drive for cleanliness or organisation is somewhere throttling their children's desire and process of just being 'them'. Why is it so important for each thing to go where it belongs right when you think it should?

1.4 Myths about Genius

Myths about creativity are deeply entrenched in our culture. Beliefs that only special, talented people are creative—and you have to be born that way—diminish our confidence in our creative abilities. The notion that geniuses such as Shakespeare, Picasso and Mozart were 'gifted' is a myth, according to a recent study at Exeter University. Researchers examined outstanding performances in arts, mathematics and sports, to find out if 'the widespread belief that to reach high levels of ability a person must possess an innate potential called talent' is true.

The study concludes that excellence is determined by:

- Opportunities
- Encouragement
- Training
- Motivation
- and most of all—Practice.

'Few showed early signs of promise prior to parental encouragement.' No one reached high levels of achievement in their field without devoting thousands of hours to serious training. Mozart trained for sixteen years before he produced an acknowledged masterpiece. Moreover many high performers achieve levels of excellence today that match the capabilities of a Mozart, or a Gold Medalist from the turn of the century. (*The Vancouver Sun*, 12 September 1998) According to Isaksen (et al, 2000), pioneer researcher in this field, 'Creativity exists in everyone'.

'It's complicated explaining how genius or expertise is created and why it's so rare,' says Anders Ericsson, professor of psychology at Florida State University in Tallahassee who edited the handbook. But it isn't magic, and it isn't born. It happens because some critical things line up so that a person of good intelligence can put in the sustained, focused effort it takes to achieve extraordinary mastery. These people don't necessarily have an especially high IQ, but they almost always have very supportive environments, and they almost always have important mentors. And the one thing they always possess is this incredible investment of effort. Pete Sampras didn't have more talent than Andre Agassi, but he won fourteen grand slams to Agassi's eight because he worked harder and more steadily. And as cellist Yo-Yo Ma once said, 'The most proficient and renowned musicians are not necessarily those who outshone everyone as youths, but rather those who had "fire in the belly"'.

When I asked Pandit Jasraj the secret to his excellence, he said in a matter-of-fact tone, 'For over three decades I have practiced for more than sixteen hours a day, the secret is hard work, hours and hours of it daily...consistently'.

1.5 Nurturing creativity

Allow children the liberty of choice

> 'For 37 years I've practiced 14 hours a day, and now they call me a genius'.
>
> – PABLO DE SARASATE
> Violinist and Composer

Research says, 'People who feel that their choice is restricted will tend to be less creative than people who have some choice in how they are going to carry out a task (Amabile & Gitomer, 1984; Hennessey, 1989).'

Give children choices. Children who are given choices show more creativity than children whose parents make all the decisions for them. Enjoying the chance to choose is an important part of being free and fosters creativity. Allow children the freedom of choice whether in exploration, decision making or taking on responsibilities. Children do need boundaries, but even within those boundaries they can exercise choice based on their inherent interests and innate tendencies. For instance, we can set their bedtime hour but they get to choose which book they would like to read, when they mess up the room they have the choice to clean up with music or in the quiet, after dinner or right then; they have a fixed one hour of screen time but they can choose how to divide it between the different modes (computer, video stations and the television). My daughter has to finish her mathematics homework before the next class but if she chooses to do so with *Salaam Namaste* playing in the background, it is her choice.

Choice empowers. Kohn, Alfie, the author of *Choices and Children: Why and How to Let Students Decide*, Phi Delta Kappan (1993): 8-20 talks about the importance of giving children a sense of self-determination through allowing them to be in control of their learning and their lives through the choices that they make. Kohn states, 'Students should not only be trained to live in a democracy when they grow up; they should have a chance to live in one today.'

The power of choice – Javed Akhtar

I asked Javed Sahab on the freedom that he allows his children. In his answers I saw that freedom is the very essence of what he is. He said, 'Just because I was born a few decades before my children doesn't mean that I am wiser than they on every account. Children are people in their own right and I know that there are certain things which they understand better than I do just as there are things that I understand better than they. Every time I speak to Farhan or Zoya or people of that age I learn something from them. We have always had a very democratic relationship.'

He continued, 'When Farhan was a kid, every year he'd make me write a skit for his school and that too free of cost (laughs) and now, when I would have gladly written for him, he went and did his own thing. When he narrated the script to me, I offered some suggestions. He heard me out very carefully and then rejected them all.' Javed Sahab, with a chuckle, tells me, 'Thank god I didn't face rejection where my songs are concerned. I still have my self-esteem left. But he has done a wonderful job with *Dil Chahta Hai*. The best part is that there's no in-breeding of ideas. I mean, the source of inspiration is not films we've seen in the past.'

The young and fresh director Farhan Akhtar decided to write the dialogues of *Dil Chata Hai* himself because he did not want the characters to speak a language that he was not familiar with. So he wrote in the Hindi he knew, which had a lot of English in it.

Javed Sahab ended saying, 'I have always asked my children to do what they wanted. At the end of the day, they make their own decisions about what they want to do.'

Practical steps to help children make their own choices:

- Apply the policy of informed decision.
- Give them information they can absorb, on whatever they have to take a decision.
- Step back and let them make their own choices.
- Allow them to bear the consequences of their decisions/ choices.
- Sometimes they will choose a less-than-terrific option and in the process learn a lesson.
- Do not belittle your child but be supportive and encouraging during such times.
- When they make good choices resulting in positive consequences, their confidence in their ability will grow.

Encourage the Socrates in every child

A sense of curiosity is nature's original school of education. (Smiley Blanton)

A friend once asked Isidor I. Rabi, Nobel prizewinner in physics, 'Why did you become a scientist, rather than a doctor or lawyer or businessman, like the other immigrant kids in your neighbourhood?' Rabi responded, 'My mother made me a scientist without ever intending it. Every other Jewish mother in Brooklyn would ask her child after school: 'So? Did you learn anything today?' But not my mother. She always asked me a different question. 'Izzy,' she would say, 'did you ask a good question today?' That difference—asking good questions—made me become a scientist!'

How parents unconsciously discourage curiosity in their children
Prerna was teaching her child about environmental pollution. She had to cover the topics of air, water and land pollution but her daughter would not let her progress beyond air pollution. She flooded her mother with questions, 'Mommy, if we pass wind, does that contribute towards air pollution?'; 'Why did god make plants take in carbon dioxide when we inhale oxygen?'; 'Can we recycle toilet paper too?'

How on earth was Prerna to finish the chapter?

Alok was busy catching the rest of the news which he missed in the morning, when his son asked, 'Why is the moon yellow?' Alok, in an irritated voice replied, 'Why do you always have a question for everything?'

'What exactly went wrong with Kalpana Chawla's spaceship when it entered the earth's atmosphere?' enquired twelve-year-old Rohan. His mother answered, 'I don't know'.

Kshitisha asked her mom how babies come into this world and her mom answered with, 'Was your school fun today?'

Every time a child puts a question—silly, intelligent, or thought provoking—and we either snub, ignore, postpone, ridicule or answer with a 'I don't know', we thwart a little of their curiosity. Our dry, tepid and negative responses slowly turn their quest into apathy.

Repeated rejections or nonchalance may make the child assume:

- I should not be thinking so much.
- Even if I do so I should keep my queries to myself.
- My parents get irritated when I ask questions.
- It is not right for me to know the answer.
- My curiosity is going to invite a shouting.
- I may be laughed at.
- They don't know the answers anyway (they don't care about the answer too).
- Or worse, I will find the answer from somewhere else (which could be dangerous).

Children ask questions, loads of them. It is because they are curious about everything and everyone around them. Out of their curiosity they develop their thinking power, imagination, logic, reasoning skills and creativity. They need our help to make sense of the questions that captivate them. It is the parents' duty to neither deny nor suppress their curiosity, but to try to satisfy and encourage it.

> 'The important thing is not to stop questioning. Curiosity has its own reason for existing'
>
> — ALBERT EINSTEIN

Ways to encourage 'why', 'what' and 'when'
Honour their questions and observations with your full interest and attention. Whenever they put a question, try your best to answer it.

Former President A.P.J. Abdul Kalam in one his speeches at the award giving function of **Shankar's International children's competition** in New Delhi said, 'Every mind is creative; every mind is inquisitive, when the children ask questions we have to answer the questions. This is the primary responsibility of teachers and parents. If this is done at a young age, creativity will be nourished and children will flourish'.

Remember to be enthusiastic while answering them, children have radar like sensitivities.

When you do not know the answer, invite them with a 'let's find out'. Encyclopaedias, libraries, internet, friends and family, there are many resources at hand. There is no excuse for, 'I don't know'.

Yes, there may be times when their 'why?' becomes exhausting. It is okay to say, 'I can't answer just now. Let's talk about it later.'

Ask them questions about their observations. New questions and perception may emerge from this process of exploration together.

Engage children in science and math experiences that start with asking questions, forming hypotheses or making guesses, collecting data, and drawing conclusions.

An investigation of 'what's inside' and 'how things work' makes a natural starting point. Let your child help when you:

Set the ink cartridge in your printer

Set the clocks

Fix a broken door knob

Read the ingredients of a cereal box/juice pack/milkmaid tin/ toothpaste tube etc.

The Nobel Prize-winning physicist Arthur Schawlow was asked what he felt made the difference between very creative scientists and less creative scientists. He said, 'The labour of love aspect is important. The successful scientists often are not the most talented, but the ones who are just impelled by curiosity-they've got to know what the answer is'. (Schawlow, 1982) Curiosity is an important element of intrinsic motivation.

You can teach a student a lesson for a day; but if you can teach him to learn by creating curiosity, he will continue the learning process as long as he lives. (Clay P. Bedford)

Introduce them to divergent thinking and generation of ideas

Thomas Edison said, 'To have a great idea, have a lot of them.'

'Sir Ken Robinson, chair of the UK Government's report on creativity, education and the economy, described research that showed that young people lost their ability to think in "divergent or non-linear ways", a key component of creativity. Of 1,600 children aged three to five who were tested, 98% showed they could think in divergent ways. By the time they were aged eight to 10, 32% could think divergently. When the same test was applied to 13 to 15-year-olds, only 10% could think in this way. And when the test was used with 200,000 25-year-olds, only 2% could think divergently. ... Education is driven by the idea of one answer and this idea of divergent thinking becomes stifled.' (From Glasgow, A conference in March, 2005, by the Scottish Book Trust)

In the 1920s, psychologist Louis Terman, Ph.D., began looking at the relationship between intelligence and creativity. In a longitudinal sample of intelligent children, he found that not all ended up developing their creative abilities. That's when psychologists started to realise more than intelligence was required–also critical is having an ability to see things from a different perspective, Simonton, another pioneer is this field says. 'You need an IQ of around 140 to learn enough physics to be truly creative in it. But once you have that minimal IQ, there's still something else that must be there for a person to be truly creative.'

The mental factor lies broadly under two heads:

Convergent Thinking: These abilities are those which are mainly responsible for dealing with given information in a logical manner to arrive at a single right answer for any problem.

Divergent Thinking: These abilities are those which enable the individual to go off in many different directions, generating new information from given information and arriving at varied and unusual solutions to problems.

Both type of thinking have their place in life, but the divergent thinking abilities consist of a very important cognitive component of creativity. Creativity has been considered in terms of process, product or person (Barron and Harrington, 1981). In dealing with young children, the focus should be on the process, developing and generating original ideas, which is seen as the basis of creative potential.

Here are some ways we can foster ways for divergent thinking
Have brain storming sessions. Brainstorming is a key part of the creative process. It's the best way to think of a whole pile of potential answers to a problem. It can be tons of fun too.

Present problems for which they have to come up with a pool of solutions
'What would you do if you came home from school and the house was locked?'
    What if you got lost in the science fair?
    Place a child in a different time and place. What if you woke up to find yourself in the deserts of Egypt?
    Encourage their curiosity on the questions that they themselves pose. When eleven-year-old Prarthna realised that the USA is just a five-hundred year old civilisation she was curious as to why they are so rich and technologically advanced. We all began thinking of possible reasons and each came out with as many as they could. There was no fear of being ridiculed for 'silly' ideas.

Ask thought-provoking 'What if' followed by an unconventional, strange, or unexpected supposition
'What if everyday gravity went haywire for twenty minutes?'
    'What if there was no telephone?'
    'What if dogs owned humans and not the other way round?'
    'What if we lived underground?'
    'What if everyone looked the same'?
    'What if people were magnetic?'

Build their imaginative skills with a 'What other ways can you think of...'
Measuring the room. First Sanaya measured with her ruler, then her hand, then her feet, then her steps, then by rolling along the floor.

Making peace with or teaching a lesson to the class bully.

Making music. Arvind used pots and pans, spoons and dishes, claps and taps, hums, and whistles.

Ask for ideas:

How would you equip a person to fly?

How many different ways can a button be used?

What if your best friend asked your honest opinion about a touchy issue? How can you be honest and yet retain the friendship?

Find most uses other than the obvious ones for every-day items like paperclips, bricks, anything that comes to mind.

Encourage wild ideas.

Encourage wild Ideas !

Involve your child in exploring activity, like making a list of as many problems as possible related to the environment, or list of things around you. Put questions like:

Name as many things as you can think of that are blue? Four year old Kartikeya came up with 'cold nose'.

Ten-year-old Chintal was asked what things might cause accidents at home. Some of her answers were:

Irritating the dog so he comes and bites

Putting one hand in the almirah and trying to close the door with the other hand

Falling down from the bunkbed

I asked my daughter what should one do if one bangs her head and a lump develops. She answered, 'Do not look in the mirror or you might faint at the size of the bump and injure yourself further'.

Someone starts a story and then each person adds a part.

- During the process of divergent thinking it is important to:
- Accept all ideas, as 'there are no WRONG ideas'!
- Withhold evaluative or critical comments or judgments about their ideas.
- Emphasise that a quantity of ideas is the goal.
- Encourage 'wild' ideas

1.6 Free play time

☑ *Reality check*

How long does your child spend in free play every day?

2-3 hours

1-2 hours

> 1 hour

> 30 minutes

No free play (where is the time?)!

Importance of free play

Play is the serious business of young children.

'Play positively impacts key aspects of childhood development such as imagination, self-confidence/self-esteem, creativity, problem-solving abilities, social skills and cooperation,' says psychologist Vikram Prabhu.

It is not just a state of mind but also a state of body, emotion, and spirit. Free play fosters the child's social, physical, intellectual, creative and emotional development. When in play they use all five senses to interact with the world around them. According to research, Kashdan & Fincham, 2002, 'There is concentration, interaction, imagination and the very sort of "regulated curiosity" that empirical research associates with creative behaviour.'

Glowing faces convey enjoyment as children come alive most when they are busy making strategies as the ace warrior; building towns and cities with their blocks, cushions, sheets, chairs; exploring the make-believe world of space, undergrounds, dragon lands, fairy lands; creating exotic sounding dishes from paper, dough. They are what they want to be, doctors, teachers, fire fighters and painters. I still can't forget when my six-year-old daughter, after watching the movie *Honey, I shrunk the kids* put on her scientists' cap and began preparing concoctions to miniaturise her dog. In her imagination the dog had even become that size and they had a whole host of fun activities with the supposed Lilliputian. Play is wonderful and an end in itself.

Children are creative not only during their play hours but, according to research, creativity increases following free play too. Fifty-two English school children, six to seven-years-old, were randomly assigned to two groups. The first group was allowed to play for twenty-five minutes, while the other group copied text from the board. All children were then asked to produce a collage of a creature, using a controlled range of tissue-paper materials. Ten judges assessed the creative quality of the resulting work. The range of colours and total number of pieces used by each child was recorded. The results revealed a significant positive effect of unstructured play upon creativity. Children produced more colourful and complex art after being allowed to play, compared to children who first followed a structured exercise. — P.A. Howard-Jones & others. (2002). The effect of play on the creativity of young children during subsequent activity. Early Child Development & Care, 172, 323-328.

An important condition for the development of creativity in children is to encourage them to socially interact with the people and children around, which happens automatically in their free play.

Factors that have made play difficult

Most of us remember the leisure evening hours from our childhood days spent in play (hopscotch, tag, and hide-and-seek, when play was mostly about fun, not bringing home a trophy), chats, fights and making up. When we see our children caught in the trap of getting A's and going for every extracurricular activity (to keep up with other kids who are trying to keep up with ours) we do feel bad and sigh with a, 'we used to have so much more fun' but that is where it all ends. Ironically we become mute spectators to the shrinking play hours in our children's lives, but vouching for playtime to be the best part of childhood. There are time constraints with more school hours and structured activities. Every available extra minute is gobbled up by the T.V., computer and video games (virtual is replacing the real).

Children today have fewer siblings to play with, neighbourhoods have smaller families.

Their physical boundaries have shrunk. Homes are smaller, many societies do not even have a provision for play areas; parks and gardens are being turned into supermarkets and office complexes.

A 'culture of fear' and 'stranger danger' has made parents apprehensive about their children's safety and so has emerged the genre of latchkey children who are instructed to stay indoors.

Whatever our individual causes may be 'Free play time' is shrinking in most households today. Even activities that have the potential for providing enjoyment and fun, such as sports, dance and music have become pressure cookers for far too many children. As a consequence they are fast losing their interest in free play. Even when given an opportunity they would rather opt for the pal-a-la-screen (T.V., computer) rather than a living, active thinking playmate. According to Sutton-Smith 1997, 'A child who is not being stimulated, by being ... played with, and who has few opportunities to explore his or her surroundings, may fail to link up fully those neural connections and pathways which will be needed for later learning.'

Decreasing play hours is resulting in psychological (temper tantrums, adamancy, depression and irritability), physical and emotional problems which the parents tackle with doses of medicines.

Encourage free play

Time and freedom
Children need unstructured time to engage in free play that is spontaneous and fun (without adult intervention) everyday, period! They need time to do what they are inclined to do naturally—play in imaginative ways. Whether they choose to play with friends, art material, fantasise, sing, dance, or engage in pretend play, they should be set free in a room without T.V. or go outdoors. Parents should perhaps quit the entertainment director's cap and leave the children alone to figure out how to entertain themselves.

When Ashna told her mom that she was bored, the mom just replied, that's sad and went about her work. Ashna sulked for two whole minutes before realising that it was no fun. She then went on a field trip to her society's common garden. She picked leaves and flowers (which were on the ground), small pebbles and began making a collage. She stayed at it all morning; hands busy, head bent low. Hours later, she returned toting an array of self-made pictures—it certainly wasn't an activity that would have crossed her mother's mind—but it had crossed hers.

Nature calling

Get them into nature/outdoors as much as possible. Studies have provided convincing evidence that the way people feel in pleasing natural environments improves recall of information, creative problem solving, and creativity.

Nature seduces one into a creative state. Children love to build. In a natural setting, they build mazes, castles, tree houses, clubhouses and hideouts. They build trenches in the sand and rock dams over streams. The play that takes place during and following the building using branches, stones, piles of leaves is filled with creative imagining.

Nature accesses a child's innate bent toward the creation of poetry and song. They make up songs, dances, poems. Sakina adopted the periwinkle plant and observed it for many days and came up with the, 'Biography of my Winky (that is what she called it)'.

Children's attention is captured by the phenomena and materials of nature: the sparkle of sunlight through leaves, the sound of the wind, the myriad hues in flowers, the endless shapes made by passing clouds, the chirping of birds. They look for images of things in smudges on walls, scribbles on sheets of paper, the bark of trees, foot marks. Early experiences with the natural world have been positively linked with the development of imagination and the sense of wonder. They also have the expanse of space where they can run like a cheetah, crawl like a snake, jump like a kangaroo, climb, throw and kick in the open.

Children can become artists in natural settings. Antara frequently takes her children to the woods and asks them to collect variations of shapes of dry leaves and stick them in patterns. They then make colour by mixing primary colours. This they repeat with various other colours in nature. They also make a colour scale with two colours. They bring coloured leaves and reproduce the same by mixing colours. Children collect different types of leaves and draw them in detail.

Materials

Children's play depends largely upon play material. They must be exposed to materials and experiences that trigger ideas and feelings. These materials can include paper goods of all kinds; writing and drawing tools; materials for constructions and collages, such as buttons, stones, shells, beads, and seeds; and sculpting materials, such as play dough, clay, and shaving cream. They can also use sand, mud, unused pots, pans, cups, cardboard frames of used toilet paper rolls. Save common household items—wallpaper remnants, fabric scraps, old magazines—for spontaneous projects, such as collages, storybook covers, or homemade photo albums. Blocks with special pieces, such as tunnels or steeples, allow imagination to flourish. Old clothes, sheets, caps, socks can be used by children to act and dress up like people they know. Then there are dolls, science activity kits and magic sets, construction toys, percussion instruments. Bring out the creativity in kids with theatre/puppet shows, cooking sets and pretend play projects such as tea parties. With supervision, older children can use real tools and enjoy developing skills that include them, in some way, in the adult world. Start a basic tool kit, and add scrap wood, hardware, and old doorknobs for simple carpentry projects.

The first tryst with destiny – Bill Gates

In the late 1960s, the Lakeside Mothers' Club (Bill Gates' mother too was a member) used the proceeds from a rummage sale to buy an interface terminal and computer time for the students at Lakeside. At thirteen, Bill wrote his first software program: Tic-Tac-Toe. With this new terminal, he and several other students could play Tic-Tac-Toe against the computer. However, this process could be considered cumbersome. There was no monitor–only a keyboard and a printing machine. Each time they made a move, they would have to type it at the keyboard and then rush over to the printer to see the results.

Although, playing one game on the computer often used their entire lunch period (compared to a matter of seconds with a pencil and paper), he was entranced with the machine. Reflecting on it, he said, 'There was just something neat about the machine.' He was fascinated that he could actually give the machine instructions and it would carry them out perfectly every time. Let them use their material the way they want to.

Sahani got the rocking doll but the Barbie came with an instruction, 'do not spoil her hair or break her legs. I will not buy you anything expensive if that happens'.

The dinky Mercedes that Arvind received got was not allowed to be rolled on the society roads. 'That would spoil the tyres'.

Says Karuna, a mother of a seven-year-old boy, 'My child never plays with toys the way he is supposed to. For instance, the toy mobile which I gave him, was taken apart in a matter of minutes. He had the batteries, the electronic chip and the outer cover in three separate trays. He used them as props for his little show. Why should he play with toys the way a manufacturer directs? I let him be free with it. He has fun coming up with wild stories and plays for hours'.

1.7 Discuss your own creative process and experiences

Children's imaginations unfold in interaction with their parents. When we talk about our own creative journeys we unconsciously give them the courage to venture on their own urges. When we talk about the hindrances we faced they overcome theirs; when we talk about the pleasure we felt when we were at sync with our selves they learn to trust their instincts.

Aparna Sen on her father Chidananda Dasgupta

Padma Shri Aparna Sen spoke about how her father, veteran Indian film critic Chidananda Dasgupta, would not only watch classic movies from all across the globe with his family but also have long discussions on the same. Aparna said, 'I had a very intellectual upbringing at home. My dad was a reputed critic of world cinema, and most visitors to our house discussed issues that initiated a lot of thought and analysis of various topics, including cinema. Even I, as a kid, was encouraged to comment on these discussions.' Aparna Sen too preferred to have her daughters around on shoots whenever their schools permitted. She wanted them to experience the world of movies not just as a finished two hour product but feel the fiber of movie making.

Scientist Chaman Lalji Gupta

I met Chaman Lalji Gupta, a scientist working with solar energy and a resident of Auroville, Pondicherry. Along with being a natural inquirer into the 'why and what' of atoms and cells, Chaman Lalji nurtures another passion, that of teaching. He has been a teacher, mentor and guide for the children at Auroville for almost thirty years now. Children keep him alive to the marvels of the human mind. He is always struck by what makes them think the way they do.'

I asked Guptaji whether it is truly possible to share my own creative process with a tender eight-year-old mind and expect her to grasp the nuances of it. Would it not demand faculties beyond what an eight-year-old possesses? He answered, 'Talk to them about your creative experiences as you do with an adult. Children may not understand everything, but then they do not need to understand everything. They will derive their own learning and that is what is important.'

He then gave me an instance from his own experience. He said, 'Till date I have never prepared my lessons which I am supposed to take up in class beforehand. This does land me in trouble once in a while. Even now after three decades of teaching, at times I am stuck and do not know how to explain a certain principle or concept. My students see me struggle and fumble; many times I give up for the day with the lesson unfinished and unexplained. But to me it is not important that they think I am a good teacher, one who never errs. What is important is that they share with me the struggle of life—that even after three decades of teaching I can get stuck and I do get stuck. Growth and learning is a difficult process. If it is difficult for them at nine, it is difficult for me at sixty. May be I can learn things faster because I am older and perhaps have the advantage of experience, but nothing more.'

Renowned Kathak exponent Maulik Shah who also runs the dance school 'Anarth Foundation' choreographed an entire dance sequence in front of us. We were witness to the creative process slowly reaching fulfillment. He composed steps, tuned it to rhythm and set it according to the competencies of us students. He also had to keep note of allowing us enough rest time between tukdas so that we could catch our breath and still have some movement on stage to keep the audience entertained. We saw the highs and lows that the creative process brings. At times steps would fit in with the parameters and we would go on to the next stage and at others he had to try out fifteen-twenty steps to make the piece look interesting as well as keep it within the reach of our abilities. We saw him persist till a high-quality result was achieved. We witnessed his frustrations, exhaustion as well as enthusiasm and satisfaction which a work well-done eventually brings.

When we share our own creations—drawings, stories, ideas, thoughts, even the half-cooked ones, we bring to life once again the excitement, the pleasure and the satisfaction that comes with the creative process,

not only for us to relive but for them to see. Our enthusiasm can be contagious and the child will appreciate the excitement and involvement that we have in an area that we feel passionate about.

We can also allow ourselves to be a little more whimsical, impulsive and spontaneous.

We all have the power to be creative. Yes, it can be tough to be creative when the baby is crying, the kids are fighting, and our brains are fogged with lack of sleep. But we can let ourselves go once a while. We can find our inner child, act curious, energetic and ask questions. We can break into a dance, create a funny voice, make those long strokes on paper and paste it on our cupboard door (on the insides for the conscious types). Creative thinking guru Roger von Oech says that sometimes we need a 'whack on the head' to jolt us out of our routine patterns of thinking. So the next time you find your child jumping on the sofa or refusing to go to bed, it might just be the whack on the head that you need.

'Creativity may breed creativity,' says psychologist Dr Barbara Kerr of Arizona State University. When college freshmen and sophomores who had a lot of creative accomplishments were asked if their family supported their ideas, Kerr said 'the reply was so strong that we had to divide the responses into yes and yes plus. It is hard to emphasise enough how strongly supported these participants felt'.

The book, *Cradles Of Eminence* documenting the childhood of more than 400 eminent personalities states: 'The parents of these celebrities are curious, experimental, restless, seeking'.

Are you?

1.8 The creative environment – The issue of exposure

Creativity cannot come out of 'nothing'. According to research, Weisberg, 1992, 'Stunning creative thought does not simply appear. Rather, it is the product of years of learning, thought, and preparation'. Children are strongly influenced by the inducement and social support that they find in their environment. They need a carefully crafted environment through a consistent exposure to a wide range of creative fields. Einstein poetically called it 'the enjoyment of seeing and searching'.

Expose children to diverse creative interests.

Jogen Chowdhary – 'Creativity is culture'

I asked the painter Jogen Chowdhary, 'How can one give the creative environment to one's child?' He answered, 'Creativity is culture. One cannot create out of "nothing", one needs a cultural connection and preferably... no certainly, from childhood itself'. Jogenda, got into his half-smile and dreamy eyes and with him I toured his small village in the interiors of East Bengal (now Bangladesh) full of pukurs, unending woods and small huts. He said, 'Since I was small, as young as five perhaps, I became an involved observer of art all around me. For me life was Pujas, Jatras and theater which came to our village ever so often. *Mahabharta* and *Ramayana* were liberally enacted. Actors and their costumes, their gait, their dialogues, their emotions and their principles were my text books. I learned from these travelling Jatras and even today you can see its influence on my work. My work has kings and queens...it is all those Jatras which I saw when I was small, but they are still as vivid in my mind as they were four decades ago'. Jogenda spoke of his fascination with the Image-makers or the 'kumbhakars' too. He said, 'These "kumbhakars" modelled images of Durga from clay. For hours on end I would observe them as they drew the eyes, shaped the arms and the body. The movement of craftsmen's hands on the idols enveloped my entire sense of self and during those hours nothing existed for me except the image and the image makers'. As these craftsmen retired for the day, Jogenda would go and treasure-hunt on their leftovers, collecting small bits of colours, chunks of clay discarded by the craftsmen. He would then fashion his own idols. 'My images were flattish and they would not stand but I revered them nonetheless and the process of creation itself thrilled me'. He continued, 'My mind was already working in a different way and it had ample resources to feed on'.

Jogenda says, 'What I got naturally because of the culture of my time and the abundance of nature around, we have to give our children through a conscious effort. But give we must, whatever be the cost in terms of time and effort. Children must be exposed to culture, through museums, books and theater. They should also be encouraged to spend time with nature.' He said, 'With my son too whichever part of the world we go as travelers, we visit the local museum, theater shows, local handicraft shops and also workshops'. He ended with another, 'creativity cannot come out of 'nothing'...it needs exposure!'

Javed Akhtar – 'One does not create out of 'nothing"

Javed Sahab too said the same thing in different words. He said, 'Ultimately whatever you create doesn't just come down from the sky. One can't be creative to write a book in Chinese. Creativity requires exposure and input. As parents it is our duty to make that input available. The input is very important, not the conformity.'

Sanjeev Kapoor – The kitchen became our laboratory

Says, gourmet, Sanjeev Kapoor, 'I learnt experimenting with food from dad. Leftover Diwali sweets at our place turned into interesting kulfi or shake under his expert hands. Dad always experimented with change and I loved watching him create new dishes. Yes, at times they were inedible but then at times we concocted novel mouth-watering items.'

Priti Patel Mehrotra

Says Manipuri dance exponent Priti Mehrotra, 'I still remember that year. I was twelve then. Patel community is generally a closed, clannish one where girls and daughters-in-law are not encouraged to work, but my grandfather was different, and I am talking of the 1960-70s. That summer he invited Guru Bipin Singhji from Bombay. The idea was to prepare a dance drama where the participants were to be the women folks of the family. It was to be choreographed under Guruji.

'With it, one of my most memorable summer began that year. Our cousins and aunts would flock in; every evening would be "party time". We learnt, rehearsed, ate delicious snacks, and connected with each other over cups of tea. Each member was given some role. My mother was not much keen on dancing and so settled to sing the recital, some took up preparing costumes, others doing the stage. We eventually performed our family dance-drama in the auditorium Kala Mandir amidst huge applause and cheers.

'After the show Guru ji approached my grandfather and suggested that I should be encouraged to specialise in one dance form and that is how my tête-à-tête with the Manipuri dance form began.

'But that summer was a revolution for the then ten-year old me. The idea that I do not need to stick to the already established norms but can forge my own pathway took root. I cannot thank my grandfather enough....'

Harvard University Professor Howard Gardner said, 'All youngsters should be exposed to such important creators as Rembrandt and Picasso, Mozart and Duke Ellington, Shakespeare and Toni Morrison.' They need to see how non-realistic art work can evoke interest, imagination and emotion: Modiglianis faces are more interesting with the 'wrong' proportions, Franz Marcs cows unforgettable with the 'wrong' colours and the immense effort can be felt by Jacob Lawrences 'distorted' runners.

1.9 Creativity requires depth

Manipuri dance exponent Darshana Zhaveri

Manipuri dance exponent Darshana Zhaveri said, 'Creativity and a feeling of not just contribution but achievement, comes only when one goes deep into a subject that he/she is enthralled with'. Darshana's achievement bears testimony to her life experience. She said, 'Our Guruji told us in the initial years itself, that we must never compromise depth for anything. Only when we know what the form truly is, how it has originated, journeyed through centuries, will we be equipped to add our own value to it. Under his guidance we started our journey not only to understand the dance form but go to the heart of its origin. We travelled all over the state of Manipur and collected the oral tradition, recorded verses from various gurus, read every piece of material published and all manuscripts relating to the dance form. We read the extant 'Vaishnav Shastras' on dance and music. We toured and read, heard, discussed and practised and then understanding dawned on what we wanted to do. In Manipuri form, till then, Ras Lilas would normally be an eight to ten-hour programme, we capsuled it in a two-hour module, keeping the elements intact. Today I can say that above all creativity requires depth.' Purna Sanskar was there, the higher values. The Zhaveri sisters have altogether authored about seventeen books and toured almost every corner of the globe with their dance form.

1.10 Ways to provide the creative environment

- Take children to museums, science fairs, concerts, theaters, art galleries, exhibitions, etc. so that they have a first-hand experience witnessing creativity. During such trips resist the urge to tell them what they should see, feel or think. You can, however, encourage children to represent their knowledge and ideas before and after they have watched an absorbing show, taken a field trip, or a museum trip through a journal, an art work or even a small speech on it.
- Many museum shops sell postcards, posters of art works and books about art and artists, written especially for children. Invest in them.

An experience that comes to mind is our visit to NID, the National Institute of Design in Ahmedabad. NID hosted a crafts fair called

'Crafts of India'. Every state presented its popular crafts and some artists were seated in front of their stalls working and we could see the creative process in action. We saw artisans from Kerala weaving exquisite baskets, embroiderers from Jammu and Kashmir making delicate patterns out of thread while creating the famous, jamawar, brass work of Orissa and *lac* bangles from Delhi; it was an awesome experience! I allowed my children the time that they wanted to spend at each state exhibit and by the end of it they were freely chatting away with the craftsmen, trying to understand their skill, complimenting them on all the beautiful things they were creating while talking to them about their own aspirations.

Another episode comes to mind. We had gone for a performance by dance maestro Padmabhushan Sonal Mansingh. She had with her the history of a car accident in 1975 after which the doctors had concluded that she would not be able to dance any more. Her conclusions were, however, different and her indomitable will brought her to her feet again. This particular performance was for over an hour (she was sixty years old then) and we enjoyed every second of it. We were not just witness to a beautiful form of art but our nerves too came alive as her passion, zeal and complete engrossment in the dance touched us to the core. ...

- Encourage diverse interests. Field trips, activities with other ethnic groups, celebrating holidays with an element of its historical importance can all be ways to gain varied experiences. There is a famous story about the inventor of Velcro, who happened to have an interest in botany. One day he was walking through a field, when he noticed burrs sticking to his socks. He wondered what made them stick and picked one up to examine its structure. Well, you know what happened...
- Children require role models to give their growth and development a fulfilling direction. Powerful role models allow children to believe in themselves, that they too can create. An eight-year-old watching a gymnastic event may fantasise about mastering the sport and start to work harder at his parallel-bar exercises. A nine-year old

who always finds himself tapping his feet or hands to give beat to music may take up tabla after watching a performance by Zakir Hussain. By exposing children to a variety of artists and to many different styles of art, from realistic to abstract, they can see how the artists used their creativity to change things and make them their own.

It is helpful for children to see how people who have accomplished personal goals 'peers, parents, family members, community members, and professionals from various fields' think about their work and refine it, whether it is a teacher sharing a piece of writing that she hopes to polish for publication, or an illustrator sharing dissatisfying first efforts as well as the ones that were chosen for publication and explaining the reasons for those choices. Read and discuss interviews of creative personalities and their rendezvous with their creative process. We heard caricature expert Laxman's interview on Radio Mirchi in which he spoke about how he reads political speeches, at times for hours before an idea strikes and he can express it in his famous witty-satirical sketches. In his interview he even mentioned that there are days when creativity just pours, but there are days when it doesn't and he cannot sketch a single caricature.

Children need adult role models who rebound from discouragement, whose work is their avocation, and who persist at a task until a high-quality result is achieved. The creative individual is challenged by ambiguity, is comfortable with multiple perspectives, and often addresses the 'same' problem across a series of works or experiments, even if these efforts are not always successful (Lindstrom, 1997).

1.11 Nurturing creativity through arts

Author and psychologist Alice Miller noted for her work on child abuse said, 'Five years after I began painting spontaneously, I started writing books. This never would have been possible without the inner liberation painting has given me. The more freedom I got playing with colours, the more I had to question what I had learned twenty years ago.'

The arts are a dynamic channel to foster creativity. Art fires imagination, stimulates memory, facilitates understanding and enhances symbolic communication. The arts come naturally to children whether they hum a self composed music tune at three, play with finger paints at five or create fantasy stories at ten. We can do our bit by encouraging them to learn in, through, and about the arts by actively engaging in the processes of creating, participating in/performing, and responding to quality arts experiences, adapted to their developmental levels and reflecting their own culture.

Provide them with resources—time, material and freedom and open up avenues—drawings, paintings, sculpture, music, singing, drama, dance that they feel inclined towards.

Allow them to experiment—Children like to figure out their own processes and designs. Yes, I itch to rearrange my daughter's collage, get hung up on the right and wrong ways to do things, but kids just want to have fun and try different things—so let them. Edison had his laboratory at the young age of ten in his cellar. His mother was in mortal terror lest the precocious experimenter below should, in his inexperience, make some awful combination that would explode and bring down the house in ruins on himself and the rest of the family. Yet she let him have his way.

Encourage their creative expressions—Display your child's handiwork, be it in an alcove in the front hallway or a wall in the kitchen. Public exhibitions show the children how much we love and appreciate them. Walt Disney's favourite aunt supplied him with pencils and drawing tablets, and a very dear old neighbour, a retired doctor, often 'bought' his drawings with little presents.

Creativity needs time and leisure. Do not rush them to finish their art time so that they can begin with the serious work of learning.

Creativity needs guidance. Children need gentle coaching and skilled guidance. An interest in music, dance, or drama can be enlivened with lessons. Lessons, rehearsal, and practice require discipline but should always be pleasurable. Perhaps the most important disposition in educators who strive to become creative teachers is, as Fritz (2002) argues, the determination to 'find the balance between stifling the students within a limited set of skills and letting them loose with endless horizons, but ill equipped with skills and knowledge to realise their ideas' (www.21learn.org/arch/articles/fritz.html). The arts have always been focused on "mixtures and balances."

1.12 Fostering creativity through reading

Narrative is a fundamental aspect of human experience. Through books children travel to distant lands, know diverse cultures, come across a range of emotions, know right from wrong (the wicked step-mom falls off the cliff), know fantasy, mystery and realism. The imaginative elements found in books help young children free their minds from a fixed way of thinking. Books reflect the throb of human life; the magic entrances, fascinates, sets alight imagination, opens doors of interest and curiosity, informs, and triggers questioning. Restless bodies become still and concentrated—thinking is encouraged, interesting and meaningful conversation ensues.

In Roald Dahl's book, *The Friendly Giant,* the giant talks about hearing the conversations of ants. Sneha started spending hours in her society garden trying to understand chatters of all non homo-sapiens. She spoke about the squirrels playing hide-and-seek, the birds playing catch-me-if-you-can, and the frogs communicating on how much tastier the newly filled water in the pond is.

Illustrations found in picture books also help improve children's creativity. Children can enact stories that they read and do role plays. They can indulge in puppetry and even come out with their own stories. They can be encouraged to make their own story books. Sneha stapled some sheets of A4 papers and used pictures from old magazines to come out with a story. Every story's last page had two different endings, a happy and a happier one. At the end she had written: Coming more from the same author in these series...wow! That was creative. Reading is dealt with in detail in the chapter, 'Books, books and more books'

1.13 Nurturing creativity through creative writing

Children love words. Encourage them to express themselves through writing. It could be stories, poems, songs, limericks, essays, plays, or journal-writing.

Aparna Sen

When Aparna Sen was about thirteen she began penning down poems. Her home had always had a stream of intellectuals, writers, film makers and poets who would come and discuss their work with her father, veteran critic and film-maker Chidananda Dasgupta. She said, 'We were never supposed to keep away. In fact my father would often invite us to come and listen to such discussion and even share our thoughts with them.' In particular Aparna remembers the instance when the celebrated poet Subhash Mukherjee had been to their residence and her father asked her to read out the poem to him. She said, 'I remember that he appreciated it and said that there was a lot of substance in it, but why didn't I use rhyme. Being asked to read my composition to the famous poet was a validation of my efforts and went a long way into instilling a sense of self in me."

On a visit to Manav Sadhna, an NGO which works from Gandhi Ashram, I met Soniya, a journalist born and brought up in London and currently working with BBC. She shared her protocol of 'The everyday analysis' which they followed religiously every evening after dinner back home for years. Since she had been about eight her father would pick issues of general interest (environment, personalities, racism) from the newspaper and then read them aloud to her. She would then be asked to pen her thoughts on the same or verbalise her analysis and the father would put it down on paper. By the time she was twelve her skills at analysis were so strong that she became a regular feature in the 'letters to the editor's section. Soniya says, 'A large part of what I am today goes to those simple discussions and debates that I had every evening with my father.'

Creative writing is a wonderful tool to help children express themselves. We can offer just enough structure and intervention to allow children to progress securely and successfully and offer enough stimulation and variety of approach so that they can establish creative links.

We can encourage our children to write down their experiences after some turnkey events. When my daughter went up to the stage for the first time to perform in 'showcase' which was a performance by the students, she went through a host of different feelings. Her hands went cold, her mind kept going blank, her heart was thumping even when she was stationary. She was excited, nervous, uncertain and enthralled all at the same time. The next day she was trying to describe the strange way her entire self was behaving when I encouraged her to pen down the feelings.

Further, creative writing can be encouraged as we become an enthusiastic audience to their creativity. Plays, stories, can be enacted, puppet shows can have dialogues written and directed by the budding creators. Their poems and poetry can be hung in a central location for discussion.

We can gift them a beautiful journal with the promise of complete secrecy (some come with a lock and key) in which they can pen down their thoughts, feelings and desires. We can equip them with a dictionary and a thesaurus so that they feel self-sufficient.

We can encourage them towards journalism. They can interview family members (extended family) and come up with newsletters every month. They should be encouraged to write letters and greeting cards. Greeting cards can be written to an ill student, teacher, custodian, mother on Mother's Day, a dear friend during the holidays, or whomsoever they like. Some suggestions to give children about whom to write to are: a friend, a cousin who lives outstation, a relative, a letter to the editor, etc. Children can even try their hand at writing advertisements for their favourite products.

It is, however, important to instill feelings of confidence so that they can make the leaps into creativity which are involved in writing. This means ignoring grammatical errors, spelling mistakes, even incoherence in thoughts, repetition of ideas in the first read. There is always plenty of time and opportunity to 'correct' later, but the first read should always, always be to understand the thought behind the writing. I still can't forget the story my daughter wrote about the moon. I was in a hurry to get over with the customary rote appreciation so that I could make her 'nite' the right 'night'. My daughter sensed it. She saw odes of enthusiasm in my 'night' and little in the way her moon played hide-and-seek with the stars. Children usually do.

1.14 Using music to enhance creativity

Music forges new neural pathways that stimulate creativity. Research shows that music trains the brain for higher forms of thinking. In a study at U.C. Irvine, researchers studied two groups of three-year-olds. One group studied piano and sang daily in chorus. The other group did not. In eight months the musical three year olds were adept puzzle masters. They scored 80% higher in spatial intelligence than the non musical group. (Newsweek Feb.19, 1996). Listening to good music, researchers emphasise, actually taps both sides (right and the left), potentially uniting creative and analytical functions in the brain/mind. It also helps implement ideas better.

Even if our children don't play an instrument, there are many other ways we can make music a part of their life.

We can play CDs of every type, be it Bollywood music, instrumental, classical or pop. Pop music can unleash a storm of creative energy too (we can push back the living-room furniture and get moving along with them to shed those extra kilos).

While listening to instrumental music we can point out the different instruments we hear. The morning air in my house is always filled with music. The children get to choose between sitar, santoor, drums, chants, piano, tabla and vocal classical. Yes, the volume is low and we go about our morning chores with music in the background.

We can also equip our children to form their own composers' corner. We can buy an inexpensive piano, an electronic keyboard, guitar, drums, xylophone and encourage them to create their own melodies. We can record their compositions or even have them give a concert for the family, over dinner.

We can invite some of the child's pals over and get them to round up all the soundmakers in the house—windup toys, music boxes, xylophones, recorders, drums. Do not forget to cover your ears while they jam.

A.R. Rehman

A.R. Rehman reminiscences, 'I was not crazy after music. I was more interested in technology.' He was first drawn to music strongly when his father bought a synthesiser, one of the very first in film circles then, from Singapore. Till then he now says, 'As a child, music seemed to be a means of earning bread and butter. I had no special fascination for if... it was associated purely with work. Yet I couldn't take my eyes away from the synthesiser, it was like a forbidden toy'. This instrument was an object of much curiosity to the young Dileep (A.R. Rehman) and caught his fancy. Dileep used to spend hours experimenting with the novel instrument. This instrument was to shape the future of this child. It was perhaps divinely ordained that the synthesiser would become Dileep's favourite instrument since it was the ideal combination of music and technology.

Shravan Kumar's gift...

I asked music director and singer Shravan Kumar on how the passion of music took root in him. He answered, 'The toys that I grew up with were the tanpura, the pakhwaj, the tabla and the harmonium. My father was a classical singer and there were instruments lying in every corner of the house.' To the ten month-old Shravan Kumar, the pot of treasure at the end of the long crawl was the tanpura, which magically came to life whenever he fiddled with the strings. With this began his love-saga with the world of nodes and beats. He often accompanied his father to the performances of great singers like Pandit Ravi Shankar, and the likes where he sat completely enthralled as he travelled to every peak and depth with their performance. He was barely six years old then. He said, '*Sangeet mujhe khichne laga or mein khichta chala gaya.*' He joined a music school and commenced his formal training. To him everything in the school was holy; the instruments, the teachers, the environment, even the other students. He was amazed to learn that in a classical form one raga can be sung for three hours, but if one makes it lighter the same can be finished in fifteen minutes. If one makes it still lighter, it can be an all of three minutes and fifteen seconds and become a movie song. This journey from a three-hour raga to a three-minute song enthralled him completely and with this he discovered his field of expertise from the vast ocean of music that lay before him.

1.15 Making creativity part of every day

- Set up an art studio at home. It should be a safe, messable place where kids can explore a variety of art material. Put up old magazines, newspapers, used greeting cards apart from the usual art materials like crayons, paints and colours.
- Create holiday-theme posters which kids can gradually fill up with their art. A few days before special occasions like Diwali, Holi, Rakhi and Christmas, Tanna pastes a giant piece of coloured paper onto the side of her refrigerator. She and her seven-year-

old daughter, Aanya talk about the festival and its significance. Over the next several days, Aanya draws, paints or does collage on the paper.

- Pencil Talk: Take a large sheet of shelf paper, some pencils, markers or crayons, and have a 'conversation' with your child. The catch: You can't talk; you have to draw what you want to say. Ask everyone in the family to join in.
- Invent-a-Machine: Give your child boxes of different sizes, glue, scissors, a variety of buttons, knobs, pipe cleaners, string and other household items. Suggest he create his own machine or other construction (older kids may want to add battery operated bulbs and motors).
- Start a family debate: One family member can propose an issue—for instance, should children be allowed to watch any T.V. shows they like—and the others can split up into pro and con camps. It's exciting to see the wealth of ideas that spring from this process.
- Become co-investigators: Use a magnifying glass to see enlarged views of waterdrops, hair, plant leaves, and other small items. You can also look at different kinds of bugs and animals. You can go on a mission. Exploring gravity, study different habitats, seeing light through water, glass, prism, other topics could be- where does the water in our sink come from, how are such tall buildings constructed, why do people get sick?
- Love activities: Try to define love. Make a list of things you 'love'. Share lists. Categorise lists (living, non-living etc.). Discuss expressions of love (hugs, kisses, smiles, winks etc.)
- Gardening project: Plant a vegetable, a flower or any other plant and let the child nurture it. For those living in flats pots can be used. Watching the process of creation and growth can be very stimulating for the child. My child and I planted a tree in our garden. Our neighbour too planted one exactly at the same spot on the other side of the wall. Both the trees grew. They bent and shot, they twisted and grew and both found their place under the sun.

- Drawing music: Put on some lively music, and encourage children to draw what they hear. Drawing squiggles and dots in time with music will nurture brain development and broaden the familiar activity of drawing to a new all-time high.
- Cooking: Take up experimental cooking projects. Let them create their own sandwiches. You can experiment with novel combinations, or possibly even playful explorations (like letting a very young child decorate pizza with sliced vegetables–an edible emoticon). Tanya wanted to have coloured idlies. So her mom made green idlies with spinach, red with beetroot, yellow with turmeric and even purple colured with black grapes.
- Make scrapbooks: Scrapbooking is a way of preserving our lives. Encourage children to put their holiday experiences and growth process in them. Children will be able to use their artistic and creative writing faculties simultaneously.
- Use common everyday objects for new uses. For example, paint with a rubber ball dipped in paint, change a book into a talking puppet, or turn a table over and make it a boat.
- Record: Provide your child with a tape recorder, dictaphone, camera or camcorder, and let her create her own 'stories' from the sounds and sights she puts together. Give her the opportunity (if she wishes) to present her production to the family.
- Use a continuing story concept. Someone starts the story and then each person adds a part.
- Ask your child to draw his own image by looking into a mirror.

SUMMING UP

In a recent interview (Cramond, 2001) with E. Paul Torrance, one of the pioneers in creativity research, Torrance talked about his thirty-year study of what he referred to as the 'beyonders,' those individuals whose creative achievement was remarkable in a particular domain (Torrance, 1993). The characteristics that these individuals shared were: a delight in deep thinking, a tolerance for mistakes, a passion for their work, a clear sense of purpose and mission, an acceptance of being different and a level of comfort with being a minority of one, and a tendency to ignore admonitions about being 'well-rounded.' Based on this research, Torrance and his colleagues (Henderson, Presbury, & Torrance, 1983) advised children to pursue their interests with intensity, work to their strengths, learn to self-evaluate, seek out mentors and teachers, and learn to be interdependent.

In a lovely little book entitled *Creative Authenticity*, artist Ian Roberts says, 'Ultimately, it doesn't matter to the world whether you paint or dance or write'. 'The world will probably get by without the product of your efforts. But that is not the point. The point is what the inner process of following your creative impulses will do to you. It is clearly about process. Love the work, love the process. Our fascination will pull our attention forward. That, also, will fascinate the viewer.'

We, as parents, can allow, stimulate and encourage creativity or we can discourage and stifle it. The choice, as always, is ours.

Hi Buddy!

· ·

It was the first time that seven year old Sanaya's school friend Preet, was coming to spend the day at her house. Sanaya was so excited that she could barely eat her breakfast. She kept breaking into a dance. Every couple of minutes she would ask, 'When will it be 10, mom?' When Preet finally came, the two girls disappeared into nooks and corners which even I didn't know existed in my house of ten years. A search team had to be deployed when it was time for lunch or milk.

Eleven year old Tanmay told his father, 'Saikat is my best friend because he tells me things and I tell him things.'

Six year old Sanykuta says, 'When everyone is busy (mom, grandmom, brother) with their work I either go to my friend's place or she comes over, and we have fun playing with each other. I do not feel lonely at all.'

Manav says, 'Everyone in both the families finds ants yucky, but Ansh and I find them fascinating.'

Anahita says about her friend Komal, 'She taught me how to play memory and mastermind and I am now teaching it to my school friends.'

2.1 Friends matter

Friends make life more fun, sorrow easier to handle, learning more interesting and growing up exciting. Usually friends go through similar situations and feelings-mothers at home who constantly drill about clean up, pick up or sober up; dads who display the I-can't believe-we-share-the-same-genes look, when they get a b+ grade; callous teachers who order a four page hand-writing practice or fifty multiplication sums a day; neigbourhood and school bullies who bring a similar sense of trepidation and anxiety. These tiny bundles identify easily with each other's good and bad experiences because they are close to their own. They naturally place their faith in each other and share their deepest thoughts, insecurities and happiness. Friends inhabit a world unique to them; we adults can only get a glance once in a while and that too, if they deem it necessary. An instance comes to mind. My six-year-old girl Sanaya had to attend the birthday party of a school friend named Harsh. I readied the birthday gift, addressed it to Harsh but before I could write 'With love from Sanaya' an ear piercing shrill 'YOU CANNOT WRITE LOVE MOM' froze me midway. Flabbergasted, I mumbled to myself that she was just six and I ought to put things in the right perspective for her when her friend Ananya quietly propped up her gift. It too sported a scratched-off 'love' message. Sanaya's elder sister Aishwarya joined in with her 'you-do-not-understand' stance, enlightening me with, 'Mom writing "love" would embarrass Sanaya greatly'. All three children then exchanged an understanding, 'We are in the same boat' look, which I so obviously was not a party to.

We have all (hopefully,) had good friends since childhood and know their worth well. We know from our memories how friends formed the base on which we could build a network of relationships which allowed us to grow up, go to school and play in our neighbourhoods and communities. Friends can make all the difference between a happy or a doomed life, especially so in childhood.

2.2 Benefits

Companionship

According to University of Maine psychologists studying childhood friendships, 'All it takes is one best friend to stave off the loneliness and depression of a child — even if that youngster is considered an outsider with the "in crowd" of peers'.

Playing games, partying, going for bike rides, walks or classes, sitting and chatting are fun when friends are around. Friends usually find the same things amusing or funny and will burst into a giggle together. My daughter's friends were all camping at our house when suddenly a bucket of water slipped from the servant's hand spilling water everywhere. I could only think of the extra work that had to be done to clean the mess, but my daughter and their friends burst into a fit of laughter.

Children find the same thing exciting and almost to the same degree. A game of monopoly can be a matter of life and death for all the players equally. They find the same things cool-a necklace with a whistle, faded and torn jeans; or irritating-insistence on eating vegetables, being asked to brush their teeth at night, or boring-museum visits.

Like adults, when children experience problems and stress they often turn to their friends for help, advice, comfort, and emotional support. Since they have the same issues they can correlate and feel one. The solace and support of friends help children cope with troubling times (family conflict, terminal illness, parents' unemployment, and school failure) and through transition times—moving up to a new school, entering adolescence, etc. Friends also have an incredible influence over one another. There were times that I knew that as a parent, my opinion didn't count nearly as much as did Chintal's, Trisha's or the many other friends who came through our door.

Social skill development

'A child playing with a friend is building an important bridge to the world beyond himself', says Jackie Mize, Ph.D., an associate professor of child development at Auburn University in Alabama.

Through peer relationships children learn the art of handling themselves individually as well as collectively. They learn to give and take, win and lose, lead and follow, argue and make up. They also learn what is appropriate and acceptable and what is not. They learn conflict resolution and the concept of fairness, not as some preferred theory from their parents, but as workable values through group play experience. They learn that their way of seeing things is not the only way and that different people have different viewpoints, needs and perceptions. Younger children especially indulge a lot in drama and fantasies. They are found playing teacher-pupil/mother-child, shopkeeper games. This involves communication and expression of feelings and thoughts.

Physical and mental development

Friendships aid intellectual and physical development. Friends usually spend time together in play which are both mentally (Monopoly, Scrabble, Snatch, Mastermind, Memory, Pictionary, Dum Charades, Life) and physically stimulating (hide and seek, catch, lock-n-key, cricket). Susan Issacs an educational expert, described play as 'the child's work'. Friends also become one of the major sources for knowledge acquisition. Children teach one another in many situations (new games, handling the internet, doing project work, new skills like tying shoelaces, use of scissors) and are generally effective in this activity. Language development happens naturally when friends communicate with each other. If your child's best buddy is a bookworm, his enthusiasm for reading may be all your child needs to get hooked on to books. Similarly, your child may strive a little harder on the playing field if he wants to emulate a friend who's a stand out at soccer.

Ego support and confidence

According to child expert Sullivan, 'Interaction with a friend is widely and duly celebrated for its potential to validate one's self-concept and enhance one's self-esteem.'

It is the first relationship that the child makes on his own and that is a great confidence builder. Children are at ease with their friends because they feel liked, accepted and valued for what they are. In the pre-adolescent years, children create their own group identity by talking or looking alike and so form a tightly knit inner circle where they feel secure.

Friends as game partners as against parents

Advantages of friends and friend-play as against that between adults and children:

The essentials of friendship are reciprocity and commitment between individuals who see themselves more or less as equals. However much we try to be the perfect game partners for our six-twelve years old it is not enough. There are innate advantages of being with the peer group. Above all, friendships are egalitarian. Interaction between friends rests on a more equal power base than the interaction between children and adults.

Most of the time children play games with their friends at their own levels. Their interests then match equally, as opposed to a parent who might under play to allow the child to win. It is also natural for the parent to lose interest or not play with total concentration. But when two children play with each other it is complete entertainment for both, where both (or more) are equally challenged and involved. Children sense the disparity (of interest, level and enthusiasm) with their parents and parity with their friends, instinctively.

Also, with friends, since everyone is learning, the process of trial and error happens naturally. But we as parents can never forget our round-the-clock commitment of improving and teaching our children. So what if it's a game where my child and I are equals? If there arises an opportunity, where I can teach a trick or two to make the child smarter or better in the game, will I leave that opportunity unused? Most of us will vouch for 'make-the-child-know-more' option. Allow me to share a personal incident.

My husband and I had just started a game of Scrabble, when my nine year old daughter trotted in and declared that she too wanted to join in. Her eleven year old friend Trisha was also with her and they made a team and took the third side on the board. They were doing very well, scoring around twenty points every round. They could mostly muster words of four letters with an occasional five letter word; but I could see that the game had their full concentration and they were stretching their minds to the utmost and were trying their best. We could make words faster and more easily; it so happened that my word was set and I had some spare moments. With their permission I peeped into their letters. They had made a word 'brands' and were extremely proud of their first six letter word ever. But I showed them a place, where they could make 'bad' vertically in a way that the 'b' would come in a triple letter score, and 'bee' would also form horizontally. They would then get six times for the points of 'b'. They would even save their 's'.

bee

a

d

My suggestion would have been brilliant from the 'winners' point of view, but is life only about winning and losing? My child lost her first ever six lettered word in my bid to win. She became less certain about the words she was forming, and began pushing the word tray in my direction so that I would come up with a better or more scoring word. Towards the end both of them simply stopped racking their brains to put a word together because I was simply much faster and better than they could ever be. When we finished the game everyone including me, was relieved. Calculating the score was no fun either. Whoever scored the most points was irrelevant, we had all somehow lost.

This is a situation we all as parents can identify with. We rush to help our naïve children with puzzle pieces, mazes, blocks, forks, spoons, information, maths, words. In our mind we are trying to be helpful, by either giving them the easy way out or teaching them something more than what they know. But we take away from them their right to trial and error, their confidence, their curiosity, their struggle, their pleasure of discovering what works for them and replace it with our 'higher learning'.

By this I am in no way implying that we should stop all games with our children. Of course when pitted against us they will stretch their minds more, learn more. But what they need is parental non-interference in their play time.

> Don't handicap your children by making their lives easy.
> — ROBERT A. HEINLEIN

2.3 The downside of friendship

The contagious negatives—when friends lead astray

Children are very impressionable and pick up each others' habits easily. Since they do not possess a fully developed ethical and moral value system they are more vulnerable to negative influences. Sometimes, they don't understand how a bad trait can later work its way into their own characters.

Ankit learnt a new way to get back in his fights, he spat at the opponent. On being asked as to where he learnt this habit, he answered, 'My friend Vivek showed this trump card to win over any fight and I have not lost since.'

Karen began to lie to get out of a tight spot. She said, 'Anahita says it works. It really does mom!'

Mahima brought home a pink eraser which did not belong to her. When questioned she said, 'My desk mate said taking away others' things which we like, when they are not watching, is the easiest way to get them.'

Rakesh told Param, 'Come on! All of us are copying the homework from him. It's no big deal.' Param hesitated and Rakesh said, 'Everyone's doing it, do you want to show that you are extra bright?' Just to feel one amongst them, Param too began copying.

Tamanna christened her gang 'the pink petals'. Admission into that gang was difficult but once in it every member had to follow certain codes of (mis)conduct. They were required to be rude, act snobbish, find fault and make fun of every other child who did not belong to the group. Nine year old Prerna felt this was wrong, but being in the group seemed more important than concerns with right or wrong. It did take her a while, she too was one with 'The pink petals'.

Negative peer pressure could be for anything from talking badly to other peers, exclude or be hurtful to others, cheating, skipping classes, even shoplifting. The need for peer approval and acceptance becomes the overriding factor; the child learns early that any deviation from the standards of the group could mean non-acceptance, ridicule

The Pink Petal Gang.

(don't be a chicken), and even rejection. Some go along because they are curious to try something new that the others are doing. Negative peer pressure impairs good judgement and fuels wrong or harmful behaviour. A powerful negative peer influence can motivate a child to make choices and engage in behaviour, that his or her values might otherwise reject.

Bossism

When peers boss over others (and the victim unfortunately is our child), it can turn our children into emotional marshmallows. It might rob them of their self esteem (I am not good enough!), their sense of effectiveness (I can't do it), assertiveness (If I assert my view I may be clobbered) and even the faculty to rationalise and think for oneself (anyway I am going to follow her). They may lose their confidence, become quiet and passive. Friendships then hurt, become unpleasant and may actually harm the child. Some real life instances from children themselves:

'Rahul is stronger than I and has hit me twice. Now whenever he wants the swing first, I let him take it.'

'Sapna, my best friend not only tells me that she is better, but actually gets better grades in every subject too. Why am I not that good?'

'If Karl wants to play cricket and I want to play football, we always end up playing cricket. If I don't listen to everything he says, he stops talking to me.'

'I do not want to go to school as Ketan always teases and picks on me.'

2.4 But parents do have the power to impact peer influence

Dealing with negative peer influence is a challenge, but there are solutions. Since children have not yet learnt the knack of hypocrisy or gullibility we can know what is going on within the private chambers of their minds, if we are just aware and involved enough. For many parents involvement begins and ends with home work done/not done; prepared for exams or not; finished your meals or not. As parents we need to keep a close watch and trace (unacceptable) behaviour to its source.

Trace the source

Ask yourself, 'Why is the child doing what he is doing'?

Are the child's basic emotional needs (to be listened to, understood, accepted) going unmet?

Anant ran into the house after a difficult day and wanted his mother to hear the unabridged version of the entire day but there were a hundred chores to be done and she simply did not have the time that his verbose recitals demanded.

Zaheera's father lost the assignment to his colleague, but eased his guilt by accusing his seven year old son, 'You play so many pranks that I never have the peace of mind to produce good work. It seems you will spell my doom.'

Every time Rangez came home with a 5 out of 10 in any paper the mother would hold her head and wonder (aloud) as to how this Dodo was born in their house.

Rahul returned home with an A+ in his class test. The father responded with a firm verbal 'well done'. Rahul came home after being teased and picked on by the class bully. His father responded with a 'learn to fight for yourself'. All Rahul wanted was a hug and an 'I love you' on both the occasions.

Children need to be noticed, needed, accepted, loved and praised for what they are. Unknowingly, parents indulge in constant belittling, criticising and shaming the child. They withhold their love and affection and at times make the child the scapegoat for things that go wrong in their lives. Unreasonable comparisons between siblings and unrealistic demands on the child, play havoc with the child's sense of self-efficacy and self esteem. Such parents then set up their kids for excessive peer influence. Children of such parents seek approval, acceptance and support (what they should be primarily getting from home) from their peers. If the parents leave an emotional vacuum in the child's life, it will be filled from outside the family and possibly in a negative way. The choice of peers is a barometer for a kid's sense of self. If the parents don't talk to them, they will talk to anyone who listens, relying on peers for validation.

How a child interacts with other children is heavily influenced by the nature of her relationship with her parents. A close relationship with a parent provides a young child with a base of security, which in turn leads to greater confidence in developing and negotiating relationships outside the family. Loving and responsive parenting helps children to see the world in a positive way and to expect that relationships with others will be rewarding. Says Kathryn Kerns, Ph.D., assistant professor of psychology at Kent State University in Kent, Ohio, 'There is a lot of evidence that kids who are close to their parents do better with their peers.'

What kind of home environment are you giving to your child?

Does your child feel:
- Secure
- Loved
- Accepted
- Wanted

The best weapons against negative peer pressure are a loving, accepting home and open communication. Make your child know that he is special and acceptable as he is! Give him the security of knowing that you are there for him, come what may.

Know your child's friends

What are the kind of friends that your child is associating with? Wise parents not only develop strong parenting skills and participate positively in their children's lives, they also continuously scan others who interact with their children on a regular basis. When they anticipate problems they intervene, guiding their children away from negative influences.

☑ Reality check

Do you know your child's friends?
1. Name your child's best friend.
2. Name your child's closest five or six friends.
3. Name those friends' parents' first names.
4. Describe those friends' relationships with their parents.
5. Describe the social and behavioural characteristics of the leading (most popular) crowd at your child's school.

Help your child pick better friends!

If your child is with good kids there will be a lot less negative peer pressure to worry about. Know the values, beliefs and convictions of

your child's friend's parents. (It's easier to enforce a half hour T.V time schedule everyday if all your child's friends have the same rules).

Help your child learn what qualities to look for in a friend. In addition to being fun, what other qualities are important? What about honesty, dependability, responsibility, a caring attitude? Talk to your child about the type of friends to avoid. Help your child sort out 'safe' situations from 'risky' ones. Discuss what behaviour would be appropriate in various situations.

Around school

If the parents can't easily control with whom their child chooses to be friends, say in a school environment, they can still make their concerns clear and lay down specific ground rules.

Radhika was worried about her son showing great affinity towards the class Junkie Harsh. She knew that Harsh usually came with unfinished work and never concentrated in the class. Moreover he needed a friend to keep him company away from class. In Anish he found that cooperative classmate. Anish's grades too began to fall. What did Radhika do? Take a peek at their conversation.

Radhika to Anish: You know that I am your well-wisher and always do what I think is the best for you?

Anish: Yes.

Radhika: You agree that I have more experience than you?

Anish: Yes.

Radhika: Tell me honestly how would you analyse Harsh's behaviour?

Anish: Cool and heady.

Radhika: Yes, but is it also right and beneficial?

Anish: No.

Radhika: You are entitled to your own opinion and preferences, yet when I feel that the same is conflicting with what I think is right, as your parent it is my duty to make you aware of the consequences. Harsh is not an OK kid for you to be with as he consistently distracts you from concentrating and lures you to play during lessons. If you will be his partner in this you will miss out on the lessons of the day, get into the teachers' bad books and will also have trouble comprehending the lesson later. Your grades are already showing the result of your association with him. I leave the decision to you.

She further added that people change and that if Harsh's behaviour improved they could be buddies again.

Radhika used a calm tone and rationalised the entire issue. She encouraged her son to think of the correctness of the entire issue. She focused on Harsh's specific behaviour rather than generalizing or criticising his character. She explained the consequences of his continued association with Harsh, but without forbidding him to play with him. This approach taught Anish to think more logically and assume responsibility for his actions. Radhika helped Anish develop his decision-making skills by permitting him to make increasingly complex decisions, and learn from the real world consequences of those decisions.

Educate your child on how to deal with negative peer pressure

Negative peer pressure is a part of almost all children's lives. You can't keep your child from feeling peer pressure, but you can give him the

tools he needs to resist bad influence. Tell the child beforehand what face negative peer pressure could wear. His friends may tell him that it is 'cool' to:

Cut class

Be mean to others

Lie to their parents or

Sneak an answer to a friend in an exam

Friends may pass negative behaviour by saying things like:

We won't get caught.

It'll be fun.

Everyone is doing it.

Explain to your child that it is natural to give in to negative peer pressure, we as parents face it too in our lives.

Encourage your child to probe into his individual reasons

Does he fear the friend's alienation? In the book *The Kite Runner* by Khaled Hosseini, Amir and Hassan (his Hazari servant) are good friends and play with each other all day. One day Amir asks Hassan, 'Would you eat the dirt if I ask you too?' Hassan shoots back, 'Would you ask me to do such a thing?' When Amir challenged Hassan's loyalty, Hassan challenged Amir's integrity.

Ask your child, 'Is your friend being a true friend by asking you to do what you know is questionable?'

Does the child give in to peer-pressure to gain popularity? Tell your child that though there is nothing wrong with wanting to be popular, there are right ways and wrong ways to become so. Here the end cannot justify the means.

Does the child lack courage and so gives in? Encourage your child to be assertive, to stand up for what he believes in. If possible share a story of when you stood up against peer pressure. Stress how positive or courageous it is to stick to one's guns in the face of ridicule when one knows one is doing the right thing. Tell him that though it is not easy to resist negative peer pressure, when one does so, one feels good about it afterwards. And the child may even be a positive influence on his peers who feel the same way—often it just takes one person to speak out or take different action to change a situation.

Does the child feel trapped because he has already given in to wrong demands in the past, and so now feels obliged to go along? Tell the child that people change, thoughts change and stances change. He has the right to change his mind and be true to his new 'Self'.

Encourage the child to search his soul

When I was once reading *Pinocchio* to my children, the character of Jiminy came up. Jiminy was Pinocchio's conscience-keeper. Whenever Pinocchio lied, Jiminy became uncomfortable. Since then we too have a name for our guiding angel. Each of us consult our own 'Jiminy'. Many a time my daughters have come and confessed, 'I was tempted to lie to my teacher but Jiminy stopped me' or 'Jiminy told me that I must not be a part of the mean prank my friends were playing on the new student.'

Encourage your child to listen to his Jiminy. Does it feel wrong or uncomfortable on the inside? If 'yes', it probably is. Tell your child to trust his gut feeling. This kind of decision making will also help the child become self-reliant and learn more about who he really is.

My Jiminy

Encourage your child to think logically

- What will be the consequence of a negative action? Will the activity get him in trouble? Will it be harmful to his health? Will his parents disapprove? Thinking about the possible consequences of the choice helps strengthen kids' convictions and decisions. One classic line which I use with my children is 'If all your friends jumped off the bridge—would you too?'
- You can even give your child some net practice through role play. Role-playing involves practising different responses to various situations. This gives children a chance to practise saying 'no' to their peers.

- Encourage your child to always come to you to talk about incidents, even if he has submitted to peer pressure in the past. Promise that you won't let your anger get in the way of listening fairly and trying to help. The more you talk with your child, supply information, and acknowledge the many feelings that may be involved, the less likely it is that the child will be pressured into unhealthy or dangerous decisions. And the more he will know that you love him.
- Encourage your child to hangout with people who feel the same way that he does. If your child is hearing that little voice telling him a situation's not right, chances are others hear it too. Just having one other person stand with your child against peer pressure makes it much easier for both people to resist.

Give your child these practical options

The child can:

Suggest a better idea—'Let us play the game in the recess instead of cutting class now.' 'Let's think of something else in which we can have fun and still not hurt the poor boy.'

Use a factual reason—'It's illegal,' 'I'll be grounded,' or 'I could get hurt.'

Buy time—They can refrain from giving an immediate 'yes' or 'no'. Some responses could be—'Maybe later,'; 'I'll wait and see.'

Return the challenge when dared- Several examples are: 'You see it your way. I see it my way.' 'No, it's just not my style.' 'If you are really a friend, then back off.' 'You must think I'm pretty dumb to fall for that one.'

Blame one's parents: 'Are you kidding? If my mom found out, she'd kill me, and her spies are everywhere.'

2.5 Building good peer relations

It is 5 pm and you can hear squeals and excited conversations of the children in your society park. But your child is sitting at home bored and teary-eyed. You go up to her and inquire lovingly, 'Why are you not playing outdoors with your friends?'

Your child answers,
'They say that they are not my friends'
'Nobody wants to play with me'
'Nobody likes me'

My younger pampered, spoilt child Sanaya said that none amongst her nine society friends ever came to play with her once they knew that her elder sister Aishwarya was out. With tears in her eyes she said, "Mummy, initially I thought it was a coincidence but now I know that they do not like to play with me without Aishwarya.'

You feel that you can handle anything in life but not your child's rejection or ridicule by her peers. You want to 'fix it' for her, you want to make her sought after, but alas you cannot make friendships happen. But you can impart good social skills to help your child navigate her world of friends successfully and happily. We can focus on giving our child the knowledge, skills, and support he or she needs to solve the problem.

Almost every child has trouble with social relationships in some way, at some time. It is normal for friends to have an argument, not agree on which game to play, tease one another or even get into the 'kitta' mode for a few minutes, at times even for a day or two. But the ratio of their differences is commensurate to the ratio of their making up (generally without parental intervention). Kids do manage to make up almost before we come to know that there has been an estrangement.

But what when such is not the case with your child? Yes, there are some children who are habitual loners. There are also some children who need just one good friend. But what if your child wants to be with friends and yet cannot? What if she is constantly ignored and ridiculed by her friends and somewhere deep in your heart you know that the problem is with the sweet, little apple of your eye. You know that a major part of what she gets is what she deserves! What can you do under such circumstances?

☑ *Reality check*

The cause behind the effect
  Ask yourself:
  Is your child habitually bossy or pushy? Or worse, both?
  Is your child a sore loser?
  Does your child turn aggressive at the slightest provocation?
  Dose your child refuse to cooperate and share?
  Does your child expect too much from a friend?
  Is your child shy, withdrawn and non responsive?

The more 'yeses' the more lonely your child is likely to be. In these cases we have to be honest with ourselves.

Children are born with individual natures and temperaments. Social skills are those abilities that allow one to initiate and maintain positive social relationships with others. These are learnt in a healthy learning environment.

2.6 Raising social I.Q

From 'me' to 'we'...develop empathy

Empathy is essentially putting oneself in another's shoes and thinking from his point of view. When we can empathise, we don't judge, criticise or react negatively. Empathy changes the quality of our lives and the lives of those around us. Children who are more empathetic tend to develop better friendships and get along better with other children, with less fighting and more sharing.

For years, scientists didn't think young children could get beyond their own feelings or needs. Now we know they can. Research shows that during the second year of life, children begin to develop concern for other people, and often try to comfort them (Zahn-Waxler & Radke-Yarrow, 1990).

Practical ways to develop empathy

Be a good role model for empathy. Children are some of the best copycats around.

Model empathy

Research says: 'Parental modelling of empathetic, caring behaviour toward children—and toward others in the children's presence–is strongly related to children's development of prosocial attitudes and behaviour.' (Eisenberg-Berg and Mussen 1978; Kohn 1991; McDevitt, Lennon, and Kopriva 1991; and Zahn-Waxler, Radke-Yarrow, and King 1979).

If you can understand how someone may feel in a situation even though it is different from your own experience, children are likely to adopt these practices.

First and foremost show empathy to your children.

I had taken both my kids for their annual ophthalmologist visit. The younger one got her eyes checked and came out with a clean chit but the older one then nine, completely refused to sit in the chair. No amount of cajoling or scolding worked. We returned home without getting her eyes checked. I was disgusted with my unreasonable daughter. When I discussed the same with my husband he reminded me that I had been skipping my own blood sugar tests for fear of what the tests might show. Bang! I found myself in my daughter's shoes. I understood that even though my fear was unreasonable, it was still there, and that the fear was enough to override the wise and knowledgeable argument of a thirty year old mind. How could I blame the poor child? I went up to her the next day and told her, 'I am as scared as you are. What should we do now?' Without a thought she answered, 'Mom, both of us will go for our respective tests tomorrow. What has to be done, needs to be done.'

Carl Rogers, the famous clinical psychologist, talks about **genuineness** as a precondition to all empathy. To model empathy we must try and go behind the psyche of the 'other' and truly understand the 'why'. We teach our children empathy when we listen closely to what they have to say and when we avoid preaching, lecturing, or offering comments that may be experienced as judgemental and accusatory. Guiding questions that we pose for ourselves are, 'Would we want anyone to speak with us the way we are speaking with our children?' 'How would our children describe us at this moment? How would we hope they describe us?'

Give simple explanations on how others feel when hurt

Reasoning with children, even quite small ones, about the effects of their behaviour on others and the importance of sharing and being kind is effective in promoting empathy and pro-social behaviour

Research says: 'When children have hurt others or otherwise caused them distress, research supports the practice of giving explanations as to why the behaviour is harmful and suggestions for how to make amends. (Kohn 1991; and Zahn-Waxler, Radke-Yarrow, and King 1979).

Provide simple, clear explanations about how other people feel when they are sad or hurt, especially when your child has caused these feelings in another-

Rangesh feels hurt when you call him names.

Kshitsha is crying, you hurt Kshitsha when you hit her.

Be firm as you explain how these feelings work.

Use opportunities to practise understanding another's perspective. Use bedtime stories, movies, theaters, plays to engage your child in an exploration of feelings about the characters and their experiences in the story. You could put questions like, 'What would you do in that situation?', 'How do you think you'd feel?'.

Teach children to express their feelings

According to reports of Clarke 1984, 'Parents encouraging school-age children to discuss their feelings and problems is positively related to the development of empathy in those children'.

Parents who fail to show empathy to the range of emotions children express by telling them to quit crying, not to be angry, etc., teach children to avoid expressing, and perhaps even feeling certain emotions.

Praise their acts of empathy

Praise your child's acts of empathy—'Gee, I see that you shared with your brother because you are such a generous person, who enjoys making others feel good.' Reinforcing the positive traits increases the likelihood that the positive behaviours occur.

Helping children develop empathy through service

Jayesh Parikh

Jayesh Parikh, founder of Sony Entertainment Television in Asia and the executive chairman of MobiApps Inc., a wireless solutions company based in Virginia made a deal with his children aged, eighteen and twenty. They wanted to watch the soccer world cup in Germany. He promised them premier seats of all important matches and in return asked them for two weeks of their life. He came to Ahmedabad with his family for the two weeks for a service vacation at Gandhi Ashram.

Jayesh came from a lower middle class family and had worked his way up the corporate ladder through years of hard work, grit and sweat. He said, I had just Rs. 250 coming in every month to manage my fees, boarding and lodging for my undergrad in electrical engineering. For years every paise mattered, but my children have had things long before they even desired them. Jayesh wanted them to see the other side of life too...a life fraught with needs, challenges, inhuman living conditions and yet full of enthusiasm and goodness. He said, 'I wanted them to learn not only the value of money but experience the joy of giving and helping someone in need.'

After arriving in Ahmedabad this family of four worked diligently with the underprivileged through the NGO Manav Sadhna which runs from the Gandhi Ashram. They interacted with the slum dwellers and other NGOs day and night imparting their skills, distributing material goods and helping link the organisations with other global giants working in the same field. The two children taught English to the 7th, 8th, 9th, and 10th graders of Rampir Ka Tekra, the biggest slum of Gujarat. They read stories to them and bought clothes and books according to the specific needs of the children. On one rainy day, they gave in to a thirty-minute impromptu rain dance with the children of the Ashram. They even visited an institute for the mentally challenged and made bags and folders alongside them. His daughter Freya said, 'The visit really changed my perception of the mentally challenged. Most of them were entirely capable of making things and holding normal conversations. At the end of the day, they're people just like us, with likes, dislikes, certain abilities, sense of humor, etc. Its funny how human nature works and how it can be changed through experiences that we have.'

On the last day at the Ashram, all of them were given special shirts to wear that said, 'Be the change that you wish to see in the World'. Jayesh bhai said, 'I think the service vacation made a deep impression on Freya and Jesal. While it may not transform them or their value-system completely, I believe it was a good start to getting an awareness on the simplicity of the underprivileged children.' Jayesh Bhai's son Jesal is planning to take another service vacation in summer and this time for a longer period!

Schools in the US and Europe have social and community service projects as part of their school curriculum, but it is not so in our country. It then becomes even more important for us to schedule some social service activities for our children on a regular basis. During such interactions children invariably get into comparing their lifestyles against the less privileged and cannot but help see the stark difference. They almost always think of, 'what if they were in those shoes'. This not only brings a sense of gratitude for what they have but also compassion, a certain sense of humility and understanding, but above all empathy.

The sweeping change in my kids...

I once sent both my daughters to help make greetings cards for a local NGO here. The cards were mainly done by children who were residents of a slum and were aged between seven and fifteen. Most worked at the NGO after school to supplement the family's income. Both my children worked diligently alongside the rest, cutting and pasting flowers as instructed. At the end of their two hour session, they were handed thirty rupees each for their work. Both could not believe that for two hours of intense work all they got was thirty rupees! They had blown up the equivalent amount a myriad times in an extra scoop of ice cream without a thought! My older one asked her neighbouring boy Anand who was twelve as to what he would do with his money. Anand worked for four hours everyday and the money meant milk for his two year old sister and medicines for his sixty year old grandfather. Perplexed, she asked Anand that if he spent most of his after school hours working here, when does he play or study. His answer brought a subtle but permanent change in my child's perspective. After school and work Anand helped his mother with the household chores, ate his supper and then tagging his tiny sister on to his waist flocked every evening to the slum square to study under the road lamp and keep an eye on his sister too. Anand told my daughter, 'Baba comes home drunk every night and things get pretty violent. So both of us leave the house then and return only after he is asleep.'

This two hour experience changed the entire perspective of my then seven and ten year olds. Even today, a year later, when my children get tempted to buy a new Barbie, we try and see it through the eyes of Anand. Many a time when they complain of having to share the same stuff we think of Anand's little sister who is happy because she gets a glass of milk that day. It is not that they have not bought a single Barbie or any luxury item since then, but every time a new desire crops up, they do give a thought to the amount of happiness its fulfillment would really bring. Many a time they have also chosen to forgo a desired gift and used the money to fulfill the more basic needs of the less privileged.

Children should be taught to help the less fortunate with their time, money and service. They should be encouraged to hand out their overgrown clothes, books and toys to those in need. Giving materials of basic requirements to the homeless and needy, such as blankets, food and clothing, should be done at regular intervals. Children can bring a smile to others by just sharing their time. They should be encouraged to visit old peoples' homes, orphanages, homes of disabled and spend time interacting with the residents. They can read stories, play some instrument or share their travel experiences. Acts of kindness and charity are an excellent way to teach our youngsters empathy. But our children must see us involved in such activities too, otherwise it will come as preaching.

Jaya Bachchan

We know Jayaji as a stupendous actor, a parliamentarian, a strong woman; but how many of us know that she has been actively involved in social service for more than three decades now? When I asked her the reason for this well guarded secret, she said in a modest tone, 'What is there to talk about? All of us have our duties towards the community, I was just fulfilling mine.' This is the way she is, simple and unassuming, tough yet sensitive. In fact she has been taking both her children Abhishek and Shweta too, since they were as young as eight, to such visits with her. 'Maybe that exposure helped them stay rooted to reality. When they were growing up, I always told my children it didn't matter how they did in their exams. It's what they made of themselves as human beings that mattered. I remember when I was a child there were always a lot of red marks on the report card in some subjects, but the conduct column was always very good.'

Sachin Tendulkar

Sachin Tendulkar invites terminally ill children home for a quiet session through the Make a Wish Foundation. He says, 'These children want a few quality minutes with me and that's not possible if I meet them in front of dozens of people. As it's their last wish to meet me, I give each of them a T-shirt or a cap of mine. It makes their visit memorable and helps me and my family look within and appreciate how lucky we are, that God has blessed us. Interactions like that bring one back to reality... It ensures that we don't live in a dream land.'

Counter–productive to developing empathy–What not to do?

Researchers have also identified childrearing practices which are NEGATIVELY related to the development of empathy:

- Threats and/or physical punishments meted out in an attempt to improve children's behaviour are counterproductive (Clarke 1984; Eisenberg-Berg and Mussen 1978; Kohn 1991; and Zahn-Waxler, Radke-Yarrow, and King 1979).
- Inconsistent care (e.g., inconsistency in parents' reactions to children's emotional needs) and parental rejection/withdrawal in times of children's emotional needs are both associated with low levels of empathy on the parts of the children (Kestenbaum, Farber, and Sroufe 1989).
- Children from homes in which their fathers physically abuse their mothers have low levels of empathy. For example, they are typically unable to recognise the emotional states of other people and respond appropriately (Hinchey and Gavelek 1982).
- The provision of extrinsic rewards or 'bribes' to improve children's behaviour is counterproductive. As with other research on extrinsic rewards, researchers have found that providing payoffs for prosocial behaviour focuses attention on the reward rather than the reason for it and that the desired behaviours tend to lessen or disappear when the reward is withdrawn (Kohn 1991).

Keep in mind

- Give them the golden mantra of 'Do not do unto others what you do not want others to do unto you'. Ask them to treat others the way they would like to be treated.
- Don't expect empathy every time–young children are still learning how emotions work, and how people get along with others. Encourage empathy–but don't expect perfection.

2.7 Anger management!

Preet lost the WWF fight and began calling his opponent a 'Motu' and a hog. 'You eat like a pig the entire day, naturally you are heavier and so have won.'

Kirti broke Sneh's truck. Sneh gave him a whack on the head.

Anu pushed Priya and went first on the slide. Now Priya wanted to give a smack to Anu and settle scores.

Ankit was being picked on by his friends for his dirty shoes and he wanted to throw mud on theirs and get even.

Sapna was left out of the *daud-pakad* and she kept tripping the children who were playing.

Karishma called Karan names. Karan answered with his hands.

At times we feel that our child's anger is justified (when she is teased, taunted or hit) and then lashing out physically or verbally seems to be the natural outcome...after all the other child was the one who instigated it. It also brings instant results (the game or the taunting stops, the other child coils away in fear) and a feeling of satisfaction in your child (see I gave it back to you). But the question is, 'is it ok'? Is it healthy for either your child or the relationship?

We have to help children understand that though anger is a normal emotion under some circumstances and can even include feelings of revenge, acting out anger and hurting others is not okay. When a child uses his fists to settle differences, the conflict either escalates to where the other child responds with an even stronger punch or a push; or he backs away in fear, or is hurt and in tears. Whatever the consequence may be, our child is the ultimate loser. If the physical or verbal lashing happens ever too frequently the child's reputation may be scarred permanently and friends may actually keep away.

Our children need to understand that their actions will have consequences, which they must face. What choice do they have then?

They have the choice to consciously step in between anger and action (with our help) and to work towards conflict resolution in a positive, non-aggressive manner. But again they must see us actively living this.

If they have already retaliated physically or in any other manner they have the choice to apologise. They can look the friend into his eyes and say that they are really sorry. A promise that they would try to check their anger in future may also help embalm the emotional bruise.

Children should be taught to forgive and forget. They should not get into the habit of holding grudges against their peers. Hurt feelings, disappointment, and transgressions are an inevitable part of close friendship; a child who is unwilling or unable to forgive others will have difficulty forming friendships and special difficulty keeping close friendships.

Anger Management is dealt with in detail in the chapter 'Dealing with negatives'.

Don't ignore mean behaviour

Our children who seem perfectly noble to us and incapable of committing any wrong consciously, could easily be playing the brat or the bully's role behind our backs. Children, known for their politeness can be

surprisingly very cruel and mean to their weaker peers, especially if they are allowed to get away with it. Their targets are usually someone who is different from the others. Wearing glasses, consistently dressing out-of-fashion, having a distinctly different accent, being overweight or being very thin are all differences that can incite a bully's ridicule

Bullying could be verbal—usually involves name-calling, incessant mocking, and laughing at a child's expense; physical-hitting, pinching, pushing etc; **subtle**-isolating or excluding a child from activities (i.e., shunning the victim in the lunchroom or on school outings) or spreading rumors; racial through racial slurs, offensive gestures, or making jokes about a child's cultural traditions that could be harmful.

What do you do when you come to know of an incident where your child has been the bully? Worse, what if you know that your child is a habitual bully? Often we condone the wrong doings with a mild warning. After all your kid is not the victim, and then cross your fingers and pray that he improves.

But such a time precisely calls for you to be wiser and stronger beyond your love for the child. We have to empathize with the victimized child. Ask yourself, 'What must he/she have gone through?' 'What if your child would have been subjected to the same behaviour?' It is only when you see the situation from the victim's standpoint that you can be fair to your child. History is full of child prodigies who were brought to naught because the parents' love blinded their sense of wisdom.

Jaya Bachchan

Jaya Bachchan said, 'I have always told my children I do not care whether they get 80% or 60% in their academics or whether they make a runway success of their careers, but I want them first and foremost to be good, caring and considerate human beings.' Jayaji, a strict disciplinarian, never condoned a wrong doing in both her children. She said, 'A parent has to be cruel to be kind. To have a healthy love for your child is to do things which are good for the child, no matter how harsh or difficult it may seem. I have always done so and today I can proudly say that both Abhishek and Shweta are good human beings...and that is my reward!'

One does not need to thrash the child to take disciplinary actions. There are other ways.

Emphasise that bullying or any such misconduct is a serious problem and absolutely unacceptable. Make sure your child understands that such behaviour would have consequences at home (time outs, losing privileges etc., though do allow the child to earn the privileges back). In the same vein, do not tolerate cruelty between siblings.

2.8 Respect others!

Teach your child to respect others!

Prarit had no tolerance for the strange turban which always sat on Harvinder's head and so made frequent cracks at him.

Snehlata and Sudha taunted Tanya by calling her a sissy because she was scared to slide down the big water slide at the park.

Tanmay was waiting for Sharad to finish his bath and in the mean time fidgeted with everything around and messed up Tanmay's order of books about which he was very fastidious.

We have to teach our children that all kinds make this world. People may be different due to skin colour, race, culture, religion, or disabilities. They must respect the differences, rights and boundaries of other children.

> Some practical tips
> - Does your child monopolise conversations? Positive reminder: 'Listen to what others have to say and ask them questions about themselves'
> - Does your child talk too loudly or in a rude tone? Positive reminder: 'Practise turning down your volume. Be gentle in your tone'.
> - Does your child make too many negative comments or talk disparagingly? Positive reminder: 'Don't say anything if you can't think of something positive to say. Compliment others when they do well'.
> - Does your child get mad when others won't do things his way? Positive reminder: 'Be willing to listen to and try out other people's ideas'.
> - All these need to be adopted by parents too. We must walk our talk.

2.9 Build your child's social skills

Help your child develop these commonly needed social skills: Waiting one's turn, whether on the swing, playing with a toy or netsurfing.

Seeking attention in an appropriate manner
Cooperating with peers
Allowing others to talk without interrupting
Sharing things and tasks
Saying 'please' and 'thank you'
Complimenting others
Greeting others, waving
Accepting 'No' for an answer
Making eye contact and smiling.

2.10 Take practical steps to help foster young friendships

Provide children with opportunities to play with peers. In previous generations, children learned social skills by hanging out with the kids in the neighbourhood and by interacting with large and extended families. Families today are generally smaller and more transient, so children have fewer siblings and relatives with whom to practise their social skills. Most children today have many structured activities and lessons, leaving them less time to simply play with others. These are contributing to highly individualistic, and sometimes selfish children. It is harder for today's children to learn through hands-on experience how to get along with other children. Try to arrange opportunities for your child to play with peers, so he can learn how to get along with others. These playdates can be held in one's home, a neighbourhood park, an ice-cream or a lunch out, an excursion to a local museum etc. Think of ways to incorporate new children into existing groups: have friends over, celebrate birthdays, let children call each other on the phone.

2.11 Share your confidence

Children often have trouble with perspective. If someone doesn't invite them to a birthday party, they react like it's the worst thing in the world. If kids are mean to them, they assume that this will always be the case. As adults, we know that circumstances change, that people grow, and that there's a big wide world outside of this year's elementary school class. So, when your child comes home crying because 'everyone' was mean to him or her, listen, empathise, try to understand your child's point of view, but also express your confidence that, with help, your child will be able to find a way to deal with the situation. For example, if a friend was uncaring or made an insensitive remark you might say, 'Maybe your friend was having a bad day' rather than 'She was mean to you on purpose because she really doesn't like you.'

Let your child know that you feel friendships are important and worth the effort. Be a friend to other adults.

Read stories or books to your child that highlight children's friendships. Ask your child what he or she thinks and what ideas the story teaches about being a friend.

Show your child that it is important to care for friends-to help them in bad times, to visit them when they are ill, to be their strength when they are weak.

Shekher Sen

Shekhar Sen, a talented singer, music composer, lyricist and the actor-director of famous monoplays like Kabeer, Vivekananda and Tulsi, places a premium on friendship and friends. His profession entails a lot of travelling and he has taken his plays to many cities in India and abroad. He said, 'My father always told me that which ever city I go to I must make sure that I make at least four friends. The moment I have friends in a city it will feel like home. The city will become mine and I will not be unhappy or lonely. And if God forbid, something tragic should happen at least I will get to my final rest on the shoulders of four friends rather than complete strangers.' Shekhar has followed his father's advice and says, 'Every word of his advice has been true. I have truly felt at home even at the farthest corners of the globe because I knew my "priyajan" are sitting in the audience, watching me with love in their heart and a smile on their face.' Shekar has decided to give the same advice to his ten year old son. He said, 'Many a time I team up with my son and his friends and we go for a movie or play cricket together.'

> 'The world would be so lonely, in sunny hours or gray. Without the gift of friendship, to help us every day.'
>
> – HILDA BRETT FARR

Young Naturalists

....

To see a world in a grain of sand
And a heaven in a wild flower,
Hold infinity in the palm of your hand
And eternity in an hour.

—William Blake

We instinctively turn to outdoor activities and nature as a way of relaxing and enhancing our well-being. Nature soothes and nurtures. Nature fulfills and motivates. Nature whispers and commands.

Are you listening?

The few times that we did, it left us in complete awe.

We have a Hibiscus plant in our garden. Every fortnight a flower blooms on it—big, bright and tender. Through the day it smiles with the sun and dances with the wind, but as evening approaches, it starts closing down. The morning after, it withers completely and by evening it falls and becomes one with the earth again. The flower comes to life only for a day, yet it does so in its full splendour. What if we too live our life, however short, to its fullest...?

We went to a rocky beach and saw the spread of the majestic ocean and the rocks alongside—carved, sculpted and shaped by the water. Water is so soft, rock so hard. Yet, as the water flows over it every day, for years; the rock gives in. It takes the shape which the water commands. Our problems are so colossal and we are so small, yet if we persist...

We saw small bits of grass popping out from concrete pavements through small cracks. It left us wondering—however, impossible things may look, there is always an opening...

Even the most reasonable of us maintain that we are somehow better endowed because we are richer, better placed. But when it rains the pure water showers on the supposedly more endowed and the less endowed equally. Nature plays no favourites...

We saw a tree bare of all leaves in the cold winter months. We thought that its chapter was over. But three months passed, spring set in and the tree was back to its green majesty once again-full of leaves, flowers, birds and life. What if we too had the conviction that however difficult things are right now, things will not be so for ever. Remember, 'this too shall pass'.

We saw an army of ants lugging a fly which was at least ten times the ant's size. They organised themselves around it, lifted it on their frail feelers and carried it to quite a distance. Their teamwork and perseverance were phenomenal. What if, we too were consistent, organised and focused...

Spider webs are delicate, yet very strong. A rainbow colours the entire sky. Oysters take in a grain of sand and open up with a pearl. Innumerable stars shine across the infinite sky. Clouds take up new shapes with every passing moment. The wind makes the trees dance with unhindered passion. Water, without a hint of ego, changes its form according to the dictates of the sun and the wind. When we see a caterpillar turn into a butterfly, a flower turn into a fruit, we experience the alchemy of nature...we touch it and become gold ourselves.

Architect Mr B.V. Doshi said, 'I built my house with borrowed money, yet I bought a plot which would allow a small little garden. I wanted my children to grow up amidst plants, trees, birds and the open sky. I can say that

> "Nature is an endless combination and repetition of a very few laws."
>
> — Ralph Waldo Emerson

subconsciously they have absorbed nature. Even today most of them sit here for hours at a time, in quiet thought. Nature is their first and most important school.'

3.1 Natural advantage

A growing body of documented medical science research shows that nature has positive, restorative and regenerative healing effects, especially in children. It leads to better psychological well-being, superior cognitive functioning, better social skills, fewer physical ailments and speedier recovery from illness.

Cognitive advantages:

Children in contact with nature score higher on tests of concentration and self-discipline. The greener the environment, the better the scores (Faber Taylor et al. 2002, Wells 2000). Exposure to natural environments improves children's cognitive development by improving their awareness, reasoning and observational skills (Pyle 2002).

The attention-restoration theory—Environmental psychologists at the University of Michigan, Stephen and Rachel Kaplan have developed the attention-restoration theory. Kaplans have taken their inspiration from philosopher and psychologist William James, who, in 1890, described two kinds of attention: directed and involuntary. In the early 1970s, the Kaplans studied the impact of a range of activities. They found too much directed attention (this could include computer tasks, homework, studying for a test) leads to what they call 'directed-attention fatigue,' marked by impulsive behaviour, agitation, irritation, and inability to concentrate. Directed-attention fatigue occurs because neural inhibitory mechanisms become overstressed by blocking competing stimuli. Stephen Kaplan explained in *Monitor on Psychology*, 'If you can find an environment where the attention is automatic, you allow directed attention to rest. And that means an environment that's strong on fascination.' According to the Kaplans Nature is an ideal example of such an environment and can be the most effective source of such restorative relief. People don't have to head for the woods to enjoy nature's restorative effects, the Kaplans emphasise. Even a glimpse of nature from a window helps.

Creativity enhancement

Nature affords unabashed freedom for a child. He can run, shout, scream, invent, discover and build. Nature provides the best playground for open-ended, timeless play that inspires wonder, awe, and the chance to marvel and imagine. Natural habitats are grounds upon which a child can be the architect. Nature's artefacts such as pinecones, stones, seashells, leaves, twigs, feathers, fossils do not come with a 'how to use' manual, children are at complete liberty to devise any use that their imaginative minds can conjure.

When children play in natural environments, their play is more diverse with imaginative and creative play that fosters language and collaborative skills (Faber Taylor et al. 1998, Fjortoft 2000, Moore & Wong 1997).

Nature helps children develop powers of observation and creativity and instills a sense of peace and being at one with the world (Crain 2001).

Early experiences with the natural world have been positively linked with the development of imagination and the sense of wonder (Cobb 1977, Louv 1991). Wonder is an important motivator for life long learning (Wilson 1997).

Stress buster

Nancy Wells, assistant professor in the Department of Design and Environmental Analysis at Cornell University, embarked on a study of 281 children in grades three to five, comparing the 'naturalness' of their home settings with the impact of stressful events such as bullying, peer pressure and parental divorce. 'Naturalness' was measured by the visibility of nature around the home, the composition of the yard and the number of plants in the house, while stress was calculated by measurements of urinal cortisol (a hormone the body releases when under stress) and parental reports of children's psychological wellbeing. The results: exposure to nature increases a child's resilience to stress – and the more stressful the event the more marked the effect.

Physical benefits

Nature is essentially outdoors and outdoors offers the expanse for children to hike, run, jump, do somersaults and play sports. A child in the open will be in continuous movement and that is bound to bring physical benefits. According to research (Fjortoft 2001, Grahn et al. 1997), 'Children who play regularly in natural environments show more advanced motor fitness, including coordination, balance and agility, and they are sick less often.'

According to Nowak 2004, 'A decrease in children's time spent outdoors is contributing to an increase of children's myopia.'

Social development

Social-emotional development is well served by natural areas.

Play in a diverse natural environment reduces or eliminates anti-social behaviour such as violence, bullying, vandalism and littering, as well reduces absenteeism (Coffey 2001, Malone & Tranter 2003, Moore & Cosco 2000).

Research at a primary schoolyard in Berkeley, CA, that changed part of its asphalt into meadow with woods, streams, ponds, flowers showed that children have more positive social relationships in such areas and more creative play (Moore & Wong, 1997).

Play in a diverse natural environment reduces or eliminates bullying (Malone & Tranter 2003).

An editorial published in a special issue of the British Medical Journal (November 26, 2005) claims that ecotherapy—restoring health through contact with nature—could be beneficial for children with emotional and behavioural problems. The BMJ points to a number of studies that show ecotherapy can help these kids overcome social isolation.

For girls...

According to Andrea Faber Taylor, a postdoctoral researcher in the department of natural resources and environmental sciences, the positive influence of nature on concentration may be more pronounced for girls (ages 6 to 9) than for boys. He said, 'For the girls, we found that the greener the view that was available from their apartment window, the better they were able to concentrate, refrain from acting impulsively and delay gratification. The greener views translated into better self-discipline.'

According to researchers, on an average, the greener a girl's view from home, the better she concentrates, the less she acts impulsively and the longer she can delay gratification. This helps her do better in school, handle peer pressure and avoid dangerous, unhealthy or problem behaviours. She is more likely to behave in ways that foster success in life.

Helps in ADHD–Attention-Deficit Hyperactivity Disorder

Attention-deficit hyperactivity disorder (ADHD) is the name of a group of behaviours found in many children and adults. People who have

ADHD have trouble paying attention in school, at home or at work. They may be much more active and/or impulsive than what is usual for their age. These behaviours contribute to significant problems in relationships, learning and behaviour. For this reason, children who have ADHD are sometimes seen as being 'difficult' or as having behaviour problems.

Groundbreaking work from University of Illinois researchers has shown that exposure to ordinary natural settings may effectively reduce attention-deficit symptoms in children. In a 2004 study published in the American Journal of Public Health, the laboratory found that children as young as five showed a significant reduction in ADHD symptoms when they engaged with nature.

Says Richard Louv, a child-advocacy expert and the author of Last Child in the Woods: Saving Our Children From Nature-Deficit Disorder (*Algonquin, 2005*), 'Direct experience in nature may be as important to children as good nutrition and adequate sleep.'

Nature connections...

When a traveller asked Wordsworth's servant to show him her master's study she indicated the garden saying, 'Here is his library, his study is out of doors.'

Science fiction author and futurist Arthur C. Clarke's budding cosmic consciousness was awakened by childhood bicycle rides under starry skies.

Picasso is reported to have said: 'Everyone tries to understand art, why don't they try to understand the song of a bird?'

Henry David Thoreau wrote in *Walden*, 'I went to the woods because I wished to live deliberately, to front only the essential facts of life, and see if I could not learn what it had to teach, and not, when I came to die, discover that I had not lived.'

Stuart concluded that nature is 'the perennial source of happiness.'

I asked Jatin Das, a renowned Indian painter, 'What is your idea of perfect happiness?' He said 'Plants'.

The 'Nature-bond'–Hemant Trivedi

Hemant Trivedi, the fashion icon of India, has always been a nature lover. His home is alive with various types of flaura and fauna, tended and watered solely by him. To Hemant who is still a bachelor his plants are his babies, companions and confidantes. Six years ago Hemant met with a near fatal car accident. For a month he was in a coma hanging between life and death. After the miraculous recovery from the coma he spent another month in intensive care and returned home on crutches after spending two hellish months at the hospital. He had no left-right eye coordination; his body was literally sewn up in places so that it didn't fall apart. Every little movement hurt, even lying down without budging an inch was painful. However, Hemant, not one to give up, faced the situation head-on.

His parents flew in from Australia to help him recover, but that was an even bigger strain on him. He said, 'They had their own life in Australia but here they were staying in the guest room trying to nurse me. I told them, "Here I am trying to get better, trying to get my brain in shape and I am worrying about the two of you as well. I have been on my own for long and I will be able to handle this. Please go home".'

First his father left. Though it was very tough to convince his mother, she too eventually gave in and left for Australia. Hemant said, 'Now that I was solely by myself, I had the Herculean task of managing my daily life and that is when I saw five images of one object. I had to consciously remind my right leg to take a step after the left leg had moved, for if I would not do so, my left leg would take another step forward and I would lose my balance and hit the ground. To make it back on the legs too, it was just me.'

Hemant particularly remembers a morning when he was walking towards the plants with a bowl full of water, balancing precariously on his broken and splintered arm. About six feet away from the plants, he lost balance and fell. He lay on the floor, completely wet, tired and in intense pain. He said, 'I asked myself, is it not better to just keep down there and wait for it all to end? But then I told myself, that if I keep lying like this and do not get up, I die, and if I die my plants die. How can I let my children die simply because I have the option to not fight back?' Hemant got back onto his feet, limped all the way to the sink, refilled the bowl and again made his way towards his babies...

☑ *Reality check*

What is your child's interaction with nature?

Your child may be an expert on 'endangered species' but does he have the time to watch the play of squirrels or the architecture of birds in his backyard?

Your child may have written pages on the perils of deforestation but can he identify trees and plants in his locality?

Your child may have encyclopaedic details on the planets and heavenly bodies, but does he peer at the night sky and form his own constellations?

3.2 The estrangement

Intense urbanisation and industrialisation have deprived children of outdoor, in particular nature-based, experiences. The experience of childhood and the social construction of the family are not what they used to be. Both have gone through a series of profound changes as a result of the emergence of postmodern culture. The contemporary child's exposure to nature is getting more and more impoverished.

For five thousand years we lived close to nature, but for the last three to four decades things have changed rapidly. We have taken the fast track from a rural to a highly urbanised culture. According to UN-Habitat, 60% of the world's population will be living in cities by 2030. Urban growth and suburban sprawl have swallowed up vast pieces of open land. Cities have become concrete jungles of glass, tar, steel bars and artificial lights. They are characterised by congested and densely clustered housing and commercial complexes with very little green space. Parks and open fields which do exist are neatly

manicured with 'do not touch' signs posted everywhere. There are no rough edges to enjoy nature, no trees to be climbed, and no rocks to be unearthed. Cecily Maller of Deakin University, after a study on the health benefits of contact with nature said, 'Never have humans spent so little time in physical contact with animals and plants, and the consequences are unknown.'

Even in areas where kids do have access to green spaces, they're accessing outdoors less. The lure of technology is contributing to this estrangement from nature. Information is increasingly imparted through books, technology and media. Their sense of wonder and curiosity is satisfied through the T.V. and internet. The virtual is replacing the real. They know more about exotic animals on Discovery Channel or National Geographic, than frogs, snails, squirrels, birds, worms, and bugs that live outside their windows.

In one study, approximately 60% of children reported that they had seen more animals on television and movies than they had in the wild. Only 40% of rural children reported they had ever spent more than half an hour in a forest, and less than 20% of urban children have seen wildlife in a natural setting. (Nabhan and Trimble 1998)

Preferences too have changed. Children can more easily relate to adventure on a computer or T.V. screen, than adventure with nature. Instead of discovering a whole universe of habitat under a rock children prefer to find better internet sites for racing games or a virtual dress-up Barbie site. Instead of reaching out in the open and making social connections they chat via e-mail and SMS. According to research, Chipeniuk 1995, T.V., nature documentaries, National Geographic and other nature T.V. channels and environmental fundraising appeals are conditioning children to think that nature is exotic, awe-inspiring and in far, far away, places they will never experience. Children are losing the understanding that nature exists in their own backyards and neighbourhoods.

Parental fears of traffic, crime, falling off tress, being bitten by bugs, flies (the omnipotent malaria mosquitoes) also keep kids indoors and away from nature. The current educational system too does almost nothing to reconnect children to earth and its roots.

Besides, longer and more strenuous school hours, coupled with tuitions and co-curricular activities is leaving children with hardly any free and leisure time to enjoy nature, even if it does exist in the close vicinity. While many children used to walk to school, interacting with neighbourhood yards or vacant lots, now many, if not most, children are driven to school. Overall childhood culture has changed. Children today go to multiplexes instead of parks, to shopping malls instead of bike rides, prefer astro-turf to green lawns, videos instead of games outdoors and go to theme parks instead of nature parks. They cuddle stuffed pets and their homes adorn artificial flowers and plants. They hate slugs, sweat and dirty clothes more than they love the openness, greenery and the sunsets. Ubiquitous air-conditioning has made homes into comfort cocoons and they keep indoors. For most children growing up in cities today, nature is simply not relevant.

3.3 Fall-outs of lost contact with nature

Research too suggests that a connection to nature is biologically innate. Our need for nature is deeply ingrained, it is a biological craving.

> To forget how to dig the earth and to tend the soil is to forget ourselves.
>
> — Mahatma Gandhi

Biophilia

Edward O. Wilson, a Harvard University entomologist, coined the term 'biophilia', referring to humans' 'love of living things'—our innate affinity with nature. He describes biophilia as the 'innate tendency to focus on life and lifelike processes.' In his book *Biophilia* he says, 'We are human in good part because of the particular way we affiliate with other organisms....they offer the challenge and freedom innately sought. To the extent that each person can feel like a naturalist, the old excitement of the untrammelled world will be regained. I offer this as a formula of re-enchantment to invigorate poetry and myth....'

Biophobia: The Aversion to Nature

However, if this human natural attraction to nature is not given opportunities to be exercised and flourished during the early years of life, the opposite, biophobia, an aversion to nature, may develop. Biophobia ranges from discomfort in natural places to active scorn for whatever is not man-made, managed or air-conditioned. Biophobia is also manifest in the tendency to regard nature as nothing more than a disposable resource.

Overall well-being suffers

The loss of children's contact with the natural world negatively impacts the growth and development of the whole child. Disconnected from nature children suffer, psychologically, emotionally and physically. Depression, obesity and attention deficit disorder are some of the problems which have been directly linked to a lack of interaction with the natural world. Disassociated with nature kids lose the ability to focus and pay attention. Many report a sense of atrophy. Says Michael Gurian, a family therapist and author of *The Wonder of Boys*, 'Neurologically, human beings haven't caught up with today's over-stimulating environment. The brain is strong and flexible, so 70 to 80 percent of kids adapt fairly well. But the rest do not.'

The environmental reason

When children do not connect with nature, it can become a fearful place.

For this generation of technocrats it is not just that nature and outdoors is 'uncool' but that it doesn't exist. And children cannot love what they do not know, they cannot miss what they have not experienced. According to Nabhan & St. Antoine, 1993, 'When children do not play in natural habitats, they tend not to know about the plants and animals that live there'. Does not knowing lead to not caring? Pyle too elaborates on the cycle of disaffection that is triggered by this extinction of experience. He says, 'As cities metastasizing suburbs forsake their natural diversity, and their citizens grow more removed from personal contact with nature, awareness and appreciation retreat. This breeds apathy toward environmental concerns and, inevitably, further degradation of common habitat, leading to the loss of rarities. People who care, conserve; people who don't know, don't care. What is the extinction of the condor to a child who has never seen a wren?' It's a loss that, in some ways, is too large to see but one that has profound implications.

3.4 Close the kid-nature gap

We have to set our children free again. We have to reconnect them to the joys of the natural world, make efforts for them to be out in the open, something which naturally came to us when we were young. But for our children this has to be an intentional, conscious choice involving time, effort and perseverance. Being amidst nature has to become natural again!

The wonders of nature are not confined to exotic places which we view on National Geography or Discovery channels. They can be found even in packed and crowded cities, all that is required is a slowing down of our pace so as to allow nature to take over our senses even if it is for just a few minutes everyday. Every inner city has its nature parks, botanical gardens, natural habitat centers. University areas are almost always the green pockets which can be accessed. One can go to sea coasts, riversides and streams. An hour's drive can lead to the suburbs of any city which offers more green and open fields. If nothing else every city has its expanse of a vast sky full of birds, clouds and stars. A sparrow can be as interesting as a bird of Paradise, the squirrel can amaze with its liveliness and playfulness, the calls of frogs and peacocks on a rain-soaked day can reach our ears. Even in large urban areas, we are surrounded by animals, birds, insects and plants; we just have to open our eyes and ears to them. The father or mother who constantly points out to a child these lovely things and tells the small, intimate facts about them, and creates an interest in them, is giving a clue to what later on will mean a great blessing. There are resources and mediums within every state and locality, though there is no one-stop source.

Shun your educationist's cap

A woodpecker perched on the frail branch of a young gulmohar tree. Shanay watched in fascination as the thin branch easily bore the weight of this beautiful feathered guest. His mother walked into the garden and immediately tried to capitalise on his attention, 'Those

are babblers, they love to eat earthworms and are almost always grey in colour....' Shanay now struggled to remember their feeding habits, his wonder fading as information caught up with him...

When with nature, have no agenda for your child except a rich contact with the world through smell, touch, sight, and sound. Control your impulse to educate the child on to identifying flowers, plants, soils and birds. Let them be explorers. Let them discover what excites them, allow them the luxury of being awed and inquisitive. Technical information isn't so important at this stage. In his *Naturalist*, Pellegrino University Professor Emeritus at Harvard University and naturalist E.O. Wilson states: 'Hands-on experiences at the critical age, not systemic knowledge, is what counts in the making of a naturalist. Better to be an untutored savage for a while, not to know the names or anatomical detail. Better to spend long stretches of time just searching and dreaming.'

Curiosity and fascination will automatically lead to knowledge acquisition.

Tarana, a micro-biologist said in relation to her children, 'As a parent, my role is that of a gatekeeper. I provide safe places and ample time for my children to explore. I am not an expert or a naturalist but I am curious and interested and that has kept my love for nature intact. If I could just pass on that love without any jargon of information I will be happy.'

Keep out the sirens of doom

Do not talk about endangered species, pollution, oil spills, acid rains, ozone layer depletion and other nature perils to children because they are not old enough to handle them. Says educator David Boel, 'If we want children to flourish, we need to give them time to connect with nature and love the Earth before we ask them to save it. No tragedies before fourth grade.' According to him children younger than eleven years are not quite ready to truly understand the bigger picture without getting overwhelmed. According to Kellert too, children's emotional and affective values of nature develop earlier than their abstract, logical and rational perspectives. According to research, Coffey 2001, 'We need to allow children to develop their biophilia, their love for the Earth, before we ask them to save it. Rather than books and lectures, nature itself is children's best teacher.'

For children even small is big

Children perceive things differently from adults. For them a moment can be eternity, a leaf the universe. A potted plant can be as fascinating as a nine-yard garden, a beetle as interesting as a tiger. They do not need the expanse of a sea coast to enjoy water, a rain bath can be for them as much fun. In our bid to provide for the real woods, rolling mountains, open fields and at least an entire day to experience it all, we miss out on the small pockets of time and nature which exist in our own backyards. To a child even fifteen minutes of nature is an experience, and that is something which we can carve out, however time-strapped we may be.

PROJECT NATURE

3.5 Gardening

Whether you live on ten acres, or on the tenth floor, you can introduce your children to a life-long interest in gardening. Children are natural gardeners. They're curious, like to learn by doing, and love to play in the dirt. Digging holes is one thing that seems to hold endless fascination.

If you do have a green patch or a backyard, convert it into a kitchen or a flower garden for your child. Help the child plant seeds of his favourite vegetables, fruits or plants. Give your child his own garden bed, keep it small though. Set him up for success. His plot should have the best soil and light. Choose native plants, which can easily grow in your climate and soil conditions. Encourage his enthusiasm by planting seeds that mature quickly and are large enough for a child to handle easily. Children lose interest if nothing seems to be happening, so seeds that germinate quickly are great. If you plant them near the edge of a clear plastic cup you can see them germinate even before they break the surface of the soil. Favourites are beans (broad or runner), which will germinate in three to four days in a warm place.

Give him good tools, not cheap plastic ones. Let the child be responsible for the upkeep of his plant. He will not only enjoy picking the vegetables or fruits right off the plant but the taste of a truly fresh just plucked vegetable can be an experience in itself.

Play a game of 'Spot a gardener's friend', by making a list of helpful creatures (for example, bees, butterflies, ladybirds, frogs and hedgehogs) and see who can spot the most. Not only will they love the competition, this will also help them learn that bugs and animals are precious and not to be harmed.

My daughter once planted tomato seeds in our small kitchen garden and tended to it everyday. Six weeks later small tomatoes appeared. When the green tomatoes turned red we had a tomato festival night at home. Sanaya prepared a salad with mint leaves and I prepared pasta. I did not have to goad them that night to finish their veggies, in fact we ran out of all preparation with tomatoes.

For those staying in apartments a container garden in small pots on the windowsill or patios can suffice. Children can cultivate herbs in a pot and eat the harvest! Children also seem to be attracted to cacti as the great variety of shapes and sizes makes them fun to collect.

Besides cacti subsist on very little tending. Seasonal flower plants will also make for great indoor gardening. Planting certain flora (bushes, flowers, herbs), will attract all manner of fauna (birds, butterflies, bugs). Plant some parsley, and a black swallowtail may decide to come visit, milkweed will pretty much guarantee a busy butterfly garden. Gardens, both backyard plots or pots on the patio, can become great classrooms where children can observe the cycle of life firsthand.

3.6 Nature walks

Above all, do not lose your desire to walk.
Every day I walk myself into a state of well being,
and walk away from every illness.
I have walked myself into my best thoughts,
and I know of no thought so burdensome
that one cannot walk away from it.

SØREN KIERKEGAARD

Take children on nature walks. Local parks, nature trails, or even your own back yard or playground can be a storehouse of natural wonders. All you need to do is go outdoors and observe what you see! Mornings can be especially fun. In the early dawn light, our vision feels sharp, hearing is keen, nerves calm and sensitivity at its peak. Nature can offer a sense of being deeply and entirely alive, and in touch with something bigger and sacred.

Allow children time to stand and appreciate the myriad-hued flowers and their bright winged visitors, the bees and the butterflies. Let them observe the dew on a spider web, direct their attention to trees, which is an entire eco-system by itself. They can go on a bug patrol and watch the animals and insects wake up. They can look under leaves, dead tree barks, ponds and streams and check out interesting things with a magnifying glass. They'll be amazed at the scurry of activity under a seemingly quiet exterior.

During winters one can go on a hibernating bug hunt! Shine a light under barks looking for hibernating lady bugs, spiders, butterflies, or cocoons. Check out holes in trees, look on branch tips for sleeping moth eggs. You can also go on a 'wanted dead or alive' walk and search for living things (insects, animals, plants) and once-living things—keep a journal or collect specimens. Distinguish between live and dead plant material and inanimate things, like stones or sand.

'The world,' says Jim Cummings, founder of EarthEar Records, 'is constantly performing for you.' Listen to nature's symphony with your children. Find a quiet spot and ask your child to close his eyes. Listen to the sounds of nature with him—call of the birds, buzzing of the insects, chirping of crickets, rustling and crackling of leaves, rain dripping from the tip of the leaves, gentle humming of the breeze, soft sound of flowing water can make nature come alive as our hearing takes center stage. Ask your child, did he hear better with his eyes closed, than what he usually does? Children can also differentiate between 'nature sounds' and 'non-nature sounds'. Try this in several different habitats such as in a field, near a pond and in a forest and compare the kinds and numbers of sounds heard.

Children can breathe the scent of fresh grass, smell the earth and the fresh air without fumes and carbon emissions. Wet the underside of your child's nose with a small wet sponge as this improves his sense of smell. Find familiar smells such as flowers to try, then go on to other things like rubbing a leaf between your fingers and smelling or scratching a pine needle. Also try moss, bark, pitch or grabbing a handful of leafy soil etc.

They can walk barefoot and feel the fresh dew. Take children on a microclimate walk. On a hot day, walk in sunny and shady areas, waterside areas, or breezy areas, and notice how the temperature is lower in the shade and even lower in shady areas with trees, or with a breeze off the water.

You could also approach your nature walk by having the kids ask you questions about what they observe. If you don't know the answers to their questions, it can be a fun activity to search for the answers.

Equip them with tools like a camera, magnifying glass, pencil and a notebook pencil in which they can record their findings, if they so desire.

My nature walk!

I was vacationing at Diu and went for a long walk on the beach at dawn one day. The lambent ocean shone with a delicate bridal orange, shying away from the gaze of the sky so open and direct. The sun, an orange ball till now,

> 'Follow your bliss, all else will follow'.
>
> – JOSEPH CAMPBELL

was rapidly acquiring its brilliant bright yellow with every passing moment. The breeze, light and swift, whispered through the trees and plants and made them dance to its whims. The early birds with their chirping provided the lyrics for the dance music. Nature was rejoicing at the beautiful morning, and I was more than keen to join in the celebration. I received my welcome in the cool soothing water of the ocean, which made a dash for my feet every now and then. The heavy, commanding sound of the waves enveloped the surroundings with its magnificence grandiose and I submitted to it by closing my eyes and listening to nothing else. There was beauty, happiness and contentment everywhere. I walked for about 100 meters and then turned back. I noticed my footprints, so distinct on the vast beach, and that filled me with a strange sense of pride. I now concentrated on making better impressions on the sand. I walked with calculated strides to leave an even gap between steps, tried to regulate the pressure on the ground with every step to bring consistency in the depth that I created...lost was the sun, lost were the waves, lost was all the beauty. After taking those seriously monitored steps I turned back once again to marvel at the impressions I had made. A big wave which untill now had been my ally tingling me, bringing me happiness, had suddenly turned foe as it took upon the ruthless destruction of my work of art, cruelly effacing all my efforts. Not to be deterred with one disappointment I tried to make a fresh set of prints, only to be washed away again. I walked a little farther up the beach to create another set; a larger wave rendered my latest work to the same fate as others. I concluded, 'if my work is so momentary against the grandeur of life, why not just concentrate on enjoying that grandeur'. I went back to the beauty of life. Familiar sensations of happiness, contentment and joy came rushing back'. Just then I spotted a beautiful shell on the ground and bent down to pick it up as a gift for my daughter and there spread out before me was my foot print, glistening, laughing, lying on the sand, one with nature. I had learnt my lesson, 'follow your bliss, all else will follow'.

3.7 Bringing nature indoors

Nature can be brought indoors for children to enjoy every hour. Tree stumps can be used for sitting especially in the children's room, wooden flooring can connect one immediately to nature, tree branches can be suspended from the ceiling. Set against a simple backdrop, curly branches become art. Potted plants can be placed in corners. Ankita filled up her child's antique wagon with potted plants and wheeled it right next to the sofa in the living area. One can even encourage children to make a creative display of seasonal flowers and leaves. My daughter brings just one flower with a few leaves and places it in a small glass on the dining table once every three to four days. Growing fragrant herbs such as lavender, rosemary, and lemon in small pots, especially on the bathroom sills and the living areas, keeps the indoors fresh with natural aromas.

Seasonal fruits can be decorated in a basket and placed on the dining table. One can create small water bodies in earthen pots and float petals and leaves. Small tabletop fountains can also be created at home. The gentle sound of trickling water is soothing and the principles of Feng Shui say that fountains create good energy. Stones, rocks, pebbles, seashells can be placed in bowls or in a ring around a vase.

You can simply bring in nature by drawing the curtains and allowing the sunlight in.

You can give your child a big empty jar (Bournvita, jam, honey) for him to put dirt in. Then send him on a mission to collect ants that can live in the new glass home. Immediately your youngster can watch the ants digging, making little chambers and compartments. He can keep them for months at a time.

Set up a bird feeder in the backyard or the balcony sill. Different types of birds prefer different types of feeders and food, so find out what birds are common in the area where you live and help your child put up the feeders that will suit them best. If you're lucky enough to live in an area populated by hummingbirds, hang brightly coloured sugar-water feeders to attract them. Show your

My Little Creatures

child how to clean the feeders and refill them every few days. You can attract even more birds by adding a birdbath, which can be as simple as a large plant saucer filled with an inch or so of water. Setting up a small aquarium is another way of bringing nature right into our living rooms.

Rearranging nature-finds is children's unique earth work.

3.8 Bird watching

By introducing our children to the world of birds we can give them a lifetime ticket to the theater of nature. We went for a day picnic to Nal Sarovar, a bird sanctuary in Gujarat. It was a chilly January morning and we set out at 5 am from our homes for a tête-à-tête with those beautiful winter guests. We reached the designated spot just before sunrise and in front of us lay the huge still expanse of the lake. At the other edge of the lake we could just about make out the still outline of the flocks in the twilight. As the sky became brighter, movements on the other side stepped up. We could literally see the still outline expanding as the massive group started spreading their wings. The morning air resonated with their chirps and then suddenly one majestic flock took flight. Thousands of birds took to the air, their wings going flip flop in complete harmony. We held our breath at the magnificent sight, but this was just the beginning of the forty minute panorama. One after the other, the groups took to the air and the sky became a riot of colours. Pink with flamingoes, white with gulls, black with coots...

This picnic took place about five years ago. My elder daughter Aishwarya was then five, Sanaya only two; but for all of us it was as if all our senses had somehow become one. We watched, heard, felt and smelt those beautiful migrants who take themselves so lightly. That was almost five years ago, but even today we just have to close our eyes and go back to that cold January morning...and the panorama begins afresh.

Bird watching can be a very soothing and joy-filled adventure. Their chirpings, flight, varied colours are a treat to the senses. Besides, these feathered aviators can teach us a lesson or two in team work and discipline, perseverance and chirpiness. Their ingenious nest building, infinite patience with their little ones, their rhythm and complete harmony with nature, their journeys running into thousands of miles on such tiny wings can serve as life lessons.

Birds are all around us, perched on telephone wires, branches, rocky ledges, lawns, just about anything that might serve as a landing site. Offering to feed them bread crumbs or chapattis may tempt some to come closer. Birdbaths can be easily set up which will ensure their visit everyday. Early morning and late afternoon are usually the best times for observation, because most birds are then active and singing.

Besides, bird watching is an inexpensive activity. All one needs is a pair of interested eyes and ears. Children, however, do need some training in careful observation as bird watching calls for a little discipline. It requires patience, stealth and quiet. Once a genuine interest in bird watching is created we can equip them with a good pair of binoculars and an illustrated bird-book. We can take them for bird watching vacations. Bharatpur Wildlife Sanctuary, Ranthambore national park, Kumarakom bird sanctuary are a few places in India which boast of a wide variety of birds. Children can observe their migration patterns, study their different habitats. Where the science text-book just gives a theoretical knowledge on adaptations, bird watching can actually connect the knowledge to reality.

Sneha's story

Sneha had set up a bird bath in her garden. Her daughter's evening milk time was always scheduled there. One evening they heard the birds raise a pandemonium. They rushed out and saw a small squirrel busily munching away at a nut, oblivious to a cat lurking in the bushes. When the bird-chirping went unheeded, one bird actually pecked the squirrel and took flight just a fraction of a second before the cat made its lunge. Sneha and her daughter will never forget this live show of interdependence and support that these tiny creatures gave each other to survive in this otherwise precarious world.

A.P.J. Abdul Kalam

A ten year-old A.P.J. Abdul Kalam was standing at the beach looking up at the sky in a small island in south India called Rameshwaram. He was oblivious to everything but the birds that flew around him. He saw their flight, how they dipped into the sea, hopped around the shore, and took off at will with a flap of wings, graceful and effortless. Kalam was fascinated. He was curious to know how birds could fly and wondered what it would be like to ride the wind... And in his heart was born a desire to fly like the birds. He did not know how or when, but knew that he would do it some day. His teacher, Mr. Sivasubramaniya Iyer explained the dynamics of flying to Kalam with patience saying, 'Just as an airplane has an engine to power it, the bird's wings work as its engine,' The teacher's ability to link everything with life, made things easy to understand. This instilled in Kalam a deep respect for learning and a dream to fly...Abdul Kalam, the 'missile man' of India is today enrolling the entire nation in his dreams!

3.9 Sky-gazing

Ralph Waldo Emerson, a nineteenth-century poet, once described the sky as 'the daily bread of the eyes.'

According to Ecopsychologist Sarah Conn, Ph.D., 'Awareness of the sky can help people under stress experience their situations in a larger context. They may be able to take that feeling of space outside themselves and translate it to a feeling of space within themselves.'

Take a sky tour with your child. The sky is full of stories waiting to be discovered. Indulge in sky gazing and let its infinity awe and mesmerize you and your child.

Predawn adventure—If you don't know quite where to start, try waking yourself and your kids for a little predawn adventure. You can just sit quietly and watch the sun come up. The brilliance with which the sun changes its hue with every passing minute is an unforgettable experience. See how the sky itself changes colour with the changing sun. You can even watch the twilight sky and the dim brilliance of the dying sun.

Night sky/star gazing—Children are often fascinated by stars. To prepare for a fun and successful night of star-gazing, you'll need a star map and a story or two about the major constellations. The Internet has many sites that provide these maps and stories. These sites include:

- http://www.emufarm.org/~cmbell/myth/myth.html
- http://www.windows.umich.edu
- http://einstein.stcloudstate.edu/Dome

You can buy a telescope when star gazing graduates into a deeper hobby. To begin with even naked eyes are, good to spot stars. A powerful flashlight could be a good aid though. You can even get a guide book or star charts to help identify constellations and planets.

The best viewing is away from city lights. Try and avoid house and streetlights as best you can. If you can, drive a little away from the city bustle and go to the quiet countryside.

You'll notice that more stars become visible while you wait the half hour that it takes your eyes to fully adjust. Children can use their imagination and come up with their own constellations.

You can even narrate spooky tales to your children under moonlight to create an ambience.

Cloud gazing—Go on a cloud-watching adventure. Encourage children to lie flat on their backs and gaze up at the sky and see the clouds sail by. Every cloud has a shape which fires the imagination... a cloud may be shaped as a unicorn and another as a rabbit. Clouds can be things, buildings and stories. The golden shafts of sunlight piercing through the grey clouds of the monsoon can be a sight to behold.

You can even support sky-human connection by taking the children to planetariums, observatories and sending them for over night camps. They can even join an astronomy club.

3.10 Nature treasure—Make your child a nature collector

Go on a backyard safari!

Kids can (and do!) collect just about anything. In fact, collecting and organising are valuable tools in a child's developing mind. Many adult scientists started out as young collectors. Encourage your child to collect natural treasures: Seeds, stones, bark, twigs, feathers, leaves, moss, berries, flowers, fungi, pine cones, shells, reeds, spider webs, native clay, nuts...the world outdoors is a storehouse of varied and interesting natural riches.

The beautifully written and illustrated children's book, *The Puddle Pail* by Elisa Kleven, tells the story of two siblings who go off with their buckets to collect whatever they find. The elder brother collects traditional items, but the younger, more artistic brother, interprets collecting more broadly. He scoops up a puddle in his bucket and then proceeds to 'collect' clouds, stars, and rainbows. Ultimately, his puddle collection turns into a beautiful display of paintings.

You can present your children with an explorer scrapbook, treasure box, cartons, to stack his finds. You can also display his collection on tabletops, baskets and recycled bottles. Your child may soon discover that the world is filled with treasures just waiting to be found. For the artistically disposed, nature finds can be the raw materials for product development. Children can make nature crowns, garlands, hand bands and be the princess or the prince of the day. They can make a whistle from a willow or basswood twig. They can make their own wind chimes. They can fashion clothes out of leaves and flowers and be the Tarzan boy or the jungle girl. They can also use pressed flowers as art supplies, or create a collage of fall leaves. They can discover their 'pet rock' and make it their slumber party mate.

3.11 Miscellaneous tips

- Send your children for nature camps
- Encourage children to keep nature journals
- Take nature vacations with your family

- Take your children fishing, hiking, boating or mountain biking
- Fly a kite
- Go swimming in a lake, pond or creek
- Encourage your child to sketch a plant which catches her/his fancy.
- Let your child own a pet. Dogs, rabbits, guinea-pigs, toads, tortoises are some animals that make excellent pets.
- Pottery and basket-weaving are some hobbies which can connect children to nature.
- Shift story time outside. Find a quiet spot under a tree and read your favourite storybooks. Reading a book outside, especially those that talk about the outdoors, helps children make the connection between the written word and what they see in nature.
- Encourage your children to join in or begin their own Guerilla Gardening. Guerrilla gardening is practised by environmentalists where they take up an abandoned piece of land to grow plants. Guerrilla gardeners believe in reclaiming land from perceived neglect or misuse and assigning a new purpose for it.

Learning the Tagore way–Shantiniketan

Rabindranath Tagore, the brilliant and prolific poet, writer and nationalist, founded Shantiniketan in 1901. It is a school where even today classes are held outdoors under the open skies and if the student's mind wanders, it dwells on the cosmos. He believed that children, with the freshness of their senses, had an intimate relationship with the natural world. He taught that they must never lose that communication, which was a vigorous, life-giving energy. According to him, students should have contact with living nature, 'to meet with life where it is most supreme.' He recalled his own experience of student life as stifling, shut off entirely from the outside world. He said, 'From our very childhood, habits are formed and knowledge is imparted in such a manner that our life is weaned away from nature and our mind and the world are set in opposition from the beginning of our days. Thus the greatest of educations for which we came prepared is neglected, and we are made to lose our world to find a bagful of information instead. We rob the child of his earth to teach him geography, of language to teach him grammar. His hunger is for the Epic, but he is supplied with chronicles of facts and dates...Child-nature protests against such calamity with all its power of suffering, subdued at last into silence by punishment.' (219-Reader—from Personality).

Sutano Chatterjee

On my visit to Shantiniketan I met Sutano Chatterjee, a resident sculptor there and winner of many national awards in the field of art. After completing his national scholarship in 1998, Sutano joined Shanitniketan as a teacher. He said, 'I have been able to give expression to my creative instincts amidst the peaceful and sprawling greens of Shanitiniketan. The open air which carries the force of Sri Rabindranath Tagore, the silent surroundings, beautiful sculptures and paintings at every junction and corner urge one to just be...This place which has still managed to retain its natural setting offers the luxury of time, space and peace, thus giving the creative urges the best opportunity possible.' I asked him on how he inspires creativity in his students. He said, 'I always ask my students to be with nature and observe the lines of nature, the spread of the foliage, the bark of the tree, the line of the twilight, the pattern of the clouds. I encourage them to merge their own consciousness with nature and then sketch or draw. There is no teacher like nature.' Sutano continued with, 'I encourage my students to visit the library and learn from the already produced great works of the past on the one hand, and learn from the forces and spread of nature which changes with every passing moment on the other. I encourage my students to create with these two forces in between.' He concluded, 'As the great master Isaac Bashevis Singer said, "What nature delivers to us is never stale. Because what nature creates has eternity in it".'

Born to Read

....

'Every man who knows how to read has it in his power to magnify himself, to multiply the ways in which he exists, to make his life full, significant, and interesting.'

—ALDOUS HUXLEY (1894-1963)

'For the next few days she was very miserable. She could have made it up with the others quite easily at any moment if she could have brought herself to say that the whole thing was only a story made up for fun. But Lucy was a very truthful girl and she knew that she really was in the right: and she could not bring herself to say this. The others who thought she was telling a lie, and a very silly lie too, made her very unhappy...'

I ended my day's reading with the following lines from the book, *The Chronicles of Narnia*. The incident which the excerpt talks about is after Lucy, the heroine, discovers the world of Narnia in her hide-out in the wooden cupboard during a game of hide-n-seek. But, when she tries to convince her friends of the world which lies beyond the cupboard, they laugh and refuse to believe her. One of her friends, Edmund sneers at her. This hurts Lucy immensely but she was not one who will betray a truth however uncomfortable it may be.

When I shut the book, my older child, Aishwarya, asked me what I would have done in a situation like this. Would I bend the truth to make life easy or stand up for what I know to be right even if it means inviting the ridicule of friends? The question made me assess depths of myself and I really did grapple with what I would have done. After a while I said, 'May be I would give in to them and say Narnia does not exist'. I asked her, 'What about you?' She said, 'I do it all the time to gain approval, but I want to be Lucy, mom.'

The subtle way a book can touch us, make us think or even relieve our anxieties is perhaps incomprehensible, but once there is a connection the written words become us and we say, 'that is me'! It is said that a good classic is one where the author bares his own soul, you see your own subtle feelings in them and know that you are not alone. *The Chronicles of Narnia* helped bring to the forefront a trait bothering Aishwarya, and yet she was unable to broach the subject to me. The book helped her not only articulate her feelings, but also gave her the courage and a platform to open the subject for discussion. The book formed the bridge through which she approached me. We learnt things about ourselves and each other as friends.

GIFT YOUR CHILD THE WORLD THROUGH BOOKS

4.1 Benefits

Books can be an entire universe by itself. Books contain excitement, mysticism, adventure, emotions, wisdom, morality and righteousness (the good always triumphs over evil). Books are good portable friends and once the friendship becomes intimate, boredom does not dare touch children.

Books stimulate thinking; children embark on a mission with Nancy Drew to solve the mystery of the missing key or accompany *The Famous Five* on their mission to save the world. Books satisfy the fantasy streak in children as they ride the broom with Harry Potter, become smaller than a thumb like Thumbelina, or experience the joys of honey through Pooh. Books spark creativity and imagination, expand our children's world as they globe trot and know entire cultures, communities, and life styles through their favourite characters, sitting right in the couch of their drawing room. As a child I remember touring south India with tales of Kannagi and Tenali Raman, enjoying the splendours of Dehradun with Ruskin Bond and being led by Don Quixote and Sancho, through the plains of Castile, white-hot in the sun, with dusty roads and inns full of adventure.

Reading improves language, strengthens vocabulary, sharpens the thought process and builds imagination. It increases the child's attention span. A reader almost always has an awareness edge over a non-reader.

Books, through their unfolding tales make children experience the world through the other's shoes. They know that the bully is as miserable and lonely as the bullied, that pets cry when their masters ill-treat them, that parents too go through their bad days as much as children do, that a cruel word which hurts them hurts others too.

Books assuage anxieties as children find their worries echoed in the characters. Books help prepare children to deal with feelings and events that they will encounter later in life. Books show children that losses and hardships are a part of life and do produce heartaches.

Books can pull people in, make them think and inquire about themselves as well as life. One good book begets the love for another and in the passion for books children can move beyond themselves and know a much deeper and varied world. Recreation for some, therapy for others, books can enrapture, enrage, envelop and amaze!

4.2 Some great readers

I cannot live without books–Thomas Jefferson

> 'Books gave me the idea there was a life beyond my poor Mississippi home.'
>
> – OPRAH WINFREY

Thomas Jefferson, the prime author of the Declaration of Independence and the third president of the US was a voracious reader. He had a personal library of about 6,700 books. It is said about him, that whenever he was not carrying out his duties as the American minister to France, he haunted the Parisian booksellers and frequently placed orders with book dealers in London and other European cities.

Thomas Edison

The schoolmaster at his school thought Edison to be an incredibly stupid and intractable boy. His mother, however, seemed to have different thoughts on the matter. Disgusted at school, she took her son out and took it upon herself to school the young boy at home. There, she exposed him to books at a far higher level than anyone of his age. Thanks to his mother's teachings, Edison's horizons of knowledge were not limited just to science, but also to such subjects as Philosophy, English, and History.

Satyajit Ray

Ace film maker, Satyajit Ray, had a penchant for the mystery genre and was a passionate reader of Sherlock Holmes. He loved reading crime fiction. His interest gave rise to his own body of fiction in the adventures of Feluda, where Feluda is the Watson solving one mystery after another with ease and confidence. Ray's plots involve murder, intrigue and adventure, all written in a racy and robust style. Even today he is considered the Sherlock Holmes of Bengali literature.

Jane Austen

Jane Austen, one of the most influential women in literature, had almost no formal education. She did go to a school in Southampton for a while, but was sent home when she came close to dying from typhoid fever. It is said that her real education began when she discovered her father's library. She became an avid reader since childhood and read the serious and popular literature of the time. Her family had a library of over 500 books. Austen later wrote that 'her family were great novel readers, and were not ashamed of being so.'

In the book *Cradles of Eminence*, authors Victor Goertzel and Mildred George Goertzel traced the childhood of more than 400 hundred eminent personalities of the twentieth century. The authors found that these 400 eminent people did have many childhood experiences in common. They said, 'They grew up in homes where excitement and love of learning were present.... The homes they grew up in were full of books and stimulating conversation and strong opinions, so that as children, they learned to think and express themselves clearly.'

☑ *Reality check*

What about your child? Is he/she a reader? Good readers are not born...they are made.

Are you teaching your child to love reading?

A-literates:—children who can read but don't

Jane Healy, an educational psychologist and professional educator for more than thirty-five years and the author of Endangered Minds has coined the term 'a-literate' to explain the new generation of kids who have fine reading skills but consciously choose not to read or read only what they need to read for school or work. Their mode of entertainment is the T.V. or the computer and they do not read newspapers, magazines, or books and have not been to a library for years. Not that these a-literates are not intelligent, in fact many do have an intellectual bend and are very creative but they have simply forgone reading as a source of entertainment, information and wonder.

Is your child an a-literate too? Go through the following questionnaire and in the answers the truth will reveal itself.

➢ How many books does your child own (apart from the school curriculum)?
  A. Less than his set of clothes
  B. Less than his toys
  C. He has a shelf full of books

➢ When was the last time you took your child to the library?
  A. I am not a member of any library
  B. About 3-4 months back
  C. Last week

➢ How often do you read to/with your child?
  A. Very rarely
  B. Once a week or less
  C. Almost everyday

➢ Are you or your child members of any reading club/s?
  A. I didn't know they had any book clubs for children

B. I have been meaning to become a member of one

C. Yes

➤ How often do you take your child to a bookstore/book reading sessions/ authors meets?

    A. Never, we spend our money on other forms of entertainment (movies, clothes, music)

    B. Once every two months, but he prefers to buy stationery and toys from there

    C. Frequently

➤ Which of the following best describes the condition of your child's books?

    A. Look brand new, you couldn't tell he has owned them for ages

    B. Flicked through

    C. Falling apart, they have been used so much

➤ How often do your children find you with a book in your hand?

    A. Never

    B. Once in a while

    C. I am a voracious reader

➤ Who is your child's favourite author? Which is your child's favourite book?

    A. He does not read much to have a favourite author

    B. He has one but I don't know

    C. Enid Blyton, Ruskin Bond, Roald Dahl, J. K Rowling, any other/s...

If you have secured maximum C's, kudos to you, keep it up.

If you have got more of B's perhaps you have started your child on the reader path but still need to buck up on your involvement.

If you have got A's, it is perhaps time to reassess your priorities and see how/where you can fit in the reading culture both in your own as well as your child's life.

4.3 Gift your child the reading habit

'Few children learn to love books by themselves. Someone has to lure them into the wonderful world of the written word: someone has to show them the way.'—ORVILLE PRESCOTT

Who is more qualified to be that 'someone' other than the parents? Helping your children enjoy reading is one of the most important things you can do as a parent and well worth the investment of your time and energy. Studies show that kids who read just fifteen minutes a day see an average of more than a million words a year. Yes, many forces in children's lives pull them away from reading—television, video games, and after-school activities—but if you make reading one of your priorities and expose your children to the world of books and pleasures of reading, getting them to become bookworms may not be that difficult. And this will be a worm that you will love to have wiggling in your home! Remember it's never too early to read to a child, but it's never too late, either.

4.4 What not to do—Two mistakes which most parents make

Read something one-level-up

For most parents it is not just about making the child a reader but a reader who reads 'good' (?) books. The 'good' could mean anything-Informative, classics, biographies, educational stuff (how things work, 'why' series, etc) and the 'good' is almost always one level up i.e. a level more complex than what the child is comfortable with, so that he stretches his mental muscles. Parents compute from the profitability angle; they conclude that if the child is going to spend his precious hours in a book, it might as well be one which offers him/her something beyond simple entertainment. This reasoning, however well meaning, backfires especially when the child is just getting introduced to the

world of reading. If children have to grapple with word-meanings, complex sentences, boring story-lines, clichéd morality lessons, small fonts, reading loses its lure. It becomes a chore, like homework. Children get put off and shut the book for 'GOOD'. They reason too, 'Isn't television more interesting and less brain chewing'?

Reading, anyway, carries a negative connotation for children as they have spent grueling hours making sense first of letters, then words and then tougher words and then full sentences at school. The tough becomes tougher especially when the mode of language is different from what the child is used to at home (even today most families have Hindi and other colloquial languages as their medium of communication at home and as soon as children join school the entire curriculum is presented in English). And so children for whom the love of books has not preceded the rote learning of reading and writing invariably associate reading with work and not pleasure. When we as parents load our own small tiny straw on them the camel slumps.

Remember nothing succeeds like success! Allow your child to taste success with whatever level he/she chooses. Refrain from trying to make the most out of the reading habit. Keep your parameters to the basics 'reading for pleasure', especially for beginners. Want nothing save that your child enjoys whatever he is reading or being read to. Remember you are trying to develop reading as a hobby and a hobby is something that is supposed to be fun, pure fun.

Dr. Marie Carbo, founder and executive director of the National Reading Styles Institute, says, 'Children's emotions about reading have a huge impact on whether or not they'll become lifelong readers. Your children will let you know what they're ready for as they get older.' Too often we see parents overriding their children's tastes and interests. Books purchased with the best intentions in the world will remain unread and unloved.

Children's author Bernard Ashley puts it in a nutshell:

> 'If children aren't enjoying and wanting books at seven, they aren't going to be rushing out and buying them at twenty one.'

Gradually graduate your child's taste and preferences

Once your child has developed the love of reading you can offer him the world through classics, encyclopaedias, *Tell Me Why's* and biographies. Don't we all repeat things that are pleasurable? Pleasure from reading will in its own time hone your child's interests, comprehension skills to the levels you want. Chances are they will surpass your expectations by a large margin. Trust me it has happened to both my children. My older daughter, currently eleven, reads up to seven hundred page novels!!!

Once the bug bites, the child stays bitten.

Aparna Sen

Aparna Sen, though an avid reader, somehow, shied away from Bengali literature. No amount of coaxing by her mother could get her to pick a Bengali novel. She reminisced about the time when she was around fourteen. Her mother picked a beautiful Bengali novel which was a love story. She read about twenty pages and just as the story had begun to become interesting, shut the book and said, 'I am tired baby, we will continue tomorrow.' Aparna said, 'No amount of imploring made her change her mind and very casually she suggested that why did I not read from thereon if the wait seemed so unbearable. I picked up the book and read through the evening and night and finished the novel. That was the beginning of my tête-à-tête with Bengali literature and I devoured it with the same enthusiasm and energy as I did the English.'

Another incident which Aparna remembers was when they were not graduating beyond Enid Blyton. Her father then got home an entire collection of Agatha Christie. He realised that if he asked them to read Dickens they would not. So he got Agatha Christie which had the thrill of mystery, but in a language which commanded their attention and intelligence. The curiosity of what will happen next rendered the complex words and the length immaterial.

Finish what you start

An adjective which frequently tags with the book *Da Vinci Code* is 'un-put-down-able'. People have actually raced through the entire 300 pages in one sitting. But I could not find the same pull and gave the book three shots within an interval of about three months. Yet I could not proceed beyond the fortieth page. Does that make me less keen a reader or should I conclude that my grey matter has been weirdly wired?

If we buy a certain novel and lose interest in it we easily put it aside, but this benefit is strictly forbidden to our children. For them even one unread book (which they themselves bought) becomes the defining line of their insincerity as a reader. Invariably it also becomes our 'Laxman rekha' as we tell them, 'till you do not finish that book I am not buying you another'.

Allow the child latitude

Allow your child the freedom to shut a book if it does not hold his interest. You will take the pressure off reading. Recommend putting the book aside and trying another. Maybe your child will himself revisit the book after some time but you must not force the child to finish a book which he does not like.

Allow your child the freedom to choose

Allow your child to lead. Give him complete ownership of choice. Naturally you need to make sure that the books are age-appropriate. Take your child to the book stores, library or book fairs and let him browse through the sections and decide on the purchase. Respect his choice. Whether s/he picks comic books, music magazines, short silly stories let him/her pick. Each child has his or her own level, like water. Let the child settle at the level and interest he/she enjoys. Don't judge his/her personal interests. If you deprive your child of self-determination, you will most likely deprive him of motivation too.

Teesta Setalwad

Social activist and journalist Teesta Setalwad was brought up in a very independent environment. She said, 'Freedom of thought was in the very air we breathed.' She had the benefit of a huge library right at home with books ranging from history, to philosophy to literature and politics. There was never a desire to influence their reading or thought process. They freely walked up to their library, browsed through what was on the shelf and picked any book which caught their fancy. She said, 'Once we became passionate readers we devoured every bit of writing at home and frequently visited libraries and book fairs too.'

The books that I too remember reading as a child and as a young adult were those that I picked myself. It is in this choice that I felt ownership of my own knowledge. In fact I got hooked onto reading with *Amar Chitra Katha* comics when I was young. For many months I only read and reread them. I remember visiting the second hand stores and buying all earlier publications (it was a monthly release), but I never once looked at any other comic or book. Only when I had exhausted reading and rereading the entire collection did I glance at other series and books. I did get onto the Nancy Drews, Famous Fives, Secret Sevens, and Junior classics, but those six months of only *Amar Chitra Katha* firmly embedded the love of reading into my psyche.

4.5 Create the home ambience

Fill your home environment with books! Surround children with abundant reading material. 'The best predictor of whether you read is whether you own books,' says Richard Allington, a University of Florida education professor. Let your child build his personal library. Give him a monthly book allowance. Affordable used books can be found at book fairs, thrift stores, secondhand book stores, and public library book sales. Many online stores like Amazon, Barnes & Nobles, Oxford, give you the power to access books across the continent just through a click of your finger tips. Consider subscribing to a good children's magazine–children love having something come in the mail just for them! Let your child have his special reading nook in his bedroom. A simple beanbag or any other cozy chair, a small table with a reading lamp and a small bookcase are all that is needed.

Super Parents! Navin and Kamna Chandra

Engineer Navin and writer Kamna Chandra have diligently put in years of hard work, set the right values by living through example and have not once given even an iota less than their 100% into helping their children be good human beings and finding their niche in life. Today with a satisfied smile they both can finally lie back and take life a little easy. And indeed they deserve it. Their three children are:

Vikram Chandra, is a well-known author and winner of Commonwealth Writers Prize for Best First Book and the David Higham Prize for Fiction. His second book, *Love and Longing in Bombay* too won the Commonwealth Writers Prize for Best Book (Eurasia region) and was included in 'Notable Books of 1997' by the New York Times Book Review. His work has been translated into eleven languages. He also teaches creative writing at the University of California.

Tanuja Chandra — M.A. in film from Temple University in Philadelphia and director of sensitive movies like *Hope* and *Aa Little Sugar* and *Zindagi Rocks*.

Aunpama Chopra — Film critic, senior correspondent for *India Today*; author of *Sholay: The Making of a Classic*, winner of *Swarn Kamal*, a national award for the best Indian book on cinema in 1995.

Navin Chandra said, 'Even when I could ill-afford a major chunk of my income, about 50-60% would go into the kids education and books. As an engineer I was a salaried employee but I always bought the best books possible from the thick encyclopaedias to small comics. Our home was always overflowing with books, books and more books.' In fact Navinji's work entailed travelling and he would never return home without books tucked under his arm for each of his children. He said, 'I would put in a pile of light books like comics etc and slip in something a little serious and heavy along with it. Children would read the lighter stuff and then would inevitably flick through the other book too. Gradually their tastes elevated.' All the three children became avid reader. Says mother Kamnaji, 'When in high school Vikram would read up to 1 novel every three days!'

Jacqueline Wilson's (bestselling author in Britain, second only to Rowling) biggest passion and/or worst vice is buying books. She has over 15,000 books crammed into every corner of her small house—and they've started to creep across the carpets. Her favourite holiday place is Hay-On-Wye the first book town of the world and has about twenty secondhand bookshops.

Have a wide variety of books

Fantasy – Fairy tales are among the oldest literature in existence, handed down and revised over hundreds of years. Choose from simple fairy tales to complex 'sword and sorcery' tales. Harry Potter series are children's favourites.

Mystery – Detective stories, Nancy Drews, Famous Fives, books by Laura Child, Secret Sevens etc can be full of fun and adventure for children.

Short reads even for tall kids – Compilations of Akbar Birbal, Tenali Raman, Mullah Nasseruddin, Aesop's Fables stories can offer children a nice change.

Mythology – Children love reading *Mahabharta*, *Ramayana* and stories of Ganesha, Shiva, Krishna, Hanuman, Eklavya etc.

Classics – Try authors like Charles Dickens, Louisa May Alcott, Frances Hodgson Burnett, Lewis Carroll, Arthur Conan Doyle, Rudyard Kipling etc.

Science fiction – Through science fiction children can get zapped to another world. Try authors like Diane Duane, Herbie Brennan, Vivien Alcock, John Christopher, Gillian Rubenstein and Peter Morwood.

Animal stories – Winnie the Pooh, Jataka tales, Hitopedesha, Top Dog series, Clifford Series.

Cool comic books – Although sometimes given a bad reputation comic-style and graphic novels are great motivators for kids who tend to get a bit intimidated by page upon page of neatly stacked sentences. Pictures give them a welcome respite from all those words, as well as visual cues for interpreting the text. Tinkle, Archie, Superman, Tintin, Richie Rich are some comics which children swear by.

Best Friends books – Children love fiction which talks about friends. Some series in this section are Lizzie McGuire, Two of a Kind etc.

Spooky stories – Most kids love being scared, but not too scared. The trick is finding books that will raise the hairs on their arms without inspiring nightmares. Roald Dahl's Witches was a real hit with my children. Vikram Aur Betal, Goosebumps are other series you can look into.

Movies based on books – *Monsters Inc*, comics (Batman, Superman, Spiderman) *Harry Potter, Ice Princess, The Chronicles of Narnia, Finding Nemo* can be lots of fun.

Fascinating facts books, World records – Non-fiction can be eyes-wide-open engaging too!

Books which deal with emotions – Some books can flip an emotional switch, allowing kids to access their inner feelings such as anger, jealousy, shyness, and fear. Some good authors for chidren's book in this category are Jacqueline Wilson, Laura Child, George Byne. Jerry Spinelli is our personal favourite.

Boarding school books – Some are *St. Claires, Malory Towers* etc.

Humour books – Joke books might seem corny, but don't overlook this age-perfect genre. Jokes can boost vocabularies, knowledge of idioms, and essential critical-thinking skills.

Travel Books – finding books that relate to a place you visit on a family vacation can get a child hooked.

Books on nature

Hobby books – on pottery, making airplanes, stamp collections, bird books, coin collections.

4.6 Miscellaneous tips

- Look for award-winning books and bestsellers.
- Ask friends, family, and teachers what books their children have enjoyed, try a book swap.
- Use book lists generated by various literacy organisations; they usually have good suggestions.
- Given at the end is a compilation of the top 100 books for children by 'NEA' National Education Association of the US.

This list was tabulated from an online survey that ran at this web site from November 1, 1999 through February 1, 2000. Visit the site http://www.cbc.org.au/awards.htm It is a site developed by The Children's Book Council of Australia and has interesting listings of children's popular books too. Another valuable website is www.childrenslit.com. This site has a listing of 150 outstanding children's books arranged by age. The books are selected for their exceptional writing, creative story lines and factual accuracy. Listings for the past several years are available. There is also biographical information on some of the authors.

- Visit the American Library Association's Web site at http://www.ala.org/ala/librariesandyou/recomreading/recomreading.htm. It includes lists of award-winning book recommendations by librarians and reading specialists. She also recommends the book, *Choosing Books for Children* (University of Illinois Press, 1999) by Betsy Hearne.

- A book titled, *Books Children Love: A Guide to the Best Children's Literature* by Elizabeth Laraway can serve as a good guide to help you stock up your child's personal library too.

- Check the book review section of the newspapers and magazines for the recommended new children's books.

- Choose books which meet your child's current interests and hobbies.

- Choose books with font size which your child is comfortable with.

- Choose books that your child can hold easily. Hardcover bound books, though tolerate wear and tear better, are uncomfortable in the child's tiny palms.

4.7 Set aside time for reading

Bina Sarkar Ellias

Bina Sarkar Ellias, editor of trail-blazing journal called *Gallerie* said, 'I remember how as a child the wet monsoon days thrilled me with the prospect of those delicious unlimited hours in the company of books. Schools would declare a rainy day and I would suddenly have the entire day at my leisure. I would settle down with a pile of books close to a window and read away. They have been some of my most beautiful childhood memories.'

To enjoy reading your child must have leisure time. With jam-packed schedules where activities run back to back children neither have the energy, nor the motivation or the peace of mind to curl up with a book and lose themselves in the pages.

Make reading a priority. Whether it is ten minutes every night before bed or an hour every Sunday morning, set aside a specific time for reading, both when you read to your child and when your child reads by himself. Try to make reading an everyday habit. Establish a reading time that your children can look forward to such as naptime or bedtime. By setting aside specific times you send the message that reading is an important enjoyment. If time is tight for some reason, pick a small book.

Many families set aside a family reading hour where everyone sits down with a book. This is their special time together where all electronics are switched off (T.V., mobiles and other landlines, computers etc) and the only sound is the soft turning of the pages of books.

Take advantage of 'waiting' time to share books on trips, at the doctor's office, in line at the grocery store. Read a lot to your children when they are ill in bed and have pretty much nothing to do. Meal times and bath times could also be used by parents to read to their young children.

Make reading a privilege. Let kids stay up fifteen or twenty minutes later at night to read.

Read to your children everyday

Woodrow Wilson

American president and the Nobel peace prize winner Woodrow Wilson was a dyslexic in early childhood and did not learn to read until he was ten years old. His father, Joseph Wilson could not wait for Woodrow to learn to read the books he himself enjoyed and so kept the boy home, read to him, and explained the meaning of what he read. He then asked for young Woodrow's reaction to the ideas of the book. Woodrow Wilson later said of his father that he was 'the best instructor, the most inspiring companion...that a youngster ever had.' He later on went on to become a skilled academic, an avid reader and a popular writer and lecturer. Like his father, young Wilson developed great admiration for English letters and history.

The rewards of reading to your child everyday will far surpass the investments in time and energy. It will plant the seeds of desire in the child to seek adventures in the pages of books rather than in computer games or T.V. channels. Experts recommend thirty minutes of reading a day.

It's not just what you read to children, but how you read that matters.

- Snuggle up together or make your children sit in your lap.
- Read in a loud, clear voice at a leisurely pace. Give them time to take in what they have heard, imagine the people and places and also ask questions relating to them.

- Follow the children's cue. At times they get so caught up in the story that they do not want stops and detours along the way. Read without pauses then.
- Let yourself go when you read! Be with the book, mind, body and soul. Your child will love it and it will be an enjoyable experience for you as well.
- Change voices. Give life to the words. Change your pitch (high and low) with the words in the story. Change your volume (soft and loud) and pace (fast and slow) as well.
- Use pantomime, finger plays and other props.

Read to your children even when they become independent readers.

Older children enjoy being read to, too. My older daughter Aishwarya though preferring to read the fiction genre herself, still looks to me for the news of the day. Every morning the breakfast table becomes her personalised news station, as I become the news reader updating her with the happenings around the globe. I show both my children pictures of events and people too. She particularly loves the common man's caricaturist depiction done by Laxman. Her all favourite sessions though are the Sunday debates. I explain the context first and then read both the arguments and counter-arguments. With the Sunday leisure it almost invariably turns into a family debate where each expresses his/her view, right from the youngest Sanaya, who is seven, to the oldest her grandfather, who is sixty-four.

Older children can also be read interesting incidents, experiences and stories from adult magazines and books. We subscribe to the Time Magazine, and after all of us have gone through it: I place it in the children's room. One issue carried the picture of the steel tycoon Laxmi Narayan Mittal (The story of the Arcelor bid) as the cover page. Since Laxmi Mittal was all over the news, in the papers, and T.V. channels, my daughter was well familiar with his name. She read the four page article by her self and asked her father to fill in the gaps of what her eleven year mind could not comprehend. Father and daughter discussed the reservations of Guy Dolle regarding Mittal's

Indian status and whether Mittal would be successful in acquiring the company. This in fact, led to a deeper discussion on racism too. Father-daughter talked about the Asians settled in the US and Europe. Since Aishwarya's cousin is studying at Cambridge she emailed him as well asking about his experiences with racism. Father and daughter transcended time and era in their discussions and Mahatma Gandhi took center stage.

Another incident which I remember was after reading Lincoln's biography. I told my children about Lincoln's vision, where just before the beginning of the Civil War he had requested the European nations to cut off all trade ties with the southern states which they did as they too supported Lincoln's call for abolition of slavery. This was perhaps one of the main tipping points which resulted in the success of the Union over the confederates. Since the southern states were left with huge produce and no buyers their pecuniary power declined. Lincoln and the Union scored victory and slavery was abolished with the US still integrated.

Through relating anecdotes from biographies, inspirational reads and classics, parents can expose children to information beyond their reading level and comprehension.

Kiran Bedi

Celebrated police officer, winner of the Ramon Magsaysay Award for government service, the Asian Nobel Prize, the Joseph Beuys Award, the Asia Region Award for Drug Prevention & Control by the International Organisation of Good Templars (IOGT), was asked if she would join the police service again if reborn, she replied that she would, 'provided I have the same parents.'

Parkash Lal, supercop Kiran Bedi's father was a voracious reader especially of books that were positive and inspirational (by authors such as the Americans Dale Carnegie and Norman Vincent Peale). Kiran Bedi said, 'He would wake us up even late at night and read us a passage that had caught his imagination. He would then go back to his bed and sleep. We, however, could not sleep. Stirred by our father, we were charged with energy to do, energy to achieve, energy to win.'

Though the family language was Punjabi, English and Hindi were also spoken, and there were always several English-language newspapers and books. This according to Kiran really contributed to a balanced growth of all three languages.

Consider your child's interest

If your child enjoys sports, pick up a *Sports Illustrated* and read a feature story together. If your child fancies fine arts, subscribe to an art magazine and show your child different works of contemporary artists. If your child has the environmental streak in him get National Geographic and other magazines dealing with the same. There is some reading material out there which caters to your child's interest. All you need is to connect the two!

4.8 Give them the Library power

You don't have to have a house overflowing with books to gift your child the magical world of books. Any library in the locality could be home to an abundance of books and many other valuable resources. Apart from housing a wide variety of children's books and magazines, libraries often lend audiotapes, cassette tapes, compact discs, videotapes, book/cassette kits of childrens' books and movies. Many provide computer and internet facilities. Libraries today even sponsor special events like reading sessions and author meets. There is a corner for every child in a library.

The British library in Ahmedabad had organised a reading programme called 'The Reading Voyage'. It was a programme channeled through schools in Ahmedabad. Children were required to read six books each and make a presentation through any medium they felt comfortable with. Parents were invited for the grand finale and we were treated to a medley of creative expression. Some narrated their stories through puppets, some through songs and dance and yet others through dramatization. Amidst claps and cheers, children enacted their favourite stories. They were so enthralled with

> 'Here was one place where I could find out who I was and what I was going to become. And that was the Public Library.'
>
> JERZY KOSINSKI

the world of books and drama, that most children who participated in the voyage forced their parents to ask for membership of the library, and have become frequent visitors to the literary temple. As for my kids, the British Library introduced them to the world of Jacqueline Wilson, of Georgia Byne and Jerry Spinelli, authors I had not heard of or ever read, and probably would not have experimented with, since the tried and tested series of Enid Blytons and Nancy Drew were readily available in the market.

We can't possibly buy every book that our child wants to read. The library is an inexpensive source of books. We can allow children much more flexibility and latitude in book choices—after all, mistakes cost nothing and can be returned. Through a library we can teach children about responsibility and the sense of community sharing too. They learn to respect books and care for them. The use of a book mark is something which I too have learnt only through the use of library books (my personal collection of books is fraught with tiny folds). They learn to return books on time and learn the value of silence during library visits.

Let your child get a library card on his/her name. It is likely to be one of the first official documents with his or her name on it. It will make them feel important and responsible like grown-ups. Take your children to the library and let them wander through the racks. A library visit will offer a welcome change from the regular malls, multiplexes and shopping centers that we get entrapped in, the city dwellers that we are.

Most schools too are a good source of books. Encourage children to regularly borrow books from the school library.

Says author J.K. Rowling, 'Trips to the library with my mother are, in my memory, even more thrilling than trips to the sweet shop, and when I got my eldest daughter a library card I felt as though I had bought her citizenship of that same fabulous world.'

Says Salman Rushdie, 'I have always loved and valued the public libraries of Britain, and I owe them a great deal (and not only in unpaid fines). If knowledge is power, then the public library system gives that power to anyone who wants it.'

Empower your child.

4.9 Expose them to book clubs/reading clubs

The moment I finished *Of Human Bondage* by Somerset Maugham I telephoned my friend and had a detailed discussion on the book. We spoke about the protagonist, his inner conflicts, unmet desires, ceaseless longing and his struggle with himself to understand his own passions. We discussed our lives vis-à-vis his. We relived not only his story but our own passions and lives. The pleasure of discussing and presenting one's thoughts on the book and listening to others' views on the same is almost as pleasurable and stimulating as is the reading itself.

How many times have you read a book or article that you itched to discuss with a friend? A book or a reading club offers precisely that, a chance for like-minded people to get together, decide on a reading, and then talk about it. Encourage your child to seek the membership of a book or a reading club. In book clubs readers evaluate stories and ideas in the book and present their views on the same. Discussions are generally informal and essentially reader driven. This helps them enjoy what they read because the focus isn't on testing knowledge. The comprehension of the text is relative to the reader. Book clubs challenge and stimulate young minds by engaging them in creative and thoughtful discussions. They facilitate communication and advance critical thinking skills in an open-minded, receptive environment. Through the discussion that takes place at book club meetings, children find larger meaning and themes in the story and consider others' perspectives on the same.

Besides, children from different backgrounds get to share their finds on interesting reads.

Further some book clubs discuss current events, and encourage children to talk about their personal lives in relation to the book...book clubs then become an avenue for expression for deep-seated emotions. Book clubs ask for a minimum commitment of reading time and the interested child almost always gets hooked on to the habit of reading. In fact, Book clubs have succeeded in motivating even the unwilling children to read.

Hippocampus, in Koramangala, has a book club where children are encouraged to read and review books. Landmark, the book and toy store, provides the books for these little critics. The best reviews are printed in a newspaper. These children can't wait for the next assigned book to devour and then analyze.

You can become a member of the NCCL, National Centre for Children's Literature (NCCL) which has a reading club by visiting the site http://www.nbtindia.org.in/MemberShipForm.asp. Most libraries offer reading and book clubs. You can even have access to an online book club, just make sure they have the right literary choice and are age-appropriate for your child.

If there are no good book clubs within the vicinity you can start one and set the ball rolling.

How to start your own book club

Your child can call or email his buddies who like to read and see if they want to get together to read and discuss a good book. If everyone brings one other person, one will have a big enough club in no time! You, too, can call up your friends with children of the same age and invite them for the first session. Posting flyers at the school, or library (that's one place where you're sure to find book lovers!), even local book stores could help children meet new kids who share a passion for reading. Eight to twelve people is about the right size for a good club.

The first meeting should be to discuss the rules or standards the club will follow. It might be a good idea to ask prospective members to come with two book suggestions.

Making the book choice is perhaps the most important factor. Try and include a wide range of subjects. The best way to make sure that the club is happy with the book choices is to create a list and then vote on which ones should be read. The more information children have on each book (author information, recommendations, previous reading experience), the easier it'll be for the club to make a smart decision.

One kid or a parent has to take up the role of the 'Secretary'. He or she will keep track of book lists and send out reminders about meeting times and places.

Anahita's parents got together with some friends and started a book club called, 'Young readers'. They went to lengths to even create the ambience for the read of the month. They created the Akbar era with snacks, decorated the living room according to the theme and each child was even gifted a cardboard sword, which the kids themselves created on session day itself. Another parent gifted each child a blank journal that he could turn into a diary. This is where kids compiled a list of their favourite books, copied interesting passages and wrote down anything that inspired them. Some even authored their own story!

Creativity in the book club can be a great way for kids to absorb the plot of the story – and it can be a lot of fun, too! Expand the activity of the book club, make it reading for fun, add a little snack, some craft work and bring to life the book that your children are reading.

4.10 Connecting reading with activities

Reading books can be a springboard for activities

Discussions and debates

After you've finished reading, discuss the book with your child. Find parallels between experiences in the book and those in your child's life.

Teesta Setalwad

I asked Teesta Setalwad about her favourite memories of reading. She said, 'Though reading is essentially a solitary act, in our household it always became a group activity. Any work which any family member read became the springboard for heated and passionate discussion.' Authors and their views, stories and their purport, all became the battle ground on which many a time Teesta and her parents found themselves in opposing camps. Teesta says, 'We lived those books through our heated discussions. We agreed to disagree and my views weren't stubbed just because my parents had the advantage of age.' Even when as young as seven she was treated as an adult and encouraged to take responsibility for her thoughts as well as her actions. She said, 'Taking responsibility was so imbibed in us that when I took up journalism as a career I knew that it had to be responsible and serious journalism. I believe that if you do serious journalism you can change the status quo. Maybe you cannot change people completely but you can at least open a window to that change.' In fact she worked as a full time journalist almost up to 1992-93, when she realised that she could still do something more. 'Given the "take responsibility" drill that we grew up with. I knew that I could take on more and that is when I stepped into activism.' Today, Teesta also runs a magazine called *Communal Combat* and this is her bid in spreading communal peace and harmony and speaking for the rights of the deprived.

Some questions which you can discuss with your child:
- What part of the story or book your child liked best and why
- What would your child have done in the same situation?
- Did your child like the ending of the story? Why or why not?
- If your child were the author would he have treated the story differently? Why? Why not?

You too, must be a frank participant in the discussion and present your views. You can even encourage your child to ask you questions regarding the same.

Professor Mote-Serendipity

Professor Mote, Ph.D. and the founding member of IIM-A spoke of a discovery which came to him, cloaked in ordinariness, during one of his training sessions at the Harvard Business School. At Harvard, the training entailed a deep scrutiny and analysis of the various companies which were presented as case studies. Students were required to read the given text, figure out for themselves what was right/wrong or how they would have done things differently and then defend their viewpoints. He said, 'Our professor would give us a live case and ask, "What should Mr. Johnson do and why?" He did not preach that one should cut costs or one should be good, but on how you would cut costs or be good.' During one such case study came Professor Mote's Eureka moment. He said, 'It struck me that the tales of *Panchatantra* is to a seven year old mind what the case studies at Harvard are to us thirty year olds. Effectually both follow the same base principle- learning through a given situation. What really are *Panchatantra*, Hitopadesh, Akbar-Birbal stories or even *Ramayana* or *Bhagvadgita*? They are case studies. They talk of a certain scenario of conflict where the characters take up their stance, follow their actions and then bear the consequence of those actions or that stance. Everything is presented through a story with an end, which shows how the effect is interminably linked with the action. Perhaps what one needs is to make story telling as interactive as Harvard sessions are. Perhaps parents should, like the initiators there, pause at the relevant point and challenge the child to take up a stance. Parents should encourage children to think with questions like:

'What would you have done in a similar situation'?
'Do you think what he/she did was right?
'What other options were available under the circumstances'.
'Do you think he deserves what he got?"

Professor Mote ended with, 'We have a wealth of such resources, used in the right way; each home could be a Harvard.'

Dramatising

Children love to dramatise. They play teacher-teacher, doctor-doctor, mother-baby games almost as soon as they can walk and talk. Since children naturally enjoy role playing, a book they have read can easily turn into their personal theatrical production. Puppets, old clothes, toys can all be used to act out the plot.

Field trips

Extend your child's positive reading experiences. A book on centipedes can be followed by a tour of the backyard with a magnifying glass. The story of *Alice in Wonderland* could be made more interesting with a wooded picnic. An adventure or a travel book can be followed by creating a map of the area. A book on Egypt can end in a museum visit. In fact, after watching the biography of Cleopatra on the History channel, I organised a visit to the Indian Museum at Kolkata. They have a separate Egyptian section with a preserved mummy dating into BC. For my children it led to the upward spiral of curiosity and information, as the museum visit led to yet more books and internet surfing on Egypt. Their curiosity and interest in the same has led us to schedule an Egyptian vacation for the coming summer holidays. My children are now busy sourcing more information on places to visit and they have taken to be our tour guides with their superior knowledge on the subject.

Movies

Books followed by movies make for a great visual treat. As we read a book we form a mental image of that red-bricked house, the endless woods, or the villain with a slightly tilted nose. Watching the characters take up face, speak the dialogues we have read (Scarlett O' Hara's fiddle-de-de in *Gone with the Wind*) or see the landscape we have visualised, add to the thrill of the story. Movies or serials make the book come alive.

Treat your child to a movie once you finish with the book. You can even use the movie to discuss whether your child liked the movie better or the book. Watching the movie, *The Witches*, which is based on a book by Roald Dahl was juicy and thrilling. Even I was at the edge of my seat as we saw how the young boy and his grandmother outwit all the witches in the world. Some books which have been made into great movies: *Willie Wonka and the Chocolate Factory, Matilda, Madeleine, Stuart Little, Arthur, How the Grinch Stole Christmas, Winnie the Pooh, Ice Princess, Harry Potter, Chronicles of Narnia.* These will always remain favourites with children.

Book cuisine

Serve a meal from a book. Make that blueberry cheese cake or your own batch of porridge for the *Three Little Bears.* Try making interesting spinach dishes and recreate Popeye, or carry a basket filled with fruits and let your child be *Little Red Riding Hood.* Not only does it make the book more real, but also induces your child to acquire different tastes in food. Says Anita Shah a teacher and academician, 'I remember wondering how scones would taste, courtesy Five Find outers who always had tea and hot scones.'

Throw a book-related party

Read over your child's favourite book and think about what elements would work at a party. Decorate his room in a jungle theme to resemble *The Jungle Book.* Create the Harry Potter theme with brooms, wizard's hats and other paraphernalia.

Make your children write to their favourite author/s

Most authors have their websites which even have the page of 'contact us'. Encourage children to visit author sites and write to them. They can ask about the forthcoming books or put in any other queries that they may have. Eleven year old Abhishek Parasrampuria wrote to J.K. Rowling asking about the release date of her seventh book. He wrote that he couldn't wait to read it. He received a reply which made it to the school's bulletin board and stayed there for about six months. Abhishek is contemplating taking up writing as a career. Some great ones to try: the home page of Jan Brett, illustrator of *Hedgie's Surprise* and other stories, the *Curious George* site, and *Suessville*, a great destination for Dr. Seuss lovers.

Take them for author visits and have their personal copies signed.

4.11 Miscellaneous tips

- Model reading—Kids learn by watching, so pick up a book for yourself instead of the T.V remote. Share books you loved while growing up. Talk to your child about what you're reading. I share interesting reads with my children through e-mails too.
- Buy your children a good dictionary and use it regularly. On my daughter's tenth birthday I presented her with a spoken digital dictionary. That has become her companion for all hours. She carries it to school and keeps it by her bedside once she is home.
- Try to get children hooked on to a favourite author or series. Oprah loved Lois Lenski while growing up.
- Give books as gifts. Give your children books or magazine subscriptions as gifts. And encourage them to give books as gifts to others. Actor, director Amol Palekar said 'For years every achievement in my house was rewarded with a book. We were always exposed to higher literature and very soon I could be satisfied with nothing less.' My Uncle gifted me a magazine

subscription to *Readers Digest* on my twelfth birthday and I still remember how excited I used to feel seeing a magazine in the mail just for me. It was like receiving a birthday gift every month.

- Throw a book exchange party. Invite your child's friends over, and ask them (or their parents) to bring five books they want to trade. Then let the bargaining begin! It's the best way to refresh your collection without spending cash.

- Link reading for a purpose. Present reading as an activity with a purpose; a way to gather useful information for, say, making paper airplanes, identifying a doll or stamp in your child's collection, or planning a family trip. Tell your child to find out a place he would like to visit in his vacation to Darjeeling. If you do have a family vacation scheduled, encourage children to look up information from the net and identify two places they would like to visit.

- Give your child his own cabinet and arrange for a small reading nook. Let the child furnish the reading corner as he desires. This will give him the feel of ownership not only of books but the space as well.

4.12 Newspapers

My husband's friend in Kolkata found an edition of the newspaper dated 15 August 1947 during his house clean up. This paper was preserved by his father and lay hidden for almost four decades amongst his father's files and archives. The front page carried the photograph of Mahatma Gandhi and Jawaharlal Nehru.

This find was a treat for all of us. We read every news bit over and over again, compared the writing styles of then and now, discussed the font type and size, picture quality, size of the newspaper itself (it was about two-thirds in length and four-fifths in width compared to the size that comes in most popular dailies today), the colour of the newspaper etc. But the most treasured were our own feelings as the folds of the pages engulfed us completely and we were transported to that memorable day which changed the life of every Indian.

My children developed a new respect for the medium and have targeted 15 August 2007 as the day when they will buy all the major dailies of the city and pack them in a bundle to be preserved with a copy of the 1947 edition.

Newspapers are called the Living Textbooks because of their current news and interdisciplinary nature. They report happenings and events across cities, states and nations. There is something for everyone-business, sports, food, music, books, automotives, spirituality, advertisements, classifieds, brain teasers, cookery, health, comics, weather, etc.

Most newspapers have either a daily or weekly section geared especially towards kids where the articles are generally short and snappy, and either appeal directly to kids or are written from a kid's point of view. Make newspaper reading an everyday routine with your child. Given below is a list of activities which you can use as a starting point to develop newspaper reading as a daily habit.

Newspaper related activities with children

- Look for a picture of a person your child would recognise (prime minister, cricketer or any other sports person, a movie star, a police officer, or singer, etc). Talk together about what these people do. Discuss why some of them became famous or why they featured in the newspaper. Telling the child about 'strangers' peeping out of newspapers, identifying them as real people is a great way of introducing professions to a child. This one is a 'politician'; someone is a 'golfer', while someone else is a 'mountaineer'. Pictures about people from different cultures and ethnic backgrounds can lead to interesting discussions on different customs and styles of living.

- Pictorial reading—Each picture tells a different story. A picture about a natural phenomenon such as tsunami, earthquake, cyclone or landslide can lead to a discussion about their causes, location and rescue measures. The recent flood in Surat due to the water released from the dams became our issue of discussion and my children looked up information on dams, rivers, even high and low tides.

- Encourage your child to be a critic. Invite him/her to review a new movie, television show, music CD, book or an event. Ask what he/she liked or didn't like. Now look for a review of that same item in the newspaper or on the Internet and compare the opinion. You can even offer open-ended sentences in response to newspaper reading. Two simple ones are 'I agree with... I disagree with...' Have your child fill in with something that he/she has read and thought about from the newspaper.

- The newspaper often reports some national and world news in a section of brief updates. Look for a brief article to read aloud to your child. Encourage your child to draw a picture about the article.

- Conduct a newspaper scavenger hunt. Give your child a list of specific items found in the newspaper and allow him a set amount of time to find them. Examples of items to find: a movie they would like to see, a frowning face or a smiling face, a letter to the editor about a local issue.

- Older children can browse through the weather forecast, currency conversion data, railway and airline schedules, listing of emergency and essential services, movie and theatre listings. They will learn that newspapers are forums for 'information-you-can-use' details, too. So the next time you suggest going out, you'll find him reaching out to the newspaper to check out the movie listings or the entertainment advertisements for concerts. They can even look for an event coming to their city that would be of interest to them – a concert, food festival, their favourtie movie star, or the release of a new book by a favourite author.

- Sixteen pages of fresh information everyday! Use this fact to discuss about how reporters get their news. Since they have to get facts and that too from all across the globe what kind of networking do they use? This can lead to a deeper discussion on networking, onsite reporters, sourcing news from different agencies etc.

- Many of today's comic strips are like miniature narrative stories, often highlighting the problems or conflicts of the characters. Laxman's caricature of the common man is legendary. Pramesh and his eleven year-old daughter look up to Laxman's cartoon of the day and do have a hearty laugh, but his daughter has become so connected with the everyday man's malaise at the hand of the government machinery that she is thinking of getting into politics when she grows up. Besides, her sense of humour is way beyond her other sixth grader friends.

- Children can look through the Travel section to find locations they would like to visit. They can find advertisements for airlines, hotels, clothes and other items that might be needed if they were to visit these locations.

- Children can even find reviews of a movie, play, or concert that they disagree with and can write a letter to the editor expressing their opinions. What better way than this to let them experience the freedom of speech? Make sure they follow your newspaper's guidelines for letters to the editor.

- Give the children a number of articles about the same story, but from different newspapers. Ask them to compare the stories from each newspaper. You could ask as to how one newspaper has dealt with the story vis-à-vis another. Is some daily biased towards one particular point of view? How much space has each devoted to the issue? How important does the newspaper see the story? (i.e. is it on the front page or in the middle of the newspaper?)

- Colour printing in a newspaper is more expensive than printing it in black and white. Have students look through the newspaper, making note of which pages have colour photography or graphics and which have black and white. As a class, discuss why colour would be used in one instance and not in another.

- Go through the advertisements in the newspaper with your child, identifying slogans, pictures or key words that attract attention and influence decisions to buy. Are any of the products advertised ones that we use at home? Which words or phrases in the ads are most persuasive? Children can even be encouraged to design their advertisement for a favourite product or a new invention.

- Project yourself into societies in which there are no newspapers. Make a list of all the functions provided by the newspaper, including such things as providing news, serving as an advertising medium, social announcements, upcoming events, critical reviews, etc. How would each of these functions be met within a newspaperless society?

- Ask your children to imagine that they are in charge of preparing a time capsule that will be opened in 200 years. They have to thus create their own daily which will tell the most about our lives today from the newspaper. They can use news articles, pictures and advertisements in the newspaper from current issues but the discerning power is theirs alone. What do they think is worthy of being mentioned and what is not?

- They can find stories from different cities and countries other than their own and then locate them on the globe. They can collect pictures from the newspaper that shows different facial expressions. Label each picture with descriptive words.

- They can be 'cut and paste' poets. They can cut headlines that they find amusing over a period of days or till they have about ten-twenty. They can then arrange them to make a poem which could be hilarious, serious or dealing with a specific issue.

- So when you reach out to your newspaper with your morning cuppa, ensure that your child gets his daily fix, too. Just take care that you or your child does not **gloss over news items that may be unsavoury or too dense to assimilate.**

Remember good readers are not born...they are made! Sure it's best to begin early. But you can encourage a love affair with reading at almost any point in your children's lives. Busy household? Just twenty minutes a day will work. With reading, anything is possible.

Sports

••

Yellow and Red House finally made it to the final of the throw ball match of our school that year. I was captaining Yellow House on the field. The entire school was divided into two factions, one supporting Yellow and the other, Red. The day of the match arrived. Faces, anxious and excited, screaming and whispering, prophesying and praying were at the windows. We players too, while sporting a tough exterior, were a bundle of nerves within. Vigour and exhaustion, grit and trepidation alternated in a frenzied frequency in all of us.

The match started in pin-drop silence. Deafening cheers resounded whenever a point was scored either way. We had to keep our nerves in check and our focus steady. We had to help the next team member maintain the same. It was a team sport and what mattered more was how we synchronized as a whole rather than individual play. It was a battle of nerves where each team tried to outdo the other. The best of three matches went on for more than two hours, during which each of us stretched ourselves, physically, mentally, psychologically and emotionally.

Ultimately, we scored the winning throw and heard the sigh of a thousand students all at once. We gave way to tears and laughter amidst hugs. The losing team was given a standing ovation for a game played well and fought till the last point. Each one of us on the field experienced the elation and satisfaction that comes from those ultimate moments in sports.

What about the benefits that playing any sport brings...fitness, agility, mental toughness, sportsman spirit, endurance? Speaking for myself, what mattered then was only the game. Today I recognise that those endless hours on the sports field, living by the 'never-say-die' creed, moulded my thinking and responses. Today I hold my nerves a little longer than I think I can or concentrate afresh on an article even though five before them have been rejected. Those sporting days taught me life's skills which I didn't know then that I was learning...

5.1 Benefits

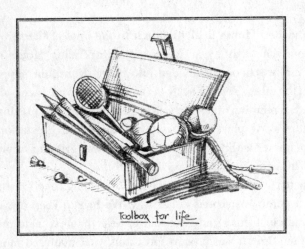

Toolbox for life

Playing a sport has an intrinsic value and offers benefits which last a lifetime.

According to the American Sport Education Program (1994), sports participation:

Builds an appreciation of personal health and fitness;

Develops a positive self-image;

Teaches how to work as part of a team;

Develops social skills with other children and adults (such as taking turns and sharing playing time);

Teaches both how to manage success and disappointment;

Teaches how to respect others.

Other benefits of sports too are well-documented.

Sports and through it, exercise, is good for everybody, but for kids, it pays double: increasing vitality today while building the foundation for a healthy tomorrow. 'Ochsner for Children North Shore' pediatrician Dr. Nancy Carter, explains that active youngsters are stronger and leaner; they have extra energy and feel better about themselves; they get a head start on lifestyle habits that will protect them against heart disease, diabetes, and osteoporosis.

There is a strong connection between academic success and athletics too. Athletes, especially in high school, perform better and remain in school more than non-athletes (Krucoff 1998). In middle school, high school, and college there is an athletic eligibility grade point average. If students don't make the grades, they aren't entitled to participate in sports. With this push in academics, students now work harder in the classroom, so they can participate.

Sports builds character. It teaches one not to react even in the face of provocation and to control panic in the midst of a make-or-break moment. It teaches fair play and the spirit of sacrifice for the team's good. It teaches discipline, the value of hard work and perseverance. British sports historian Peter McIntosh stated emphatically that, 'the real justification for the... school system' of sports 'was sought in character training.' The slogan 'The battle of Waterloo was won on the playing fields of Eton' became popular. The victorious British general, Arthur Wellington, had acquired certain 'character' traits while participating in sports at Eton; these stood him in good stead in his victorious battle against Napoleon at Waterloo.

Participation in sports equips one with the right skills, attitudes and tools to succeed in the business world. Team work, perseverance, problem solving, personal management, communication skills, belief in oneself are attributes strengthened through sports; they come handy in boardroom negotiations. Sports teaches integrity and the capacity to commit to a goal or purpose. Corporate firms have long realised that a good contest on the football field also prepares one for the fight for market share and boardroom battles that lie ahead. Skills gained through sports are *transferable* beyond the sporting context, which can be put to good use in every kind of workplace and at every level of responsibility within an organisation. Branche, who attended Howard University Medical School, credits his involvement in sports for much of his success as a surgeon. 'The structure and discipline that sports give you transcend into life,' says Branche, who played basketball and tennis in college. 'I know for sure I wouldn't be sitting here now, were it not for sports... These are things that translate into the operating room, the business arena, any successful profession.'

In 2004, the European Commission's Directorate General, Education and Culture, conducted a survey on the educational and social values of sport in the European Union. When asked about the importance of sports and the values that it develops, survey respondents most frequently identified team spirit (52%), followed by discipline (46%), friendship (38%), effort (36%), self-control (33%), fair play (32%), respect for others (32%) and sticking to the rules (31%). (European Commission, The Citizens of the European Union and Sport (Brussels, Belgium: European Commission, November 2004, Special Eurobarometer 213/ Wave 62.0–TNS Opinion & Social), p. 19.

Sports and Me–Dilip Vengsarkar

Dilip Vengsarkar says, 'Sports taught me everything. It taught me patience, it taught me tenacity, it taught me to stand by myself, despite myself. I would see the wickets tumble and knew that I had to stay put on the batting ground. It taught me to give my whole self, mind, body and soul to the moment at hand on the field, because I knew that even if one wavers, I fall. Sports gave me character.' As I saw Dilipji, retracing his cricketing days, his stance changed; he seemed almost in a trance narrating stories of his love story with this beautiful game we call cricket. He continued, 'One innings I would score a hundred and in the very next a duck. Cricket taught me humility.' In those days cricket was more of the five-day matches. He said, 'Cricket taught me that playing long innings is a matter of habit and practice. It taught me to be tough.'

Atul Kasbekar

Through--out his student life, photographer Atul Kasbekar had been a passionate sports person. He played team sports like cricket, basketball and football and also individual games like tennis. Sports to Atul was, 'singularly crucial' in making him what he is today. He says, 'I am only as good as my stylist, my model, my makeup artist or my production guy is. So essentially a shot which you call perfect is nothing but a moment of perfect tuning where each member gives his best while still keeping in harmony with the whole. Now how can I get my team to give its best? How can I recreate that perfect tuning every time I shoot? I do so by making them feel that they are a part of the process and that their mastery can make or break the shoot. I give them freedom to give their best while believing in the fact that they will give their best. I can do so because this is what I have done all through school and college as captain of the cricket or basketball teams which I led. Team sports taught me that I am not a self contained unit and I have used that training to create that magical moment with my camera. My expertise is the expertise of synthesis and harmony. Team sports taught me team management but it taught me one more thing, it taught me how to separate my efforts from the win-loss trap. I learnt that factually you win some and lose some but if you have given your best, fundamentally you are a winner all the way!!!'

Vandana Agarwal

Vandana Agarwal, a qualified architect, has taken up social service as her life mission. She currently works with an NGO Manav Sadhna which runs from the Gandhi Ashram. Her son Amish, an ardent sportsman though played a variety of games when young took up tennis seriously around the fifth grade. He was the state champion for Gujarat and represented the state at the national levels. Vandana says, 'The most important skill which sports taught my son was to understand the difference between confidence and over-confidence. He understood through experience the delicate balance between not allowing the negative thoughts to cloud his psyche which would harm his performance and yet not under-estimate what he is put against or take the game lightly at any point in between.' Amish secured 93% in his board exams and is currently doing his civil engineering at Michigan University US, which is one of the best institutes in the world for this stream. Vandana says, 'Sport not only taught my child life skills, but offered the much needed respite and relaxation from his intense study hours during exam times. He could lose himself in the ball and would come back to his books refreshed and replenished.'

Brandy Johnson

Brandy Johnson (America's top gymnast in the late 1980s) after her retirement, said, 'Through gymnastics I've learned how to be disciplined and how to make sacrifices. How to use good judgment and how to make decisions that will affect the rest of my life, not knowing if they're good or bad, but having to take a chance.' *Parade* Magazine, April 7, 1991

Billie Jean King

Tennis legend Billie Jean King said, 'It's about learning your craft... It's about making decisions, corrections, choices. I don't think it's so much about becoming a tennis player. It's about becoming a person.' *Sports Illustrated*, April 29, 1991

5.2 Sports and your child

According to National Association for Health and Fitness, U.S. children should accumulate at least sixty minutes, and up to several hours, of age appropriate physical activity on all or most days of the week.

☑ *Reality check*

How long does your child spend in sports (structured and unstructured) on an everyday basis?
    Two hours and more
    One hour and more

Less than 1 hour
Less than thirty minutes
An hour or two on weekends
Zero sports activity whatsoever

The 'No Sport' child of the twenty-first century

For centuries, games have been used for enjoyment, enthusiasm, and activity. Children take to sports as duck to water. Why then this conscious attempt to make sports a part of a child's everyday life?

A steady decline in active play has overtaken us. Less free time, increased academic pressure, and the advent of T.V. computers, play stations as means of entertainment are the prime reasons for this shift from outdoors to indoors. Youth today, exercise their minds in complex mathematical sums; fingers and thumbs are frantically punching buttons on the key board or on the myriad remote controls.

Lack of space has played the devil too. In most metros and cities, children are cooped up in isolated houses and cramped residential colonies with little space to play. Housing societies hardly have facilities for mass sports like football or for other sports like volleyball, basketball, track and field. Very little, or no land is allocated to sports clubs where indoor sports like chess, badminton, table tennis, can be played. Small neighbourhood parks, within walking or biking distance from home, have been gulped by commercial complexes. Even if there is a park nearby, safety concerns make them non-usable, as many parents do not allow their children outdoors, unsupervised.

Schools in India too, do not really emphasize on sports, as most want to make their mark through academic excellence. Kids receive one paltry thirty-minute PE class per week or an annual sports day with a mere twenty days practice. This simply isn't enough even to get them excited about moving their bodies. Many schools do not even have a playground! The message is clear, 'Let us produce child prodigies in science, mathematics, even performing arts but if one must opt for sports...one had better be brilliant, otherwise...? The stakes are simply too much. We are essentially a cerebral nation after all. The tragedy is that our bureaucratic planners have made sport an afterthought; but our children are straining at the leash, with all kinds of horrific consequences.

The 'organisation' of sports at too early an age, in affluent circles, however, is one of the main reasons which has developed an aversion for sports in general in children. In the early twentieth century,

sports and games were spontaneous, unstructured, and without adult involvement. During the latter part of the twentieth century, 'free play' or unstructured games primarily gave way to organised sports. This is reflective of parents who try to 'manage' every aspect of their child's life, in a mindless chase for perfection. Today, the situation is such that we have organised sports programmes for even four year olds. Organised sports are created along grown-up models with elaborate drafts, year-round specialisation and repetitive training sessions. In some cases, organisations shift the focus to goals that are not necessarily child oriented, and it is about how good the sports academy is in churning out potential Tendulkars or Sania Mirza's. The result is that more than two-thirds of children quit organised sports by the time they're thirteen, either burned out or bored silly.

It is payback time!

We are paying a heavy price for this disinterest in sports in our children.

More youngsters are overweight. A survey conducted by the Bangalore Assisted Conception Centre, showed that of the 1000 children between the years 11 to 18 years, 15% came under the obese category with another 20% being classified as overweight. Obesity was found to be very much more prevalent in the upper socio economic group (nearly 80%) and practically all of these children admitted to not having much exercise on a daily basis. Sedentary lifestyle and obesity is leading to heart disease, hypertension and poor muscle strength/tone. Says nutrionist Suman Agarwal, 'Something like 80% of overweight children become overweight adults, so I think it really is quite a medical time bomb... just waiting to happen.'

Besides, unfit children develop low opinions of themselves and are prone to build up antisocial attitudes. They become introverted, depressed and de-motivated. They often become the subject of bullying and prejudice in childhood and adolescence, the effects of which can be seen even in adulthood.

The threshold of tolerance in our children too is coming down steadily and coping with failure is something they seem to be quite ignorant of. This is a life skill they are not taught.

Negative sports experiences often lead to negative emotional reactions in the child, such as low self-esteem.

Exposure to violence on television and in computer games, coupled with the lack of participation in sports, is slowly making kids more angry and violent with no positive outlet for this volatile energy.

Playing sports is a great stress reliever and its absence builds stress.

Lack of sports is a prime reason for children becoming dull.

Because children don't play sports on a regular basis, they seem much older, they do not know how to relax, how to have fun and how to get along and solve differences.

5.3 Parent's role

However much we may respect and admire our sports heroes and heroines (Sachin Tendulkar, Sunil Gavaskar, Sania Mirza, Mahesh Bhupati, Anju Bobby George, Geet Sethi), once it comes to our children, academics becomes the defining stance. The measure of a child is not how agile she is with her legs, but how fast she is with her numbers; it is not about winning chess moves but whether he can use that intelligence to be the *numero uno* in his class, it is not about his powerful backhand but how proficient he is with the various languages taught at school. A (academics) after all comes much before S (sports).

And so, at best, sports remains confined to the P.T classes at school or an hour here and there in the society's playground once in a while. At worst, we push our children to excel. We do sign them up for all popular sports be it tennis, karate, skating, basketball, cricket, badminton; but if the coach does not find any edge in the child, or the child himself withdraws, he is branded as unfit for sports.

Yes, there are parents who dedicate their lives to developing their child's probable sports careers and we see these parents religiously sitting in the stands for hours, driving down their kids to practice sessions and sacrificing their social lives so that their children can be up and about at the crack of dawn for the fields. But for these parents, sports is, what is for others academics—a springboard to career and

economic security. For these parents, sports 'is' if the child 'has it' in him and its form is strictly 'organised'. But is there a negative side to this over-kill?

Consider the scenarios given below

Sanjay came home after an interclub football match and his father asked, 'Who won?' Should he have asked, 'Did you enjoy the match?'

It was already forty minutes and Sneha's mom was still walking undeterred back and forth the swimming pool edge with the timer as Sneha swam. Sneha had taken to swimming with a lot of interest and enthusiasm but all that she now worried about was whether she could bring the satisfaction on her mom's face with her increased speed or not.

Rangesh's precocity with skates turned out to be his bane. His parents ordered one of the best quality skates from Mumbai (they never let an opportunity pass to mention the same to Rangesh), they put him on to individual coaching and their vacation was sacrificed to provide the money for it, and he found himself up everyday at 6 am to the smiling and determined face of either mom or dad with, 'Come on son. Skating time, something that you love so much'. Rangesh is not sure anymore. Does he love skating or hate it?

Karan asks his dad before stepping onto the field, 'Will you love me even if I do not win?'

The design behind

The trade-off—The stakes are high for the parents. They themselves are under great pressure as they have invested too much in their kid's sports' success. Kids can't just be good academically and athletically. And so, if it is not academics, it has to be sports. The 'gifted' child becomes the focus of attention as the parents put in their resources-time, money and efforts, and at many a time even stretch beyond what is reasonable. Simple enjoyment is passé. The more the parents put in of themselves, the more exacting they become of their child. Yes they give their 'best' to the best in their child, but the payback had better be in best too. But whose best? The child's best or the best of the best players in the country or across the globe?

Logistics—For some it is simple reasoning. Kids need to be specialising in one sport early on because that will give them a jump. The earlier they start and more earnest the parents, the better will be the child's chances.

Old dream, new opportunity—Many parents live out their failed sports experiences vicariously through their children in hoping to experience success through them. So it is, 'I could not play at the International level, but I will make sure you do'. Fathers, typically, get over-excited about their children's sporting talents because they abandoned theirs too early—or discovered them too late.

Validating one's worth—In many homes non-working women go through severe identity crisis and to make sense of their lives focus their energies into promoting the sporting career of their child. Chauffeuring the child to practice sessions (and if the mother has to wake up early for the child to make it to a 6 a.m. class, the demand for returns is even stronger). She does not let anyone forget that she is forsaking her precious morning sleep for the apple-of-her-eye or waiting alongside for hours to gently nudge the child whenever his concentration wavers. These make for tremendous deposits in the 'I-am-doing-something-worthy' account.

What about sports for sports itself?

What about sports without any strings (career, fame, money) attached? For the simple, yet precious pleasures that it invariably brings—the fun, excitement and adventure; the almost trancelike state where one is one with just the sport at hand; the relief in the release of excessive energy when one runs as fast, jumps as high, stretches as much, hits the ball as hard as one can. What about hours of unstructured sports-neighbourhood cricket, kabaddi, volley ball, badminton, carrom that we spent the hours in when young? When losing and wininng were secondary to the fun and thrill of the game itself. When the hours spent on the field did not have to be justified in terms of perfecting strokes or hitting harder, heaping up trophies and certificates of the same or gaining recognition as a potential player in the professional sporting world. Weren't we a bunch of kids doing every evening what kids are supposed to do...play?

Do our children spend even a tenth of their after school time on the fields like we did?

5.4 The backfire

According to research 70% of kids drop out of sports by age thirteen and parental pressure is one of the top causes for this. Overwhelming parental support which may seem positive at first turns detrimental in most cases. Potential stars are lost because the pressure whether tacit or overt, gets to them and sports becomes a chore. They quit. Kids are turned off by bad experiences at an early age and resign themselves to a sports-free passive life. Precisely when budding adolescents need the physical and mental benefits of sports participation, they are at the greatest risk of quitting and becoming sedentary.

The ill-effects of pressure are many

Depressions

Parents see things through rose-coloured spectacles and feel that their children are better than they really may be. When the demands of a sport exceed a child's cognitive and physical development, the child may develop feelings of failure and frustration. When children do not or cannot meet their parent's expectations they feel inadequate and get subsequently depressed. Self esteem in many cases suffers immensely too.

Boredom

With too much pressure, expectations and routine, the fun goes. Kids stop playing for themselves and begin playing for their parents. Too much time is spent on perfection and not enough free time (fun time) being a kid and exploring new adventures. According to Doug Gardner, a sports psychology consultant for ThinkSport, based in Lafayette, Coliforuia, 'Kids, no matter what era, are striving to really be good at their sport. Where it has changed, obviously, has been with the adults and the parents. When the sport itself becomes more of a job, more than it is about fun and improvement and getting better, once that line is crossed, it's hard for kids to understand. Kids don't understand what they're getting into because it's a business model. These are adults running all of this stuff, and kids aren't used to such cut-throat business. They want to play their sport. They're not used to the stakes involved that a lot of adults have created.'

Parents find out that they can force their kids to play at a young age, but when they become old enough to make their own decisions, 'pressured' or enforced sport is rejected.

Burnout

Burnout has been described as dropping/quitting of an activity that was at one time enjoyable. With excessive structured sports fatigue sets in, both emotional and physical. The fire and enthusiasm leave. Children get sick of playing tournaments and matches round the year. Criticism from coaches, parents, and other teammates, as well as pressure to win can create nerve-wracking anxiety or stress for young athletes. Stress can be physical, emotional, or psychological, and research has indicated that it can lead to burnout. Noted sports psychologist Jim Loehr says that early success has its downside. '... the ones who have the most difficulty are those who have the greatest success earliest, because they're always defending turf and having to live up to all these phenomenal claims of genius.' *USA Today*, July 17, 1996.

Health costs

Warning signs abound from pediatricians and trainers about specialising too early – overuse of muscles, over-stress on joints and mental fatigue are screaming from all quarters. Children who are expected to train too much or too often can develop overuse injuries such as stress fractures and damage to growth plates. 'We are seeing more and more stress fractures in children and more and more injuries caused by repetitive use,' according to Dr. Carl Stanitski, chief of orthopaedic surgery at Children's Hospital of Michigan.

5.5 Reversing trends

Milind Deora

Milind Deora, the youngest MP, *Economic Times* Editor and a management graduate from Boston University, said, 'If there is one thing I could rewind and live again, it would be my participation in sports.' Milind was interested in the guitar and so avoided sports. He said, 'I regret, that I found excuses to escape sports and I regret that those excuses were allowed and accepted. I wish I had taken up sports more seriously.'

Taking matters in hand

We, as children remember being on the field all day running and playing preferring it to the X-box. Today it is wishful thinking that the pull of the playground will eventually prove stronger than the lure of the channels (Pogo and cartoon network), computer and video stations. Rising obesity in children bears testimony to our flawed assumptions. Leisure, to our children no longer means outdoor games. It is wake up time for us. Unless we step in and give them the gentle push to step out, chances are they will be bundled up exercising just their fingers on the remote controls/key board/ or their eye muscles as they shuttle between the T.V. channels. We may not accept that our child is grossly overweight till the first sign of physical collapse.

We can be the missing link connecting children to sports. We have to build the right climate for sports participation, whether it means handling structured sports better or encouraging our children to be out in the fields for informal sports. We have to put the fun back and take the pressure out.

Dr. Ranier Martin, a researcher in Human Kinetics states: 'Youth sports are not inherently evil nor are they inherently good—they are what we make of them.' Sport is like a double-edged sword. Swung in the right direction, the sword can have tremendous positive effects, but swung in the wrong direction it can be devastating. The sword is held by adults who supervise children's sports. Whether a sport is constructive or destructive in the psychological development of young children greatly depends on the values, education and skills of those adults.

Let us go to beginning-the right know how for sports participation for our children

5.6 The science of sports

The Age Factor

Not every sport is appropriate for every age. Attempting to teach a one-year-old to read is futile and frustrating to both teacher and infant

because the child at this developmental stage does not yet have the mental or physical capabilities to do so. Within the sport context, one can similarly argue that unless children are prepared physically, cognitively, and emotionally for the demands of competition, they will experience frustration, benefit little, and possibly suffer a great deal. It's important to select a sport that is safe and suited to the child at hand. According to Sally Harris, M.D., M.P.H., a pediatrician in the Department of Sports Medicine at the Palo Alto Medical Foundation in Palo Alto, California, the pace of development varies widely in children and it's impossible to specify sports-readiness ages with precision. 'We go mostly by common sense and experience,' Harris says. But she does suggest some general guidelines for the following age-groups:

- **2 to 5 years.** Children are just learning fundamental skills like throwing, catching, running, and jumping. It's best to stick with activities that use these skills but don't combine them in a complicated way.
- **6 to 9 years.** Children put the fundamentals together in moves related to actual sports: throwing for distance or accuracy; rearing back to kick a ball. Better memory and decision-making enable them to deal with basic strategies of simplified forms of baseball or soccer.

- **10 to 12 years.** Youngsters can master the complex motor skills they need and have the cognitive ability to learn strategies for 'adult' forms of most sports, including football and basketball.

Says Paul Stricker, a pediatric sports medicine specialist in San Diego, 'Kids develop sports skills in a very sequential manner, just like they do sitting up and walking and talking. Parents and coaches just don't understand that sequence. They feel that after they're potty trained, if they practise something enough, they'll get it.'

The Issue of Specialisation

Three months of football, a couple of months in cricket, badminton in winters—that's the way it used to be for many of us when young, but the children of today (parents?) pick up one sport and stick to it exclusively. Early specialisation is one of the most striking features of modern sports. Since international-level participants appear to be getting younger, specialisation in sports such as gymnastics, figure skating, tennis, and swimming at an early age has become predominant.

Does early specialisation really make a difference down the line? Contrary to popular belief of parents, research shows that it may not. According to The American Academy of Paediatrics, children should be discouraged from specialising in a single sport before adolescence to avoid physical and psychological damage. They said, 'Those who participate in a variety of sports and specialise only after reaching the age of puberty, tend to be more consistent performers, have fewer injuries, and adhere to sports play longer than those who specialise early.' Waiting to specialise until the age of twelve or thirteen, when children are more emotionally and physically mature, helps ensure that they are pursuing an activity that really interests them, rather than trying to fulfill a parent's or coach's dream.

An early maturing child may be better during childhood, but research indicates that late maturing children may have greater potential of reaching international standards in a specific sport during adulthood. In fact, in their quest to dominate the athletic world, the former communist nations of Eastern Europe switched, in the 1980s, their preference to select talented children for sports, from early to late maturers. Their prior decision to select early maturers has only seldom met their expectations. Late maturers, however, had more consistency and in most cases achieved higher performance. Late maturing children start into their adolescent growth spurt at a later stage of development than early maturing children and, in most cases, their growth spurt lasts longer.

One interesting study conducted by Barynina and Vaitsekhovskii looked at athletes who began specialising in swimming early (at seven to eight years), met the criteria for a USSR Master of Sport at age eleven to fifteen, took part successfully in high-level competition, joined the USSR national teams, and achieved results at a national and international levels. After some time had passed, (between two and twenty years after their sport careers ended), they asked how early sessions in a sport had affected the social, psychological, and medical aspects of the athletes' lives. They found that the earlier the athletes began specialised training, the shorter their stay on the national team and the earlier they left big-time sports. Among the reasons for leaving big-time sports, these swimmers cited psychological fatigue, general health, and loads that were difficult to withstand. (Barynina II, Vaitsekhovskii SM. The aftermath of early specialisation for highly qualified swimmers. Fitness Sports Revue International 1989;6:21-23.)

An increase in injuries of child athletes has also been linked to early specialisation. Physical-Children specialising in a single sport run the risk of overusing muscles, causing stress fractures and fatigue. Says Brett Oden, MD, director of Buffalo Hospital's Sports Medicine Center, 'As children specialise in one specific sport, they run the risk of muscle imbalance, damage to growth plates, and overuse injuries such as tendonitis.' Injuries in one's youth can also increase the risk of injury in the future. For example, knee injuries in childhood have been shown to increase the likelihood of adult arthritis by as much as four times (Lord 'Dangerous Games'). In girls, secondary amenorrhea, or cessation of menstrual cycles after menarche, can occur as a result of intense athletic training. Prolonged amenorrhea may cause diminished bone mass from the associated decrease in estrogen secretion, augmenting the risk for stress fractures and the potential for osteoporosis in adulthood. (American Academy of Paediatrics. Intensive training and sports specialisation in youth athletes: Policy statement. Paediatrics 2000;106:154-157.10.)

Psychological—Specialisation actually, most often leads to a tremendous increase in pressure, which can lead to burnout. Intensive sports participation may take time away from normal social and developmental activities and can lead to isolation or other problems, including depression, anxiety, conversion reactions, and eating disorders. Steven Anderson, University of Washington sports medicine professor, asks, 'How many kids need to get frustrated and burn out to produce every Tiger Woods?'

The Competition Frenzy

When should children begin competitive sports?

While just about any type of sports program can be found for children of just about any age, a critical question concerns the proper time for them to begin competitive involvement. The fundamental purpose of youth sports is to allow children to learn and enjoy a sport without the anxiety of having to keep score or care about winning or losing. Competition at an early age robs children of the fundamentals of sporting. Children below seven do not fully understand game rules, including the concepts of winning and losing. Competition at this stage can lead to stress and can be detrimental to the children's self esteem. Evidence suggests that coaches and parents provide most of the stress for the kids.

According to Steven J. Anderson, MD, clinical professor in the Department of Paediatrics at the University of Washington in Seattle and chair of the American Academy of Paediatrics (AAP) Committee on Sports Medicine and Fitness, 'Even in early elementary school, the emphasis should be on learning basic skills and rules, without the added pressure of competition. Equal participation rather than winning, should be the goal at this age.'

According to Dr. Jerry May, a Reno-based sports psychologist, who works with Olympic and professional athletes, 'In early school-age years, kids should be committed to mastering the skills of the specific game, not to winning.'

According to Sally S. Harris M.D M.P.H, 'Prior to age ten, most children do not have the cognitive ability to understand and remember complex strategies required for competition. Additionally, they are not able to master complex motor skills required for most competitive sports. Throughout childhood, skill development, fun and participation should take priority over competition.'

Research, (Brustad, 1993a), has focused on children developing attributional capabilities, with the finding that until about 10, they are not accurate in distinguishing among ability, effort and task difficulty as causal factors in determining sport outcomes. Consequently, success or failure may be easily misattributed to lack of effort when in fact it may be a consequence of task difficulty or deficiency in skill. Consequently, when the child fails he might try harder, but experience the same failure because the task is extraordinarily difficult, or he lacks the necessary skills to be successful. Inevitably, frustration leads to discouragement, lowered self-esteem, and ultimately withdrawal.

5.7 The psychology of sports

The Fun Element

For children, playing a sport is not about winning or training better, it is about having a good time. Never let go of this perspective. Check on the sports compass. Align the true-north to 'fun'. Ask yourself,

'Is my child having fun?' If your answer is 'yes', he is in the right direction.

SPORTS COMPASS

Choose a sport which is fun for your child. In a summary of many different studies on the subject, the Journal of Physical Education, Recreation and Dance found that children consistently had multiple motives for participating in sports, and those motives defined as intrinsic were unanimously the main reason for participation. Intrinsic motives, which were cited most often, include 'having fun, learning skills, testing one's abilities, and experiencing excitement and personal accomplishments. Getting awards, winning, and pleasing others (known as extrinsic factors) were consistently rated as having the lowest relevance to participation' (Brady). In a similar study done by the Institute for the Study of Youth Sports, children said the number one reason they participated in sports was 'to have fun,' and they rarely cited reasons like 'for the challenge of competition' and 'for the excitement of competition' (Wolff 'The American...').

Picking a sport in which the child's other friends are into, can make the experience more fun and increase the likelihood for the child to stick to the game longer.

The 'Choice' Element

Let the child sample several sports before he settles down to one or two.

Sachin Tendulkar

For the great master blaster, Sachin Tedulkar, cricket was not the only love in his childhood. There was a private green at the front of his building where he used to spend all his spare time playing football, volleyball, hockey, cricket and a lot of tennis too. In fact, his friends and family called him 'Mac' for he had styled himself after the great tennis hero John McEnroe. He grew his hair long and made his father buy him the same headbands and sweatbands too. It was only around his early teens that Sachin settled for serious cricketing and not before that.

Expose your child to a variety of sports through stories, movies, television, demonstrations, sporting events, or the Olympics. Watching people compete and seeing new possibilities for activities may spark a child's interest too. According to Dr Laskowski form Mayo clinic, 'The more that children can try different sports and activities and find something they're good at doing, the more they'll enjoy the activity.' You might have to go through a whole list before the kiddo latches on to one. It may not be easy to find out, but the search will ultimately be rewarding. There is a sport activity out there that can create interest and motivation in your child.

Natural Bent and Passion

Allow your child to lead you. Children who excel in sports are those who are passionate about it. And for them the drive comes from within. We think of Sachin Tendulkar and his world class style but do we also know of his undying passion and the endless hours of practice which he put in day after day and year after year, on his own accord? He had to change his school and opt for one close to the cricketing ground, which meant forfeiting the friends he grew up with. The decision was left to him and he did not take very long to reach a decision, 'cricket was more important'. Sachin said, 'My only dream was to wear the Indian cap and the Indian colours. When I was a child, somehow I always knew I would play cricket for my country. There was never even 0.1% of doubt. I was so much into cricket that I did not miss anything else. There were times when I felt like going out for a movie with friends, but I could not do that often, because I used the time for practice, even with a rubber ball, when it was raining heavily. I used to be looking forward to 3 O'clock in the afternoon. I really used to enjoy playing cricket for three or four hours.' His coach, mentor Mr Achreka too, said about him that, 'Since childhood, whenever he had any problem with his batting, Sachin would go on practising for hours till he rectified it. And we all know, 'Practice makes a man perfect'.

The phrase 'eat cricket, drink cricket, sleep cricket' began to ring true for Sachin. Even after he broke into international cricket, Sachin was known to talk—cricket, of course!—and walk in his sleep. And the phrase he uttered most often in his sleep? 'Take two!' (In Marathi—'Don-ge').

Child's Emotional Makeup

Would your child prefer a team or an individual sport? If a child enjoys solitary activities, karate, swimming, track and field, and gymnastics are sports that involve a good deal of independence. If your child loves to be around people you can opt for team games like cricket, basketball, football, etc. The health and fitness benefits of physical activity will be experienced whether an individual or team sport is chosen.

Does your child prefer a fast-paced game? You could go for football, basketball or running. But if he prefers leisurely activities, it could be throw ball, golf, etc.

Is your child comfortable with group-training or individual-training routine? A child with a shy temperament may need some one-to-one coaching before he/she is ready to face the group.

☑ Sports organisation checklist

Once you have zeroed down a sport appropriate to your child's interest and abilities, it is time to check out the available coaching institutes and classes.

Go through the following checklist:

Is the playing field free of hazards?

Is there a plan for handling injuries or medical emergencies?

What is the student-to-coach ratio?

Is the coach really knowledgeable about the sport?

If he is knowledgeable, can he also teach well based on individual child's ability and nature?

Does the coach treat the participants with dignity, emphasizing encouragement and positive feedback?

Does the coach teach participants to cope with negative feelings like embarrassment, anger, frustration and fear?

Is the coach fair and consistent in his coaching?

Does he insist on warming-up and cooling-down times to help prevent injuries?

Most importantly, is playing there, fun for your child?

Is the coach pleasant and positive? For a serious player, his coach's words are the law. The coach influences not only the child's game but also his development and attitude.

Miscellaneous tips:

Always remember a coach will take more interest in your child, if you as a parent do too. Interact and exchange notes with the coach about what your child shared with you after the game.

Make surprise visits during coaching.

5.8 The right sports parent's attitude

Some parents use their children to validate their self worth or goals. Some miss the big picture because they want their child to be a star. Do any of these apply to you?

The 'You-must-win' syndrome

Sneha Kapadia, a sports parent, said, for many years, her son's cricket team beat its archrival, a team from a neighbouring town. The first time her son's team lost, she was upset and asked her son if he was sorry about the loss. She says, 'I realised, for my son, the game had ended ten minutes before. I was the one who was wrapped up in the emotional rivalry.'

Parents enroll their children into a sport for all the right reasons- to improve fitness and coordination, learn new skills, build character. But watching their children compete, brings out an unfamiliar intensity of emotion in parents. As the whistle blows and the game begins, parents start to think, 'If you're not a winner, you're a loser'. Goals change, expectations go awry and the child becomes the 'product' which the parent is developing to be a 'success'. Healthy encouragement becomes obsessive involvement.

The tricky business of parental support

Take the pressure off
The pressure to succeed can shift children's focus away from their enjoyment of an activity to fulfilling adult expectations. Sport psychologists point out that the attitude of a parent can make or break a child's athletic experience. Learning to take risks, to fail and to feel OK is as important as winning all the time. We live in a competitive

society, and sport simply reflects other major institutions in which individuals are tested against one another. We cannot do away with the competitive frenzy (especially at an early age) even if we want, but we must keep our perspective in check. We can say to ourselves and our children that:

Winning isn't everything or the only thing, and

One does not need to win to enjoy the magic of sports.

Dilip Vengsarkar, 'I did not have to prove myself. That is exactly why I proved myself.'

Gully (by-lane) cricketing made Dilip Vengsarkar the cricketer that he is. Vengsarkar reminisces on his school days when he would return home, fling his bag in a corner, catch a quick bite and then run to the by-lanes with his bat for his 'gully cricket', only to return after sunset. There was no pressure to perform and he had the luxury of leisure. He said, 'We did not have the T.V. culture and our parents were not obsessively involved trying to manage every moment in our lives. We were left pretty much to ourselves and this allowed cricket to develop into a passion from mere interest.' He did not go to any coaching or extra curricular classes, but spent a lot of time observing the then famous batsmen. He says, 'When we were not playing cricket we were watching cricket. And that is how we improved. We used to watch players like Sunil Gavaskar, Manjerekar and Amaranth, studying their every move in great detail. We would watch them play at close quarters, their leg positions, arm drives, the position of their eyes, even the way they walked up to the ground to bat. And then we would practise those moves ourselves. We played for hours, working on ourselves, improving ourselves.' He ended with, 'I did not have to prove myself and so I proved myself.'

Sania Mirza

Imran Mirza, Sania's father said, 'As we came from a sporting background, we knew very well the kind of pressure that built up in competitive sports, particularly at an international level. So we tried our best to toughen her up mentally. Right from Day 1 we tried to teach her that as long as she was doing her best on the court, winning and losing did not matter. I think that a major role we played in her evolution was to build the right match temperament.' Sania Mirza, in an interview, said, 'Parental support is very important in this area. Kids don't mind what others say, but when parents criticise them, it really hurts them.' *The Rediff Special/*M D Riti February 07, 2005

Remember for every success story like Sania Mirza there are numerous prodigies whose promise fizzled under pressure.

Have realistic expectations

A positive approach starts with realistic expectations. Get to know your child's capabilities. Talk to the coach about her/his expectations for your child. Your child may or may not be a sports prodigy. Though it's natural to compare your child to others, it's dangerous to have expectations based on what someone else does. If your child isn't an all-star, accept it.

Manisha Basu

Says Manisha Basu, a TT champion herself, 'My younger son Abheek once during a game of TT at the national level came upon a profound discovery about himself. After winning the game he came up to me and said, "You know what mom, seeing the pain of loss on my competitor's face breaks my heart. I do not think competitive sports is for me." Her son excelled in technique and exuded stamina but was not emotionally suited to "match temperament". He still plays TT everyday but for his own pleasure and exercise.'

Besides, what really are the chances of reaching the level where one plays at the national and international games? Very little. According to research, less than three percent of children will make it to the top brackets. And when they do so, it is at a big cost. We see the fame and glory of popular sports but we cannot see or know the years of hard work, turmoil, sweat, missed playing hours, being with friends and enjoying simple moments doing nothing. Ericsson and Charness (1994), in a comprehensive review of the literature on elite performers, concluded that specifically, it takes a minimum of ten years of intensive practice to reach world class levels of performance. During this time, a performer's psychological, physiological, and physical attributes are shaped to the activity in which she or he is engaged. Hence, while peers may be engaged in play and recreation, the child who strives for excellence must start early, and maintain a strict schedule, which provides for practice under the guidance of knowledgeable coaches. More than innate talent, according to Ericsson et al., it is the sheer magnitude of this deliberate practice which accounts for differential performance among individuals competing at different levels. Maybe your child does have the star potential, but he may still not want to make sports his sole focus. Remember to 'let be'. The child is playing for his enjoyment, not yours.

Emphasise efforts

Do you have a young goalkeeper on your team that may let in one too many goals but still gives 110%?

Applaud the effort. Don't give false praise, but always try to find something to compliment. 'Good shot,' 'Nice rally'. A quiet pat on the back or a simple 'well played' can do the trick too. For Karen the awareness came when she took up skating lessons herself. Trying to improve on her balance, and yet not lose on speed, made her realise just how tough it is for children to learn everything from scratch. She felt like a ten year old, wanting to cry or stomp off each time she lost her balance and fell. From her skating lessons she learnt something even more worthwhile than the art of balancing on wheels and that is, the difference that positive encouragement can make. For days after not being able to roll backwards, when her coach cheered 'great speed in front rolling,' she turned her defeat into the desire to try again. Children learn to appreciate the ability of others, to win and lose gracefully.

Do not reward their efforts through bribes-ice cream treat, I-pod, computer, etc. Kids who 'play for pay' tend to burn out quicker and take less pleasure in playing.

Acknowledge the good effort of the children playing against your child-they're not to be blamed if they do something well. Let the children see your pleasure in witnessing their ability to compete.

Handle their disappointments tactfully

Install emotional support and positive messages. Tell them, 'Win or lose—if you are having fun, that is what matters'. Tell them, 'There is always another chance. No matter what the score is for you today the sun will come up again tomorrow.'

When speedskater Dan Jansen lost a race at age eleven, he cried on the car ride home. But his father helped him put it into perspective by telling him, 'There are more important things in life than skating in circles.' *Chicago Tribune*, November 9, 1994

> Take the emphasis off defeat by asking question like:-
> - What was the best part of the game?
> - Do you think you gave your best?

- What is the one thing you have learned from this match?
- Remind them of their sporting heroes and ask 'Did he/she ever finish second?'
- Talk about the difference between winning and the satisfaction of personal achievement.

  Criticism—overt or tacit, should be avoided at all costs

  Some parents sigh and say very diplomatically, 'You were good, but you could have been better'. And a time which the child could have used to share joy and pride in his or her team's performance – or freely express his or her thoughts and feelings after a rough game – turns into a post-game critique and criticism session. The child's experience no longer matters. The parent's experience and emotions take center stage.

- Listen, especially after a disappointment. Give your child a chance to express feelings in an atmosphere of unconditional love and support. Do not lecture or talk. Just listen.
- Says, Trupti, the mother of skating champion Apoorva, 'I may be disappointed, but I know my child will learn from any loss.'
- Never encourage your child to blame anyone else for his/her defeats.

Give them breaks

Children need breaks, both physically as well as psychologically. Swimmer Matt Biondi, who earned gold medals in three consecutive Olympics (1984, 1988, and 1992), started swimming at the age of five, but trained only three months a year until he was fifteen. 'A lot of parents have a strong drive to get their kids to be the best at ten years old. I'd rather see a kid be the best for ten years, rather than the best at ten,' he said. (*Rocky Mountain News*, July 5, 1992.)

Children's bodies need time to build up muscle and therefore need time between exercise, to repair the minute amounts of damage that comes from regular exercise. Dr. Suzanne Tanner, a physician at the University of Colorado's sports medicine clinic, recommends some down time. 'Taking a summer off can be the best thing some of those athletes can do for themselves. It allows for them to catch up on growth and gives their bodies time to recover fully from any injuries they might have. I don't recommend year-round participation.' *Boulder Daily Camera*, July 28, 1995.

Does your child strangely develop a headache or a tummy ache just before his football coaching? You dismiss it by saying, 'I know these are your excuses.' Well, try and go behind the reason for the excuses. Can a visible physical injury be the only reason for your child to miss his coaching? What about a punctured interest? What if your child, emotionally or psychologically, does need a break?

Allow them 'other' time too

Don't let training become all consuming. Organised sport should not eat away all the free time of the child. Children have other interests which should be respected. Life is not just about training all day long, at school for academics and at home for sports. Children do need their leisure time, lone time, and time with family and friends when they don't have to 'perform' or do anything in particular.

Support the right way

Brush up on the fundamentals of the game your child is playing. Learn the rules and fewer happenings on the field will look wrong to you.

Teach the concept of 'fair play' by not boasting when your child wins, by avoiding criticism of other players and coaches, and most importantly, differentiating between right and wrong.

Teach children to set personal goals rather than competitive ones. For example, swimmers can think in terms of personal bests rather than races won; skaters can focus on learning new jumps rather than competitions won; tennis players can aim for better control rather than matches won.

Finally, what if even after doing everything right, the child loses interest and wants to quit? According to Mr. May, a sports psychologist, Before quitting, ask the child to last for an agreed amount of time, say a certain number of weeks. Then it's OK to quit at that time ... for the child to say, 'I just don't like it.'

5.9 Unstructured sports-less structure and more freedom

Silken Laumann

Olympic rowing medalist, Silken Laumann said, 'Play was really a big part of my life and the foundation of how I became an Olympic athlete,' she explained. 'I don't see kids having the same opportunities to fall in love with sport, to be able to play on the streets in neighbourhoods, having sport and play as part of life. I'm passionate about reconnecting play and sport in the community. The time has come for us to take back the streets and parks so that our children can be active, and ultimately healthier, again.'

Organised sports is not the only avenue to reap the benefits of sporting fun. In fact, even if children are into structured sports, informal outdoor sports still deserves a place in their daily calendar. There is a delicious sense of ownership in the unstructured, unorganised sport that children take up by themselves. They get to pick the game, decide on the teams, formulate rules and set the pace of the sport exactly as they enjoy it. They settle their 'disputed calls' fast, as no one wants to miss out on the fun time. There is flexibility in choice as they switch from one game to another depending on whether they are having fun or not. There are no coaches, no fans and no parents, no tournaments, no trophies. All this translates for them as 'no pressure'. When kids get together for an evening and kick a soccer ball with friends or play road hockey or gully cricket, it is not exercise or a chore or learning, but pure fun. Informal sports allow children experimentation and creativity.

It is 'Pricket' mom!

For my children, Aishwarya and Sanaya, cricket was the reigning flavour one summer season. The society's common plot served as their personal Eden Garden where they spent most of their evening hours playing matches. One day I had nothing much to do and so went up to their playground to watch their cricket. I saw the children bowl 'one over each' in alternate precision, consequently, they also batted 'one over each'. They scored runs but never got out. They dived for catches and again, more runs were added into the catchers account and the 'batsgirl' did not lose her wicket.

I was aghast. They had, to my mind a quack knowledge of the game and as their mother, it was my cardinal duty to show them the right way. I butted in and said that they had the rules all wrong. I began my narration with the appropriate authority to convey my right knowledge and understanding of cricket. After a ten-minute non-stop harangue, I asked them to start afresh and this time the right way. I offered to be their referee to make sure that they played with the right rules. My children, however, had other plans.

My elder daughter said, 'But mummy, we are not playing cricket but a new game called "Pricket".' She further taught me the rules of her pricket.

Rule1: No one gets out.

Rule 2: They play an over of six balls each, so no one really needs to wait endlessly to bat.

Rule 3: They just have to make more and more runs.

Flabbergasted, I mumbled, 'How does the game end and who becomes the winner?' Now the superior understanding was in their eyes and they began. 'We stop playing when we tire, add both our scores and compare them with the last session. Both teams win if the score is more than the last match and we both lose if the score is less."

The 'but-that-is-not-the-way-it-is-played' would not go away in me and I began once again only to be stopped short after a meek 'but...' as they said, 'It is just a game and games are meant to be fun and we are having loads of fun.'

Infallible logic! Great wisdom! I concluded, these kids are brilliant only if we allow them to be so.

Informal, unstructured and unorganised sports is not only pure fun, but can teach our children a hoard of skills which they unconsciously learn. Independence, endurance, decision-taking, problem-solving, strategising, organising and fair play are the tools of the trade which they become adept at to survive on their own every evening where everyone is an 'equal'. Above all, they get the much needed physical exercise which keeps the body lithe and mind alert. They can scream their lungs out, hop on one leg, run, jump, fall on top of one another and they find a release of energy in the way which works best for them. (They also sleep well once they hit the bed).

Research shows that children who are most active are those whose parents have encouraged them to be so. We have to provide children with resources time, a safe place and friends and then just give that little push and wait for the momentum to take over.

Make play-time a part of your child's daily calendar by slotting in at least an hour everyday for sports. Set the protocol of 'evening time is outdoors time'. Make it a habit to send them down to the society's play area, or the neighbourhood park in the evenings. Suggest outdoor play as a release for children when they are feeling restless or anxious. This will encourage an early involvement in sporting activities. If you have a backyard you could install a jungle gym or plant a tree, put up a basketball hoop near your garage. It could make for great sporting hours and also build creativity, imagination, social skills, strong bones and muscles. If you don't have facilities near your house, take your child to the nearest field, park or clubs. Get your child to meet other children. Soon they will get together and begin to enjoy themselves.

When it's time for gift giving, choose activity oriented gifts like balls, cycles, hula hoops, roller skates, skateboards, swing set, jump rope. Akash saved for a year and gave his son, Nikhil, a club membership on his ninth birthday. The smart card bearing his name and photograph was all that Nikhil needed. It is three years since then and Nikhil has practically used every sporting facility of the club.

Make your children join after-school sports clubs. They will enjoy make friends, socialise and also get to flex their muscles.

Send children for sports camps. Camps are a great place to learn about teamwork Consider enrolling with friends to make it more fun.

Get active in your society/building or colony. Chip in and buy a TT table or a carrom-board, install a sporting net where children can either play badminton, volleyball, throw ball or catch. Have Sunday-special tournaments of jumping rope, hula hoops, skating, basketball, cricket etc. Take the initiative and mobilise other children and their parents.

Consider starting a sports club in your locality.

Incorporate physical activities into birthday parties, family gatherings, and when your kids' friends come over to play.

Make T.V., academics, tuitions an absolute no-no during the evening hours.

Harsh Neotia-Family sports

Harsh Neotia's grandfather lived up to the age of hundred and till ninety-eight, he walked upright. Harsh Neotia said, 'I remember that even till about ninety-five years of age, he would play a few hands of bridge everyday with a group of friends, who were about seventy. My grandfather remembered his cards well and gave most other players, even though twenty years younger, a jog for their memory.' They had a TT table and his grandfather played that too, regularly well in his nineties. Harsh said, 'Sporting came very easily to us. I can't think of a situation where we didn't want to be out on the playground playing some sport. My children, too, have by now sampled varied sporting activities from swimming, to cricket, to tennis and of course TT.'

Make family sports a regular activity

Children love it when mum and dad join in their games. Throw a Frisbee or ball together, fly a kite, play hide-n-seek or hop-scotch together. Strap on those inline skates or that rock-climbing gear. Practise your tennis or racquetball swings together. Remember you're never too old—or uncool—to learn how to skateboard.

You don't have to play with your child every day, but on your day off, make a point of sharing in an outdoor activity with your child. A little is better than nothing. We have a once-a-week cycling programme where my two daughters, my husband and myself go cycling on roads in the early hours of the morning. They love the thrill of being on the, otherwise restricted territory and we get to teach them road cycling rules too.

Tanisha purchased a pedometer for each family member and her entire family logged in their steps and miles daily. They got into the 'winners of the day' contests, calculated steps from everywhere to everywhere-to the mailbox, park, school and other destinations. They learnt geography, honed their math's skills and enjoyed the sport of it all too.

Share your favourite sport with your child. Play catch, football, basketball, cricket. A game of footy in the backyard will get the blood flowing! Play together as partners. Have skipping rope, hula hoop tournaments. Swimming too can be a good family sport.

Use nature for sports. Introduce nature and to make things a little bit more fun. Take children trekking and on to beaches. Go hiking,

fishing, camping, boating. Make a treasure map of a park and have your friends find the 'hidden treasures'. Go bird or wildlife watching with binoculars.

If you are dropping and picking up your child from coaching, or sitting and watching, it is a good idea to enroll yourself as a student too. You probably will not get to play with your child, but still will be involved in each other's game and learning.

Growing up, winning, losing and learning are tough enough without parents confusing the issues. The beauty of all children is that they are all different. Some can hit better, some can swim quicker and some can just play a sport better than the majority of other children. Whether children are brilliant or just average, the games they play will help them grow. All children are different in ability but the same in their basic desire to play a game. Don't let them lose that desire. Less than 3% of children who play competitive sports will ever reach an elite level, but 100% can have a chance to enjoy and grow through it if we would just let them. Let children be children.

The Confident Child

Prarit felt he could conquer the world and Sarang had doubts about reaching the corner store to get the butter his mother asked for.

Eight year old Tanya walked into the new art class, nervous yet smiling, Kiran, however, wore a somber, almost solemn expression; she was certain that no one would want to befriend her.

Tanmay forgot his lines in the recitation competition but filled out the form once again in the next season promising himself, 'It would not happen again'.

Arthik stammered a couple of times in the same and swore that he would never participate in another competition, 'I am likely to repeat my bad performance', he concluded.

What makes one child have faith in himself where another quivers and cracks at the slightest challenge? What makes one keep on where another gives up? What makes one raise his hand to risk an answer even when he is not sure, while another fears 'what if I am wrong' and sits quietly even though he has the right answers? What makes one feel secure, worthy and effective while another concludes that he is unfit, worthless and would never amount to anything?

Genes? Is it a genetic lottery? Are the attitudes of Prarit, Tanya and Tanmay a reflection of their heredity?

Partly yes, but we know today that we are as much a product of our environment as we are of our genes. 'Nature' and 'Nurture' together determine who we are. New research, in fact, shows a tilt towards 'nurture' over 'nature'. Scientists now believe that genetic inheritance contributes less to behaviour than was thought at one time; environmental factors count for more. In McGill University in Montreal, Canadian scientists have conducted experiments which would suggest that a child's personality traits are influenced more by the parents' behaviour than by genes. Dr. Sushma Mehrotra, a psychologist from India also states her belief that if parents give the right kind of stimulation even an average child can excel. On the other hand, if there is a lack of stimulation, even a bright child will not reach his full potential. While we may not have control over what genes we pass down, we can influence the environment that our children grow up in.

What kind of environment are you giving your child? Having the best of intentions may not necessarily translate into best parenting strategies. In fact many a time, well-meaning parents consciously/unconsciously undermine their kid's faith in themselves without even realizing that they are doing so.

☑ *Reality check*

Answer the following questions:

Do you indulge in insults and name calling? Do you label the child 'stupid', 'dumb', 'useless', 'nitwit'?

Do you play the great future reader and pass statements like, 'You will never get it right' or 'I knew you were going to spill that'.

Do you ask for impossible standards of performance? And then say 'you do not measure up?' 'You should be good in school's basketball, cricket, debate, elocution, GK etc...'

Do you hit your child? Pinching, pushing or pats on the bum (however small) qualify too.

Do you withhold your love from the child or say things like 'You can't be my child if you did that'?

Do you compare your child unfavourably to others (siblings, friends, and your own younger self)?

Are you generally critical about everything? 'Your clothes are so dirty'; 'Your room is a mess'; 'you are such a picky eater'; 'you have no manners'.

Do you criticise your child in front of others? 'She's got two left feet' or 'He has no brains for mathematics'?

Do you use sarcastic comments? 'Of course, Queen Victoria can't keep her plates back in the sink'. 'Well, you sure made me look like a perfect idiot on the field today'. 'You have brains, right? Why not use them?'

Do you take all decisions for your child, usually giving him no options or choice?

Do you consciously/unconsciously adhere to 'Gender' stereotypes? When parents endorse the stereotype that mathematics is a male domain, their daughters underestimate their maths ability. A son who shows empathy is labelled as 'feminine'. In both cases, self esteem suffers.

Do you reproach your child's past mistakes time and again, leaving no space for error?

Do you rush to show your child the easy way out, the solution to the puzzle?

Do you react badly if your child doesn't do well?

Do you make your child feel guilty for the slightest of things?

Do you order, prescribe and command and the child has to do it because 'I said so'.

The more 'yes' you score, the more 'no' it is for your child's sense of self-worth and efficacy.

We can undermine our child's confidence and self esteem day in and day out and be completely unaware of it. Most parents justify their actions with:

'I have my child's best interest at heart'

'In this over-competitive, hard driving world it is only fair that I be pushy, demanding, critical and strict.'

'He doesn't know what is good for him/he does not know his own mind and so I have to take all the decisions for him.'

'Yes, at times I blow my fuse too. I am under great stress too in my bid to carve a space for my kid in this fast paced mad world. So he becomes the punching bag once in a while. So what?'

6.1 Self-esteem and the child

At its core, self-esteem is the way the child views, values and feels about himself. The way he feels about himself affects the way he acts and perceives the world around him. In her book *Your Child's Self-Esteem*, Dorothy Corkville Briggs, educator and child counsellor, says:

Your child's judgement of himself influences the kind of friends he chooses, how he gets along with others, the kind of person he marries, and how productive he will be. It affects his creativity, integrity, stability, and even whether he will be a leader or follower. His feelings of self-worth form the core of his personality and determine the use he makes of his aptitudes and abilities. His attitude towards himself has a direct bearing on how he lives all parts of his life. In fact, self-esteem is the mainspring that slates every child for success or failure as a human being.

Parents are the primary and by far the most important influence on a child's sense of self-worth and self-esteem. It is of course, not only from parents that the children get their self-esteem. Many other factors like peer relationships, success and failure at school, positive or negative experiences like death or other tragedies, also do influence a child's sense of Self but the parenting effect is the most powerful and far-reaching. Parents are the mirror through which a child sees himself. The way in which parents behave with the child remains in the child's psyche and becomes a part of the child's own perception of himself. The child needs the parent to believe in him as he learns to believe in himself.

According to a research by Nicholas Emler (London School of Economics), 'The strongest influences upon self-esteem are the individual's parents'.

Steven Vannoy in '*The 10 Greatest Gifts I Give My Children*' said, 'If I could give my child no other gift in the world, my top choice would be self-esteem.'

WAYS TO BUILD THEIR SELF ESTEEM AND CONFIDENCE

6.2 Love

Love them. You do. In that case make sure that they know it too.

Parental expressions of love and enthusiasm provide vital emotional nourishment for a child's developing sense of self-esteem, and stimulate the growth of new neuronal connections in important areas of the brain.

Kiran Uttam Ghosh

Designer Kiran Uttam Ghosh's childhood was not a bed of roses. They lived in a small two bedroom flat and finances were always strained. Moreover her parents divorced when she was in her teens. She said, 'Despite all our problems, ours was a family of kisses and hugs. Though money was tight, love and warmth flew in abundance. Though my parents could not get along with each other, love for me was never an issue. I knew that both loved me deeply. They made me a part of their problem whether the issue was incompatibility between them or pecuniary constraints. My mother would tell me, "Dad and I have fought but it does not matter, we love you equally". She would tell me, "I have Rs. two hundred; I will give you Rs. Ten and the rest I will use for the house". They would share their problems and I always felt one with them. Though I came from a broken home I did not carry within me the bitterness of it, for I knew that I was deeply loved....'

Wave the I-love-you flag whether they come home with an 'A' or an 'E' in their exam papers; whether they stand first or manage the last position in their school sports; whether they get the centre stage in the drama or become the inconspicuous part adding to the general flora created in the play.

Love is an unconditional gift from the heart. The security of having this love makes the child's confidence blossom. Life is full of races, competitions and exams. Your child will get a chance again to prove himself. Don't for one minute let his accomplishments be the weathervane of his worth. Ask your child, 'Do you know that I love you irrespective of every failure and weakness of yours?' What is your child's answer?

Express your love often

Use touch therapy. We are touch-a-holics. We are attachment junkies. By simply touching, we can express love, approval, comfort, security, support or any number of feelings. The child at the receiving end of this high-touch style of parenting develops self-worth. Hug, cuddle, pat, kiss, run your hand through your child's hair, exchange butterfly kisses, nose-to-nose Eskimo kisses, shoulder massages, foot rubs...there are many ways you can use touch to reinforce that the child is loved.

Create a secret word, sign, or gesture of affection that only you and your child share. Harsh's father had invited one of his business colleagues over to dinner and the evening was turning out to be extremely boring. Harsh's mother knew his plight and so she blinked her eyes twice which meant, 'I hate it too, but together we can see this through'.

Don't forget to say, 'I love you' to children of all ages!

Do you enjoy getting notes from people you love? So does your kid. Tuck a compliment or a love note in his lunch box. You can slip little love notes, jokes, poems, and words of encouragement into your children's backpacks, or next to their beds (if you leave before they wake up), just to let them know you're thinking about them all day long. You can even e-mail or mail the love note. On nights when you creep in way past her bedtime, stop in your child's room, rub her back and give her a kiss. She may have a moment during her most dreamy state when her subconscious registers your affection.

I let my daughter touch me with her creations. My daughter was into one of her I-live-for-origami-only moods. She decided that her bride for the day was me. Now the bride had to have many jewels and so I got a ring, three necklaces, bracelet, bangles, anklets, (not to mention the minuscule bindi's which she took the longest to put on me) all made out of coloured wrinkled paper. I displayed it proudly through-out the day (first on myself and then on the dining table, under the pretence that I did not want them torn).

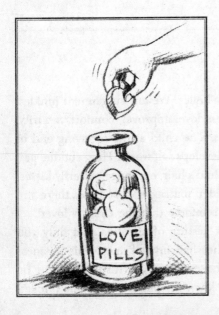

Sneha came up with the PILL BOTTLE. She took an empty bottle and labeled it as 'Love-pills take one as needed'. She filled them with messages saying, 'mommy is crazy about you'; 'you are the best thing to happen to us'; 'my life was so dull and lonely before you came along'.

Love is good for self-esteem.

Love equals time

One SMS (short message service) that I received, read, the best way to show someone your love is by giving that person your time, because when you give someone your time you give him/her a part of your life that you will never get back. Give your children 'everyday' time. Share the small pleasures of

> 'The work will wait while you show the child the rainbow, but the rainbow won't wait while you do the work.'
>
> — PATRICIA CLAFFORD:

life. The relationship between a child and her parent is built on little moments, not on the edifices of deeds and duties.

Create an only-me-and-you time with your child. No phone calls, no chores, no worries, no newspaper, no television, no planning (in the confines of your mind too, as children do sense it) during this time. Children will deduce, 'My parents want to be with me. I am worth their time and attention. I matter.' This feeling is integral to their self-esteem.

Jaya Bachchan

Without as much as a second thought Jayaji gave up tinsel town after hits like *Koshish* and *Guddi* and joined in again only eighteen years later, after her kids had grown up. Jayaji says, 'Motherhood means everything to me.' She came from a middleclass family in which her mother had always been around. She says, 'I became the person that I am because of her. I learnt my life values-honesty, commitment, respect for others by observing her in day to day matters from simple things like the way she treated the servants or the way she cared for our grandparents. Naturally I wanted my children too to have all the advantages which I received when I was young. I remember that for years all that both my children wanted once they were back from school was to be with me and share their day's experiences. They felt loved and wanted.' Jayaji, says 'I don't care what the world thinks of me as far as my children have faith in me.'

I met Jayaji at the Leelavati hospital where her mother in law Teji Bachchan was admitted and her condition was critical. Jayaji spent most of her time at the hospital. I told her that she is indeed lucky to have a daughter-in-law who is so committed and affectionate when Jayaji said, 'Oh. She does not even recognise me. She does not know that I am here, sitting outside.' Instantly I said, 'But then, why this....?' Before I could finish Jayaji said, 'Maybe she does not know who I am anymore but I know who she is. She has a family and we are it. How can her family leave her alone at a stage like this?'

Abhishek and Shweta even today, are watching their mother tend to an ailing person with sincerity and love even though the person being tended to would perhaps never know of this care. As Jayaji rightly said, 'You can't teach children the right values just by telling them what is right or wrong, but you can hope that they will learn their life values by watching their parents live with integrity.'

Yes, we are over-stressed, time-short and children are great time robbers. But we must remember that our little ones grow up quickly, and very soon they will shift loyalties and prefer their friends over us for their games and questions. We will never be able to get that time back, once it is gone. It becomes ever more difficult as children grow, to try and repair the cracks in the parent/child bond due to missed opportunities.

In his book, *The Seven Habits of Highly Effective Families*, Stephen R. Covey writes:

'To those who would say. "We don't have time to do these things!" I would say, "You don't have time not to!" The key is to plan ahead and be strong ... Things which matter most must never be at the mercy of things which matter least.'

Ways to spend only-me-and-you time
- Take a long walk together at your child's pace
- Read together
- Play games together
- Discuss challenges and important issues.
  The evening meal at super cop Kiran Bedi's childhood home was

the time when each daughter had the opportunity to share her day with the parents. The talk would move from one challenge to another, encountered both at school, home and the extracurricular activities that they attended. Her parents, great listeners and posers of questions, would pay attention to how their girls had applied themselves, confronted and resolved problems, and handled stressful situations. The sisters would ask each other how they could have done more, or better. Kiran came away from these and other family talks reenergised, challenged to do more, and determined never to give up, turn back, or complain. She learned to assert herself in the service of right and to always respect the rights of others. When asked if she would join the police service again if reborn, she has replied that she would, 'provided I have the same parents.'

- You could do activities like painting, singing, gardening together.

Children love it when they are entrusted with some responsibility and treated as adults. Involve them in kitchen chores. When you are getting dinner ready, instead of making it a rushed, slapdash affair, consider inviting your children to assist. Even really young kids can help you measure, pour and stir.

- Plan for a holiday, a birthday, or any special occasion.
- Eat meals together without television, newspaper or books.
- Share hobbies together.
  One can start up on collections of stamps, coins, bottle caps, bay-blades or any other fascinating objects. Parents and children can pursue hobbies like candle-making, pottery, dance, Golf, carpentry together.
- Make bath-times special. Give your children a nice oil massage and stay with them and laugh at all their chatter. Share some of your silly thoughts too.

6.3 Communication

'You never listen to me'. Mom accused her eight year-old son Tarang.

Tranag retorted, 'We are quits Mommy, because you never listen to me either.'

Most children love to talk. They have this innate need to report anything as trivial as, 'Today I sat next to xyz in school' to something deeply moving as 'I feel no one loves me'. They need an interested, loving, excited, understanding and an ever-present ear for their encyclopedic narrations. They want to speak about:

Trivia and daily happenings

Fears, doubts, insecurities, challenges, difficulties

Their happiness (Mani gave me an éclair today), triumphs (I am not scared of the cockroach), creations (I made another poem), learning (ask me the spelling of hundred) and every other thing which has happened to them

Questions that intrigue them, from 'where do babies come from' to 'why is the sky blue'.

How much can we listen to? After all we are:

Short on time.

Short on energy.

Short on sincerity.

And they have a surplus of it all.

The gap between demand and supply is too much. Communication slips!

Communication is our most critical parenting tool. Children begin to form ideas and beliefs about themselves based on how their parents communicate with them. They feel valued when they are heard. They deduce, 'What matters to me, matters to them. I am worth their time and attention. I am worthwhile'. And if they continually sense apathy or disinterest in their parents' eyes they may also conclude, 'My parents do not listen, understand or have time for what matters to me. Do I matter?' It then might take manifold our time, energies and efforts to convince them that they do. In some case the slip may become irrevocable as the child shuts himself completely from his parents.

Besides, when we communicate well and effectively with our children we not only help raise their self esteem but uncover layers of understanding as they reveal their psychological world through their conversations. They express their hopes, dreams, problems, ideas and opinions and we discover the dynamics of their thoughts.

By simply communicating well with them we can share their joys and their disappointments and in the process build bonds of trust that last a lifetime.

Natasha Finlayson, ChildLine's Director of Policy and Communications said: 'Talking to children—and listening to what they have to tell us—is absolutely vital to their safety and well-being. It might take fifteen minutes of casual conversation when they suddenly speak about how the driver tried to touch them at a place where they felt uncomfortable.'

Besides, as children get into their teens their preference for their audience (friends, friends and more friends) is most likely to shift. Have you not heard parents of teens complaining that the children hardly ever want to spend time with them? According to research children aged 12-15 are almost twice as likely to enjoy talking to people their own age than their parents (89% vs 47%) and would rather watch T.V.

(88%), play video games (58%), eat sweets (50%) and even read books (50%) than strike up a conversation with mum or, even more unlikely, dad! Feel lucky that you still have some precious years left.

Listen

Father: 'I hear what you say.'
Son: 'Yes, but you're not listening.'

Have you ever tried to tell someone about something, only to realize the person isn't listening? Isn't not being heard one of the most frustrating experiences?

How often does your child begin telling you something and you 'tune out' as you mentally move on to the other things you have to do today?

'Listening is the most underrated yet most important skill in parenting,' says Kathy Thompson, an associate professor of Communications at Alverno College in Milwaukee and a former executive director of the International Listening Association.

☑ *Reality check*

Remember, we grown ups too crave for attention, a listening ear. Do you listen and listen well? Answer the following questions for a more realistic appraisal of your listening skills.

1) Do you look your children in the eye when listening to them?
2) Do you listen patiently to all that your children have to say before you start talking?
3) Do you stop what you are doing when your children have something important to tell you?
4) Do you listen in a way that encourages your children to express their real feelings?
5) Do you try to understand how your children feel instead of thinking how you feel about what they are telling you?

6) Do you control raising your voice in anger at your children even when they interrupt you while on the phone or when you are entertaining guests in your home?

When our children speak we are busy working, thinking, organising, gossiping or adept at multitasking do all of them together. Their idle chatter, little joys, small hurts, big insecurities, complaints, their news of the day, elicit a maximum of 'hmm...', 'okay', or a 'really' from us. Besides, we think how would they ever know that our minds are elsewhere? But the kids do know. They do realize that behind our half-hearted response is our half hearted attention.

Become a 'yeah-tell-me-I-am-all-ears' kind of a listener

Be available

Be available to your children when they are most likely to talk. Children may feel chatty once back from school, but again they may not be so too. 'A lot of things happen during a child's day,' says Adele Faber, co-author of *How to Talk So Kids Will Listen and Listen So Kids Will Talk*. 'Often a child has not processed the input of the day when you first greet him. Your best response is a hearty "welcome home; glad to see you." Then be available when the child is ready to talk.'

Try not to postpone the conversation

When a kid has spoken, that is the right time. Put down the newspaper, turn off the T.V., ignore the phone and if you feel the need, arrange for privacy. If you are in the middle of something that couldn't wait, say, 'I really want to hear about it, but I have this thing to complete can you give me—minutes?' Remember there will be plenty of time to read, cook, clean, work but only a few fleeting years of having daily conversations with your children.

Be attentive

Fulfilling children's attention needs is a key component of instilling high self-esteem, and helps cement the parent/child bond. When Shreshta began her days' chatter, mommy listened to the first few lines and got the gist of what was coming. She went on with some chores. Shrestha said, 'Mommy, will you stop what you are doing and listen to me'. Mommy replied, 'It's okay. I can do both together'. But for Shrestha too, the content of the matter was not important. Having her mom's complete attention was.

Hear your child out completely

On the first day of his skating lessons Prarit refused to put on the wheels. His mother assumed this to be the beginner's fear of falling down. She dug into her repertoire and used every tool (reward, anger, encouragement, explanation) to convince her child, but to no avail. When he refused to skate on day eleven, she confronted him outright with, 'Why don't you want to skate?' She had exhausted all her resources and was all ears for her son's explanations. He said, 'The coach told me that once I learn to skate she will make me race with others children and that will be fun. I don't think racing is fun and I don't want to race. If I don't learn to skate I will not need to race.' She immediately shot the impatient question, 'If I ask the coach not to make you race will you give skating a try?' He said, 'Maybe, yes.' She asked the coach not to bring the race issue, six months have passed since then and Prarit skates for about an hour a day.

Hear your child out completely. It's a basic rule of engagement. Avoid cutting children off before they have finished speaking. It is easy to form an opinion or reject children's views before they finish what they have to say. Young children have a limited ability to immediately put thoughts into words. With limited vocabulary and experience in talking, children often take longer than adults to find the right word. Listen as though you have plenty of time.

Move beyond your need to be Mr. /Ms. Fix-It

To discipline, 'Stop biting your nails when you talk'

To correct, 'You shouldn't feel that way',

To offer suggestions, 'I think you should ...'

To be a problem solver, 'I will speak to Rohit's mom and make her correct her son's behaviour'.

To preach or moralise, 'If you are going to behave like that you are sure to...'

To correct pronunciations, 'It is not...'

MR. FIX IT!

The value of listening is in the listening itself.

Validate their thoughts and feelings
Children feel as much and as intensely as adults do, they think as much and as often as adults do, though not about the same things. But often we suppress their feelings, thoughts and opinions. For instance girls are often taught that being mad is not nice or is unfeminine and boys are taught not to cry because it's not manly.

The study of the human psyche reveals that all of our emotions – even the so-called negative ones – play pivotal roles in our emotional health. Therefore, our children need to have all their emotions validated (supported), when expressed in appropriate ways, to ensure their proper development. Children who are allowed to feel their feelings; and helped by their parents to identify their feelings and learn from them, are learning skills to deal with life in a responsible way. Also, when children 'tune in' to their true feelings, to know what makes them happy, sad, fearful or angry they are much more likely to understand what it is they really want from others, and from life.

Researchers at the Emory University Center for Myth and Ritual in American Life studied the conversations of Atlanta-area families and came across some noteworthy findings. Parents who encourage their children to talk about feelings, like anger and sadness, were more likely to raise resilient kids. The researchers took special note of family conversations concerning negative events such as a death. In these instances, kids struggled to understand what happened. When parents didn't shut them down, children felt accepted and acknowledged. More than that, these children had better self-esteem and were more socially adept.

Let children know it is normal to feel hurt, sad, confused, happy, scared and angry. Validate their fantasies. Let children know that they're not crazy to think or feel the way they do. You could use lines like, 'You have a right to feel that way. If it happened to me, I would probably feel the same way.'

Label their feelings. Young children, especially, often need help in describing how they're feeling. Sentences like, 'I bet you must be mad';

'It must be frustrating to just sit there and not be able to answer as fast as the others were doing'; 'You're feeling really sad!'; 'that must have been embarrassing'; validate their feelings, and give them words to use in the discussion.

Acknowledge their feelings with a, 'Mmm', 'Really', 'Oh', and then wait.

Help them express themselves verbally: 'I'm upset because...' or 'I feel happy when...'

You can even acknowledge their conversation with a, 'Oh, you went to the park today. That's great!' They will know that they have been heard.

I am what I am–Sanjeev Kapoor

Sanjeev Kapoor of the *Khana Khazana* fame, chef extraordinaire, T.V. show host, author of best selling cookbooks, restaurant consultant and winner of several culinary awards says, 'My parents believed in me right from the beginning. I could share my deepest feelings, doubts and anxieties with my father, however trivial or profound, with the faith that he would not sit upon judgment or tag me as wrong or right. I knew that I have an attentive and a willing ally in him and also a mentor who would guide me handle my delicate feelings.' Sanjeev's father worked in a bank and so they often moved cities. During one such transfer Sanjeev had to join a school in a new city midterm, sometime during the 6th grade. Sanjeev, a precocious student had been given a double promotion in the third standard. He said, 'I had always been looked upon favourably in most schools that I attended, but here a shock awaited me.' After a half-hour interview with the principal, Sanjeev got the distinct impression that the principal was not 'impressed' with him, and gave him admission more out of favour than his academic merits. This upset Sanjeev terribly.

Sanjeev's father read his mood and asked him about it. Sanjeev said, 'Since the Principal did after all give me admission, my reservations on how he judged me could have very well been looked upon as silly or overdrawn. But I knew that my nuances were as important to my father as they were to me.' After listening to him patiently his dad said, 'Yes, may be the principal thought of you less than what you would have wanted him to think and this fact must be distressing, but does this make you any less of the person you are? The reality is what you are, not his perception of you. You have created a perception in his mind in this half hour that you had, and maybe you could have created a better impression, but you do have ample opportunity to work on it and change it to what you think is more deserving of you. But whether you succeed in doing so or not, it still does not change "you".' Sanjeev said, 'Since then I knew that irrespective of what people think I am, I am what I am.'

Show respect for your child's feelings even when you do not agree with him

As you listen to your child you may realise that you will not be agreeing with him/her on so-and-so. Nevertheless, don't stop listening. You can't always let your children have their way, but you can show respect for their desires and feelings. Remember that all feelings must be accepted, it is the actions which have to be limited. Why not give our children the same courtesy we give to our clients, business partners or political rivals, that is, 'agree to disagree?'

Some examples:
'Yes, I can understand that you are really angry with your friend. But tell him how you are feeling not with your fists but your words.'

'Yes, I know you want to play with the new Swarovski dinky car but it is expensive and may break. Why don't you play with the yellow car instead?'

'So you think granny's house is boring, but we are the only ones she has and she really looks forward to these Friday evenings.'

Soften your reactions even if you strongly disagree or disapprove of what your children are saying. Otherwise, they may decide to never truly say what's on their mind. Kids, like adults, have a tendency to tune people out if they sound angry or defensive. Express your opinion without putting down theirs.

Don't let your feelings block your ears

Many emotional 'triggers' stop parents from listening. Talking about difficult issues or embarrassing subjects can be difficult, but remember if your child does not get the right information from you he might access his friend for the same and settle for perhaps half-baked and inappropriate information which might prove to be dangerous for your child. When you feel angry, worried or anxious about what you are hearing, make a conscious effort to control your feelings and listen.

Encourage the child to talk by:

Making him feel comfortable.

Maintain eye contact to show that you really are with the child.

Invite, and extend conversations. Use statements like:

'I'd like to hear about it.'

'What do you think about ...'

'Would you like to talk about it?'

Ask your children for their ideas and opinions regularly. If you show your children that you are really interested in what they think, feel, and opine; they will become comfortable in expressing their thoughts. Arnold M. Kerzner, M.D., a child and family psychiatrist in private practice in Belmont, Massachusetts, suggests that, 'In parent/child conversations the most important thing is to develop the relationship, not get the facts. Don't start from the inquisition mode. Start from the feelings mode. Make a statement like, "it's so nice to see you home," to create an atmosphere where the child will feel special, unique, and wanted.'

Listen to non verbal messages too

Ten year old Shresta had developed a new passion, internet. Through it she befriended a much older boy and in her naivety gave her new internet pal details regarding her school, residence etc. A few days later her friend Trisha mentioned an incident where a minor was abducted by a person who befriended the child through the internet. The abductor apparently invited the child for an ice-cream and that is the last anyone ever heard of the child. For Shresta, the ground slipped from under her feet. She was petrified and couldn't stop thinking of what she may have brought upon herself. In her mind the internet pal was a sure hoodlum. She knew that she should tell her mother everything but she couldn't find the words or the courage to do so. But her behaviour and demeanor did the talking and her mother picked up the cues. Shresta stopped going out of the house alone altogether (even within the society's compound), would burst into tears at the slightest provocation and bore an expression of perpetual anxiety. Her mother at an opportune moment, asked Shrestha whether she was okay. The nudge was all that Shresta required, she confessed to the entire story between sobs. It took both her mother and dad a month to convince Shresta that no one would break into her home and abduct her. Finally Shresta understood that though she had made an error it was not fatal or irrevocable.

Though Shresta wanted to speak to her mother and seek help she did not have the courage to bring up the discussion herself. She gave ample non verbal cues for it though. As parents we must never be too busy to pick up on these cues.

The meaning of a message is in the non-verbal packaging as well as in the words. Try to keep an observant ear and eye on both. Non-verbal messages are communicated through the posture, facial expressions, change in behaviour patterns etc. Though the non-verbal code is difficult to read, it often indicates the truth more than the words do. One can often tell more from the way a child says something than from what is said. This is especially helpful when verbal communication is blocked by a language or any other barrier. It is important to catch these non verbal cues, which could easily be a child's desperate SOS call.

Golden rules:
- Parents should use their ears and mouth in proportion – listen twice as much as you speak.
- Taking the time to listen is much more important than getting to soccer practice on time.
- When you tell your child he can talk to you about 'anything', you've taken a huge step towards communication with your child.

> But honour the 'anything' they may come up with, and do not
> rebuke him for it.
> - Understanding your child's resistance is enough to make it go
>   away. Children resist their parents simply because they don't feel
>   heard or seen.
> - 'Conveying that you've understood the problem is much more
>   valuable than trying to solve it,' says Laurie A. Segal, a Sands Point,
>   New York, certified social worker and founder of a psychological
>   wellness program for families. Solutions come later.

Talk

Watch what you say to your children. Children are usually very sensitive
to their parents words. What kind of linguistic climate are you giving
your child? Do your expressions and tone reflect your faith and respect
in the child, as much as your love?

Since we so want our children to be successful and better than
best we often become critical, nagging, demeaning, sarcastic and
insulting. We hit them hard with our words, tone and looks, at times
within limits, but often we lose control over our own state of mind and
become much harsher and more cruel than what the situation calls
for. Language that embarrasses, humiliates or hurts us, embarrasses,
humiliates and hurts children too. Cruel words, foul language, harsh
tones, derogatory accusations can take away their feeling of self-respect.
Negative remarks wound and destroy.

No labels! No put downs! No insults! No commands!
Some labels we very generously tag our children with:
Bad
Lazy
Troublemaker
Dumb
Slow
Clumsy

Stupid
Cry baby, etc

Put-downs/Discouragements
'You will never amount to anything in life.'
'How could I have borne an idiot like you?'
'I knew that you were going to fail.'

Insults
'Get out!'
'Shut up!'
'Brainless!'

Commands
'Come here right now!'
'You do it because I say so!'

Labeling is definitive; once we say it, it holds meaning. The danger of continuous labeling and put-downs is that children tend to believe what is said about them and live up to that negative expectation. Commands take away a child's right to opinion and thought.

Stephanie Madon, an Iowa State University psychologist, investigated parents' expectations about their children's alcohol use. She discovered that when both parents believe that a child will abuse alcohol, in fact, the child is likely to drink more than expected. This holds true even when signs, such as past alcohol use and friends' behaviour, suggest a teenager is at low risk. The findings support the social theory that prophecies are especially self-fulfilling for stereotyped groups. But Madon notes that her study also offers hope. If one parent has positive expectations about a child, the child is protected from the other parent's negative belief. http://www.psychologytoday.com/articles/pto-20050422-000006.html.

Respect your children by using kind and respectful words. To know whether or not something you have said to a child is disrespectful, ask yourself, 'Would I say them to a friend or my friend's child?' If not, it was probably disrespectful.

Apologise when you do resort to such behaviour

No matter how much we love our children we are bound to goof up sometimes and say things which we may regret later. A hard day at work, too many errands waiting to be completed, a fight with a colleague, or a simple let down by a friend could very well put our children at the receiving end of our sour mood. The best remedy then is to apologise in earnest. It's best to immediately admit this and say to your child, 'I should never have said that. It was an unkind thing to say and I don't mean it.' Apologising shows integrity and respect and encourages our children to do the same when they make mistakes.

We had started a family card game called 'Pinnacle' which is played in teams. I teamed with one child while my husband with the other and every evening we played two-three rounds of the same. Pinnacle is a complex game which requires alertness and strategy-building skills. My kids, who had never played cards before, had difficulty even in separating the spade from the clubs or holding the twenty-four cards dealt all at once in their small palms. Naturally, developing expertise had to come slowly. Though I knew this and I did remember my own months of slow learning, I ended up calling my child 'dull' and 'slow' during one game. I could literally see her face turning red as the words 'dull' and 'slow' hit her like a slap. I felt that her eyes were asking me for my final verdict, 'you know me more than I myself do, am I really dull?' I rushed to her, picked her up in my arms and apologized profusely. Though the apology salvaged her self esteem, the hurt was still very much there. I then told her that both of us know that she is neither 'dull' nor 'slow'. It was just an irritation of the moment which took up an exaggerated untrue over-generalization.

I got away with it as I saw the familiar sense of self-belief making it up again into her psyche. I thanked myself in solitude while chiding myself for the same, but what about the children for whom such episodes are a daily occurrence...?

Separate the child from the behaviour

Your child broke glassware and you react with, 'You are so careless!'

Your child is feeling tired and you say, 'You are so lazy!'

Your child's attention is distracted and you say, 'You can't concentrate on anything!'

Your child forgot an errand that you had asked of him and you lash out with, 'You can't remember anything or you are so dull?'

Your child and the younger sibling had a fight and you accuse your child with, 'Why can't you ever behave lovingly towards your younger brother?'

Often times without realising we attribute an undesirable behaviour of the child to a 'faulty you'. The mistakes are not only magnified but generalised and spill over the entire personality of the child. The child and his mistakes become one. It is no longer, 'What you did was not good, but, you are not good' or 'Not, I do not approve of what you did, but I do not approve of you'.

A handout of such messages on a regular basis plays havoc with the child's sense of self-worth, self-efficacy and righteousness. The child's self-confidence dips, leading to worse levels of performance which in turn invites more reproach and ridicule leading to yet stronger self-doubts on his abilities. The child gets trapped into this downward spiral of falling self-esteem and deteriorating behaviour/ performance/action.

Children depend on their parents to correct them and to show them what is right and appropriate but while doing so they must remember that the child is not the action. Parents can denounce or **label a behaviour as 'bad', 'wrong', or 'undesirable' but not the child's character or personality.**

Do not discipline the child in the presence of others

Your child makes a mistake, behaves unruly, gets into a fist fight, makes excessive demands for that chocolate or toy, endlessly in public; and you scream, slap, threaten or punish the child right there to put things straight.

Remember the time you committed an error and your spouse pointed it out in front of others and that hurt your self esteem more than anything else? Well, just like adults, children are deeply embarrassed when they are disciplined harshly or their mistakes are pointed out in front of other people. They are then more worried about how others are thinking rather than about whether they should have done so and so or not.

It is important to discipline children but in the right manner. Establish rules and set limits beforehand. Determine the consequences if the rules are not followed. If the child knows the rules and breaks them, a simple comment on your part should suffice. You can use gentle physical contact rather than grabbing or slapping. It is also important to watch your tone. Avoid a gruff demanding voice– replace it with a more direct, firm, but respectful voice. In addition, gently taking the kids aside for discipline keeps their self esteem intact and maintains their respect for us.

Mrinal Sen

It was Saraswati puja eve and Mrinalda's son Kunal, then ten, had spent most of the day at the pandal sight. Since it was past dinner time, Gitaji, Mrinalda's wife, requested him to fetch the boy so that he could have his bath and dinner and retire for the day to be fresh for Puja celebrations next morning. Kunal, at the time of heading for the pandal had categorically stated that he would be home only once the image of the Goddess had arrived and was placed on the beautifully adorned stage on which they had been working on for days. The idol, however, was to take four to five hours more to arrive. Gitaji wanted Mrinalda, to make the little boy see reason and not wait endlessly.

Mrinalda, left for the Pandal site immediately. He said, 'Just as I entered the panadal area I saw a gentleman deal a sharp slap to his son deriding him for not coming home all through the day and evening. The little boy stood terrified and began wailing. His other friends too fearing more backlashes crouched behind one another.'

It was then that Kunal too saw his father. With that, began a game of hide-n-seek. Kunal went and hid behind people, structures and friends to escape his fathers searching eyes. Mrinalda kept following him trying to get him face to face. Mrinalda said, 'Every now and then I met people and had to make small talks about the puja, decorations weather...though I did follow the curtsies, my mind was only on my son. I was wondering what could I say that would drive the point home without using fear or any other aggressive tool.'

After a half hour of this cat and mouse game, Mrinal da finally managed to catch hold of his agile son. He bent his tall stature to level with the ten year old and whispered in his ears, 'Your Ma wants you to be home, get fresh, have dinner and go to sleep. If you do not come home with me right way, I will go up to the stage and start dancing. I too will celebrate the puja in the way that I want.' On hearing this Kunal just turned around and ran all the way home.

When Mrinalda reached home his wife shot her concerns with, 'What did you say to the poor fellow, he is most distressed.' Mrinalda told his wife about the small conversation that he had had with his son. Gitaji turned up to Kunal and in a consoling voice said, 'You know your Bandhu (Kunal and Mrinalda referred to each other as Bandhu only) would not do that, he was only teasing you.' At that the ten year old wiped his tears and said with all his conviction, 'Ma, you do not know Bandhu, he can very well do what he told me he would. Where would it have left me? I would have never been able to face up to my friends if he were to have started dancing on the stage...it was better to come home and not take any chances.'

Mrinalda dealt his serve and left the ball in Kunal's court. The ten year oldused his reasoning and took the call he thought to be right. Mrinalda did not have to compromise of the boy's self esteem and yet could make him do what Gitaji wanted. Mrinalda with a chuckle added, 'You know Raksha, the best part was that my son had full confidence in my idiosyncrasies....'

Share your thoughts and problems with them

For communication to be effective, it must be a two way street. Talk to your children about your experiences and thoughts, your challenges and struggles, adventures and learning. Were you hopeless in math?

Did you once score a crucial goal against your own team? It helps a youngster to see that Mummy and Daddy weren't perfect either, yet they turned out okay. In your childhood (or even today) did you keep a brave face even when you were all pieces inside? Tell your children of the same and they will know that everyone experiences fear, anxiety and trepidation, yet one must stick out.

Share your thoughts with your child. For instance, if you are puzzling over how to rearrange your furniture, get your child involved with questions such as, 'I'm not sure where to put this shelf. Where do you think would be a good place?' Asking their opinion almost always makes them feel respected and valued.

Keep conversations brief

The younger the children are, the more difficult it is for them to sit through long speeches. Avoid Filibustering. Do not take the conversation ball and run with it, silencing your child.

Parents can look for clues that their children have had enough. Some clues include fidgeting, lack of eye contact, distractibility, etc. Parents need to know when to communicate with their children, but they also need to know when to back off, too.

Dr. Kerzner warns, 'parents all too frequently move into a goal-directed relationship with their children. They want to get information when they should be developing closeness.'

Harsh Neotia

According to entrepreneur Harsh Neotia, meaningful communication in any relationship whether, boss-employer, father-daughter or husband-wife, always happens one to one. He says, 'Intensity of communication is not possible in the collective. Let us say that I want to speak to my mother and my father is around, it doesn't work because bilaterally the relations are different. I connect to my son differently than how I connect to my daughter. My daughter is supersensitive. Whenever I have to reprimand her on something or talk of any important issue it requires a physical closeness. I hold her hand or make her sit in my lap, my words are more gentle. But if I want to speak to my son regarding the same issue I have him sit across and speak with more sternness. This sensitivity is unique to each. How does one do it collectively? Even with my colleagues I use the same philosophy. Of course, general talk can be held and is held in the collective. But whenever I want to penetrate a learning, I always switch to the one-to-one mode. Only then can I modulate my perspective to the other's receptivity. Otherwise it falls short on one while going hard on another.'

Mr Balkrishna Doshi

Mr Balkrishna Doshi, architect, thinker, educator, academician and founder-director of the School of Architecture, Ahmedabad, School of Planning, said, 'My children (he has three daughters) could come up and talk to me about anything. They could do so without feeling scared, guilty or worried about how I would judge them, for I never judged them. And to me this was my success as a father.' His architect daughter Radhika Kathpalia, winner of the National Award for low cost housing said, 'I have never lied to my parents or hidden anything from them, for I knew whether they agree or disagree with me on any account, they would allow me my perspective and that too without ridicule or indifference. Ever since I can remember, I have known respect as an individual in their eyes.'

How many of us inspire this kind of belief in our children that they can come and tell us anything...just anything? To me this is the epitome of parent-child communication and relation!

6.4 Space and child

Sanaya loved to discover secret nooks and corners to finish off her school work. Her latest haunt was our store-room, which was claustrophobic, uncomfortable and cluttered as generally store-rooms are, though this one was well lit. I found her nestled on a pile of mattresses and was about to ask, 'How can you work in here' but she shot out, 'It's perfect, mom!' The mattress was uneven and would not support her writing and the room reeked of pickles. I knew she would not last long out there, but I kept quiet. I allowed her the space of her choice. She worked for about thirty minutes and finished barely the amount of work which she would have otherwise wrapped up in ten minutes. After which she flocked back to her regular study table and continued her work there. Her speed and efficiency increased once again and she declared that her latest find was not that great after all.

Children need space to work out what works and what does not. As children grow, so does their need for space and privacy. Respect that right. Allow them their space. 'Mother' don't 'smother!'

Children learn to set boundaries around their bodies, ideas, and possessions. It is not that they want to be secretive, but there are some thoughts, feelings and 'treasures' most of them want to reserve just for themselves. Parents sometimes may be suspicious of a child who tries to hide a part of himself or may make light of a child's private time, thoughts or toys. But a child who is never allowed his own space may have trouble figuring out who he is apart from others. Respect a child's right to his person and belongings. Give your child the security that his 'space' will not be invaded.

Privacy is a two-way street for parents and children. There are certain communications that truly are confidential. One of the greatest ways we can show respect to our children is by respecting their private writings. You do not want children to read your journals, let them have the right of privacy to theirs. Do not encroach upon their mails, emails, letters etc. Encourage brothers and sisters too to respect each other's requests for privacy.

You want your children to knock before they walk in through a closed door, well, give them the same respect.

You don't want your children to eves' drop on your conversations, don't do so on theirs. Children talk about different things when parents aren't listening. They need enough freedom to be themselves without feeling like every word will be weighed and judged by their parents.

Give children mind-space too

Radhika took her son to the slums and did not say a word. She gave him the mind space to take in the condition of the underprivileged as his senses permitted.

Let them make their own choices

Rahul did not want his mother to help him with his homework. Yes, he would make a few mistakes, be messy probably and not have very good handwriting, yet he wanted to do it himself. His mother gave him space.

Let them say 'No'

Six year old Ananya said 'no' to any pair of pants which did not have pockets; Kish rejected shoes without Velcro. Their moms gave them space not because Ananya would not wear pants without a pocket or Kish with laces but because they respected the child's right to say 'no'.

Let them decide their interests

Ketan was on a zoo visit with his mother. She kept showing him the tiger, he kept watching the line that the hundreds of ants were making. He wanted to know where the line began or ended.

Vikram Chandra

Celebrated author, Vikram Chandra finished his schooling from Mayo with distinction in every subject except one. He joined Xavier's college with pure science and Mathematics. The dream of every parent then was to see their child become a doctor or an engineer and Vikram's academic record endorsed the possibility for the same.

One morning even before the first month of the new semester, Vikram announced that he wanted to change his stream from Science to Arts. His father Navin asked him for the reason and Vikram replied by saying that he was not enjoying the subject and it had been a mistake to opt for it. Vikram wanted to change to literature. Mr Navin Chandra said, 'I have taught my children to think and question on what they really want to do with themselves. And when Vikram said that he wanted to quit Science I knew that he must have had his deep reasons for wanting to do so and I respected those reasons. Yes, Literature in those days was not looked upon as a field with which one could have had a sustainable and lucrative career. Besides, I myself was an engineer and so his decision to change should have had me worried. But we have always believed in giving our children the tools of thought and not the thought itself. I said "yes" but did tell him that what he owes me is giving his best to whatever he is changing to.' Vikram's mother Kamnaji, a writer herself, was doubtful though. She said, 'For me writing was okay because the burden of running the home was on my husband's shoulder, but Vikram being a man had to sustain himself. When I put my reservations about the same to him, he said that he could not serve under anyone. He said, "Trust me I will find my niche". And I trusted him. Despite what my head said I knew that

I must support his interest and I did.' She further continued, 'Our children had always seen us give our 100% to whatever we did and the fact that we never shied away from hard work. I knew that whenever Vikram was convinced of his interest he would give it his all. I didn't want to take away his power of choice and belief in himself.'

In fact, Vikram gave the Chandras' faith in him a real test run when only after a year of studying literature he decided to quit that too. He wanted to go to the US to pursue his education. The Chandras' were hesitant but not because of Vikram's change of mind but because of what the cultural climate of the country would do to a relatively impressionable eighteen year-old mind. Besides, it was a financial strain too. But between them they discussed that, 'After all, Vikram was only asking for education. As always, respect for his interest and our belief in him won and despite everything we made arrangements for him to go to the US.'

Kamnaji said, 'I have allowed each of my children their space to grow and decide and each has found his/her niche...I am happy enough for that. Their success is just a bonus.'

Delicate balance between space and control

Most of us agree that it is important to respect the space of others, but when it comes to our children it becomes a challenge to find the balance between allowing them their freedom and still keeping control of the situation. We can teach our children correct principles and values by modeling the same ourselves and then trust them to follow the same. Only when they break that trust, our responsibility as a parent becomes more important than the child's desire for privacy. If we believe that our child is in serious trouble with lying, cheating, stealing we have an obligation to intervene, set things correct and perhaps supervise closely from then on. But that too can be done in a respectful and trustworthy manner.

Allow them space to decide their own pace of learning and growth

Do you allow your child his pace to learn and grow or do you decide 'the right pace' for him based on the activities of your neighbour's, friend's or relative's child who happens to tell you what their child has done (who perhaps has based his measures on another set of children)?

John Holt, American author and educator, one of the best known proponents of home-schooling and a pioneer in youth rights theory says, 'The human animal is a learning animal; we like to learn; we need to learn; we are good at it; we don't need to be shown how or made to do it. What kills the processes are the people interfering with it or trying to regulate it or control it.'

Here is a personal example where nature and the desire to learn proved better than my need to show the world that my child was not a sissy.

Sanaya learns to swim...

For urban mothers, summer time, especially during the vacations, is 'I-have-to-teach-my-kid-to-swim' time. The pool areas in most clubs carry an all too familiar scenario: Mothers alternating between threats and pleas to lure their children into giving-in to the coach's orders; kids running, crying, kicking, hiding, sobbing, trying to convince their moms that they do not want to learn to swim; coaches screaming, threatening and pushing the kids into the pool in a bid to rid them of their fear.

How could I have been any far behind? And one summer vacation, I too landed up in the club with my sleeves rolled and a determined expression through which I wanted to convey that just-learn-it-and-then-we-can-move-on.

The sessions began and the all too familiar cries, screams and sobs began to fill my otherwise peaceful mornings. Many a times I found myself on the verge of giving up to those innocent, pleading water-filled eyes of my kids, but the senior moms (for whom it was the second year) helped me hold on to my nerves. They even shared some tricks to help me ease my conscience. I thus mastered the art of looking away every time I sensed the kid was going to look at me for yet another mercy-request, inside I was as much a wreck. Why is nature so cruel, why does keeping afloat on water translate into so much pain and hardship for the a-floater? It was then that my particular a-floater decided to give up on learning being afloat. She stated categorically, 'I will not do what the sir asks me to do and I will not do what you ask me to do!!!!' Nothing that I said or did made her budge. The coach, at that point, came up to her and said that she could do anything that she pleased on the condition that she would just hang around in the water during coaching hours. My kid agreed. Sir left her all alone in the shallow and went about his business with the others.

The scenario changed completely

My kid was left alone for that day and the day after. She just splashed around while the other kids went about their coaching and on the third day most of the other kids swam the width of the pool with either little or no help from the coach. Suddenly my daughter too wanted to paddle, kick, jump and swim. She asked me hesitatingly whether I would want her to join learning again. The coach and me feigned indifference and she was further ignored for another day. By the end of the fourth day she was screaming to be a student which she informed me was her fundamental right. Who was I to go against the constitution of India, I gave up and she learnt how to swim.

6.5 Keep your promises

What are politicians infamously famous for? Promises made with a passion and forgotten with even a bigger passion once the elections are over. Yes, we seem as heartless and indifferent to our children when we go back on our words and refuse to follow through our promises made to them. Worse, they stop believing in us.

Naina screamed at her mom, 'Why do you think I should trust you again? Your actions speak louder than your words. I'm second to your friends, to your house work, to your naps.'

Say Kayle, 'My dad never keeps his promises, like he says he will take us on holiday for Diwali, but then changes his mind and has an excuse why we can't go. Now I know he will never do what he says and I don't bother to get excited any more.'

Yes, we as parents make well-intentioned promises but life conspires against our desire to carry them out and we have to use one of our regretful explanations:

Don't you think I want to do that too...

Baby, I didn't know this would come up...

I will make it up to you next time...

Life is like that, it doesn't always go as you plan...

I just said we would go, that wasn't a promise...

I asked a bunch of kids about what they felt when parents went back on their words. Some answers that I received were:

'I feel sad!'

'She breaks most of her promises made to me. I don't believe her anymore'.

'He always does so! I am not as important to him as his nap, shuffling channels on T.V., or meeting up with friends!'

'I count hours and days for the planned programme and then it doesn't happen. I feel so angry and frustrated!

Yes, we can overwhelm them and sidetrack our little promises/ trysts planned with them under our larger "adult responsibilities." We can even justify ourselves with a, 'I must have that nap' or 'I deserve that movie' after a hectic week at work, but it still leaves a child who is DISAPPOINTED! Broken promises break the child's trust, spirit and lower his self worth. The small everyday promises made to our children which we wriggle out of because, 'the situation was so...' may seem inconsequential to us, but, over time, become a child's judgment of us and themselves too. This makes for unresolved dilemmas and insecurities in the child. As these accompany the child into adulthood, we have a recipe for disaster-a resentful, insecure child.

Thirty-five year old Sneha Tyagi reminisces of how her father somehow always found an excuse to scrap the Sunday afternoon outings with a 'next Sunday, we will definitely do it'. The next Sunday would be yet another next Sunday. She said, 'I promised myself that unless there is a fire or any other such life threatening situation my commitment to my children stayed...nothing else took priority over it'.

☑ *Reality check*

Question yourself. Do you treat promises made to your children as less important than ones made to adults?

When we do keep our promises the message that we send to our children is:

You are important to me

I mean what I say. If I make a promise I keep it. I am reliable.

I honour my commitments. I am trustworthy

You too should keep promises. Be trustworthy

Individual experiences for a child are like the continual dripping of water upon a rock. Eventually the individual drops create a groove down which all the water that follows will flow. It's possible to change the course of the water, but only with effort. It's the same with patterns or 'grooves' of behaviour. It's possible to change them, but much easier to create the desired grooves in the first place. In the lives of children, these drops consist of tiny, individual moments, moments that may seem inconsequential to us, but, over time, become a child's character. Each child develops differently. Some realize the disappointment and swear never to repeat it as adults while some become adults doing the same things they experienced as they grew up.

> **Remember:**
> - Do not make rash promises. It is much better to say you will try (very hard) and fail, than to outright promise and not follow through.
> - Never make promises that you don't intend to keep.
> - Once you do make a promise, keep it when you can for there will be enough times when you can't or when it is hard.
> - When you find yourself in a situation where you really can't (You've promised to be at your daughter's swim meet, but end up stalled in traffic while she's racing toward the finish line) you must explain the scene with full honesty and look for the first opportunity to make up to the child. Remember not to blow it the second time around.
> - Promises made to children should be taken seriously because the children take it seriously...

A young woman named Cynthia vividly recalls one of the high points in her life. It took place when she was twelve years old. Her father promised to take her with him on a business trip to San Francisco. For months the two of them talked about the trip.

'After his meetings we planned to take a cab to Chinatown and have our favourite food, ride on the trolley, and then have hot fudge sundaes. I was dying with anticipation,' she remembers. When the day for their excursion finally arrived, Cynthia waited eagerly for her father to finish work. At 6:30 he arrived, but with an influential business client who offered to take the father and daughter out for dinner. 'My disappointment was bigger than life,' she says.

In a never-to-be-forgotten moment, her father simply said to his client: 'I'd love to see you, but this is a special time with my girl. We've got it planned to the minute.' Together father and daughter did everything according to their plans. 'That was just about the happiest time of my life. I don't think any young girl ever loved her father as much as I loved mine that night,' she says.

That true story is reported by Cynthia's father, Stephen R. Covey, in his book *The Seven Habits of Highly Effective Families*. Clearly, Stephen Covey knows that one ingredient common to closely knit families is the ability to make and keep promises.

6.6 Encourage their innate strengths

Maneka beamed, 'My child is a natural at music. His hands would tap rhythmically with the beat even before he could understand a word of the lyrics.'

Pankaj said, 'My son is really a 'hands-on-guy. As a 6-year-old, he took apart an alarm clock. At nine, he helped his dad fix the lawn mower. Boy, that boy is a natural engineer'.

Shilpa said, 'Abhishek is a born batsman. Makes most runs in every match whether in the society or at school'.

Tarana has a natural eye for colours. She matches unusual but extraordinary combinations.

Nachiket is brilliant with numbers. He can solve any mathematical puzzle and always scores full marks in the subject.

Yes, most of us know what our children are naturally good at...and so we channelise our energy into other areas where they need help. In our attempt to be 'good' parents, we tend to focus on bettering

the weaker side. In the trade-off to make the child 'over-all okay' we ignore the already existing strength and inclination.

Drawing on his pioneering research and his work with thousands of students, Dr. Levine author of A MIND AT A TIME, says, 'It's taken for granted in adult society that we cannot all be 'generalists' skilled in every area of learning and mastery. Nevertheless, we apply tremendous pressure on our children to be good at everything. They are expected to shine in math, reading, writing, speaking, spelling, memorisation, comprehension, problem solving...and none of us adults can' do all this'.

Mrinal Sen said to me, 'However famous one may be, one is always aware of his/her mediocrity in certain aspects.'

Competence builds confidence

'The most important thing for a parent to remember is that confidence comes from the child's experience of mastery,' says Arizona State University West professor of psychology Paul Miller.

People feel good about themselves when they know they are good at something. Whether our little tykes practicing at their aim with their guns the entire day would turn out to be future medalists in Olympics or not; whether the kid who never misses a show on outer space is preparing for his career as an astronaut or not; whether our children's interests and passions become their careers or life or not we must support and further that 'gift'. Not only does uncovering their interests and aptitudes define them as individuals; but finding something they enjoy doing and are good at, is a big boost to their self-esteem. Children high on self esteem make for responsible, caring citizens of a compassionate universe. Home stimulation and support of interests is vital to the development of their talents.

Shreya Ghoshal

Singer Shreya Ghoshal's dad is an engineer and her childhood has been spent in Rawalbhata, a small town about sixty kilometers from Kota which is a base camp for nuclear reactors. Rawalbhata is essentially a government colony, mainly of engineers and scientists. A heavy academic environment enveloped the entire colony and children in most homes studied hard to become engineers, doctors and scientists right from grade one.

And here was Shreya who found *nodes*, *taal*, and *sur*, more consuming than formulas, grammar and mathematics. Shreya said, 'I knew that I was intelligent and could do well if I concentrated but I just could not bring myself to enjoy academics as I enjoyed music.' Shreya's father too was impressed with her grasp of 'sur' and 'lay' as she began taking her lessons as young as age 4 from her mother. Her father recalls the time when Shreya participated in the All India level music competition of a group called Sangam and was selected from the Rajashthan chapter. To quote him, 'When I heard her on stage at Kota, a chill ran through me. Her voice was so melodious and soothing that I developed goose pimples all over. I looked around and saw that others too were genuinely enjoying her song. It was not my prejudice or love for her but it was her talent.'

Shreya's parents supported her interest in music in a place which was completely cut off from civilisation in the sense that only government buses ran private services and roads were not accessible to other public vehicles. In fact, her first formal training began at the age of 6 and the sir would come all the way from Kota. Shreya's father organised three-four more children from the colony to form a large enough group for it to be viable for the music teacher to commute all the way sixty kilometers and back. Mr Ghoshal said, 'I saw in my daughter not only a talent but an interest and ever since I have done everything in my capacity to support that talent and interest.'

Shreya said, 'Yes, I enjoyed music and did show a propensity for it too, but for that "gift" to become my life, the consistent support and stimulation which I received from my parents was vital.' According to Shreya there were five major factors which played a key role in this.

Shreya was asked to follow discipline only in music. For everything else, academics, sports, extra-curricular activities she was left to decide on her level of interest and involvement. Through-out her schooling career she had been an average student and that was fine by her parents.

She said, 'Not once have I been beaten emotionally or otherwise for not scoring higher marks'.

Her teacher Mr Bhatnagar's enthusiasm and belief in her infected her. She said, 'He believed in me so much that I too began believing in myself!'

Her teacher maintained her interest by keeping a balance between classical and folk music. Since he ran both the forms parallel in her training, the boredom which usually creeps in while doing only classical was kept at bay and her training never became torturous.

Her father made sure that there were enough instances for her to perform, be it competitions or colony get-togethers. Shreya said, "I always got an audience which enjoyed and appreciated my music and it was a reward which helped me maintain my intense interest and riyaaz."

The environment at home, for Shreya, was neither excessively strict or permissive. Her parents followed the golden mean and she was given space as well as guidance and support.

Ask yourself—Am I giving due attention, respect and support to the competence/gift/talent that I find exists naturally in my child?

According to research, problems may arise if nurture and nature aren't on speaking terms—if a child's environment doesn't permit or encourage expression of his natural tendencies. That may happen when children's abilities don't match their parents' expectations; when their genetically-influenced temperament clashes with that of their parents; or when their environment offers them few opportunities to express themselves constructively, as is often the case with children who grow up in severe poverty. Research has shown that a poor person-to-environment match can lead to decreased motivation, diminished mental health, and rebellious or antisocial behaviour.

6.7 Breaking the myth of the 'gifted' child

Many of us look upon child prodigies like Mozart, and sigh at the ordinariness of our own children concluding that they will not amount to much in life.

According to David G. Myers, Ph.D., professor of psychology at Hope College in Holland, Michigan, 'Today's intelligence researchers emphasise that nearly all children-not just the celebrated 5% have special talents.'

Studies at Harvard University too bear this out, suggesting that kids can display intelligence in many different ways—through words, numbers, music, pictures, athletics or 'hands-on' abilities, and social or emotional development. Dr. Howard Gardner, professor of education at Harvard University, developed the theory of multiple intelligences in 1983. According to Gardner, we possess not one but eight distinct forms of intelligence: linguistic, logical-mathematical, spatial, bodily-kinesthetic, musical, interpersonal, intrapersonal, and naturalist. This particular theory is supported by current research in neuropsychology, psychological testing, and child development, as well as cross-cultural studies and biographical accounts of exceptional scientists, artists, musicians, and other highly skilled individuals. Dr. Gardner says that our schools and culture focus most of their attention on linguistic and logical-mathematical intelligence. However, Dr. Gardner says that we should also place equal attention on individuals who show gifts in the other intelligences: the artists, architects, musicians, naturalists, designers, dancers, therapists, entrepreneurs, and others who enrich the world in which we live. Unfortunately, many children who have these gifts don't receive much reinforcement for them in school. Many of these kids, in fact, end up being labeled 'learning disabled,' 'ADD (Attention Deficit Disorder,' or simply underachievers, when their unique ways of thinking and learning aren't addressed by a heavily linguistic or logical-mathematical classroom. Mr Gardner says, '(I)t's very important that a teacher takes individual differences among kids very seriously... The bottom line is a deep interest in children and how their minds are different from one another, and in helping them use their minds well.'

Claude Monet

At school, Monet absolutely hated to sit through hours of classes. To pass the time, he caricatured his teachers on pages of his copy books "in the most irreverent fashion.' (Seitz 11). Although his teachers considered him to be in, disciplined and unlikely to succeed, it quickly became evident that what Monet might have lacked in scholastic intelligences was supplemented by his spatial intelligence (Sheff 1). He developed a solid reputation for his caricatures and began working for a picture framing store in Le Havre. Overall, like Picasso, Claude Monet's artistic abilities appeared to be enhanced by a fruitful asynchrony between his spatial and other intelligences.

Andrew Carnegie–The Gold in every person

Andrew Carnegie, who was at one time the largest steel manufacturer and the wealthiest man in America, had forty-three millionaires working for him at a time when millionaires were rare. A reporter asked Mr. Carnegie why he had hired forty-three millionaires. He responded that those men had not been millionaires when they started working for him; they had become millionaires as a result of working for him. The next question was, 'How did you develop these men to become so valuable to you that you have paid them this much money?'

Andrew Carnegie answered that men are developed in the same way gold is mined. When gold is mined, several tons of dirt must be moved to obtain an ounce of gold. But one doesn't go into the mine looking for dirt; one goes in looking for gold. He had learned to look for and develop the best qualities in those working for him.

6.8 Find the gold in your child!

Every child has a profile of strengths—it's our job as parents to draw attention to them.

Expose your child to a broad spectrum of experiences. Create opportunities for children to explore different objects, activities, and people. Discuss news and events to spark interests, read books, take them for shows and exhibitions, expose them to multimedia, etc. Help them explore their areas of interest and strengths. Encourage children to try new things. This may activate latent talents.

Gayatri, a mother based in Ahmedabad recalls, 'My youngest daughter studied bird books when she was only eight years-old. She spent hours drawing and correctly colouring specific species. Now she works for a vet and raises birds in her own aviary. She has a real gift with animals.'

It is important to:

➢ Let the child discover her own interests, even if they are different from ours. We may even have to bypass what all the other kids in the neighbourhood are doing in favour of something that is more suited to our child.

Mr Balkrishna Doshi said, 'Look at any gardener. He tends for his plants, nourishes the soil with fertilisers, regular care and pruning, but after grafting does he ask the guava tree to bear him apples or the banana tree to give mangoes?

Sitar ke strings se uski hi aawaz aayegi, usme se shehnai ki awaz nahi aayegi. So has been my philosophy with my children.'

Mr Doshi continued, 'In fact, when we pressurise our children we are actually creating defense and that defense mode which they get into makes it even more difficult for their inherent interest and passion to flower.'

His youngest daughter Manisha showed a keen interest in painting. She would draw on the walls in the house and would paint all day long. One day she drew a big cock and Mr Doshi was impressed by her lines. He said, 'The best way for us was to give her the chalks and paper and we gave her ample of those. I stopped drawing myself because I did not want her to be influenced by my drawings. I wanted nothing to come in the way of her individual flowering.' Mr Doshi even asked Manisha not to go to college, but pursue art; however, she completed her B.A because she wanted to be a graduate.

Anup Jalota

Singer/musician Anup Jalota said, 'The first memory that I have of my parents in relation to us five brothers and sisters was that they never forced their profession on us. My elder brother found his niche at tabla, my sister took up dance, and in me they saw a madness for music, specifically for vocal music and each of us was given the latitude to pursue our own passions.' Even as young as seven, Anupji would insist on accompanying his father Purushottam Das Jalota, renowned bhajan singer, to his concerts; irrespective of studies, exams and school. He said, 'I would play the tanpura sitting close to my father and the audience would ask my father to let me sing a few lines too. I would take the mike and sing something too for which the audience would kindly clap and cheer. Those cheers meant more to me than anything else. I am forever grateful to my father for such an experience at that young an age.'

During one of his final exam papers in the fifth standard, Anupji rounded off a three hour paper in an hour and then rushed home to practice music to perform with his father for a concert that night. He got a solid scolding from his father to which he empathically stated that he had written enough to score 45% which was the pass mark. He said that he did not need to secure a first class since he wanted to be a musician. In fact through-out his school career Anupji never scored anything more than 45% and would at times be screamed at by his teachers as well as parents. I asked whether that affected his self esteem negatively. Anupji said, 'Though they did chide me every now and then for not working hard at school, they nevertheless honoured my love and commitment to music. And before long I had started winning trophies for my school at inter-school music meets. In fact many a time my teachers were at the receiving end where I would tell them that I would leave the school if they deliberately failed me.'

Music gave Anupji his sense of purpose, confidence, faith and of course he never had a self esteem issue.

Ask yourself, am I consciously/unconsciously piling my own passions/expectations on my children?

Many parents want to continue their journey through their child. Parents who wanted to be let us say a doctor, engineer, sportsman, actor and could not be or could not attain the success they had hoped for, begin seeing their children as vehicles on which they can ride to their own destinations. The child becomes a source through which they want to fulfill their bruised or a still desiring ego.

Parents then start moulding the child according to their desires. They forget that the child has his individuality and his own inner growth to unfold. And they think they love the child...they love only their ambition!

➢ Watch for the things that each child loves to do. Listen to the child. The things he cares about most may provide clues to his special talents. Free-time play too can say a lot about where the gifts lie. Ellen Winner, a professor of psychology at Boston College and the author of Gifted Children: Myths and Realities (Basic Books, $16), explains that if you want to identify where your child's potential lies, simply take note of the activities she naturally gravitates toward. Winner says she believes that if parents recognise and nurture a child's inborn abilities, the child will be able to build her confidence and self-esteem much more than any IQ or other standardized-test result ever could.

Jamini Roy

Jamini Roy, one of the most celebrated artists of modern India, showed his inherent interest in representational arts from his boyhood days.

He would stand for hours among the village potters and emulate their doll-making. His subjects were taken from rural Bengal, celebrating the peasant woman, bold yet modest, in her simple yet colourful surroundings, an embodiment of Indian womanhood. He used strong, vibrant colours in their full glory, never diluting by shading, applying each colour uniformly, which resulted in flat two-dimensional pictures. Yet the dynamism of his studies of rural India, hardly a popular subject of art at that time, was path breaking, making him one of the great artists of modern Indian painting.

Ask yourself: What does your son/daughter focus on most naturally? Identify what he/she really enjoys.

➢ Believe in your child and be patient

Scientist/professor Chaman Lal Gupta said, 'Parenting requires two things, faith and humility. Faith that every child is an evolving soul as a whole personality and not piecemeal. And humility, that the parent is not responsible for the child. Of course the parent is responsible to provide love and joy-things which help growth most.' He said, 'There are many digressions and confusions today because of the world we live in but one must never lose faith.'

Bina Sarkar Elliyas said, 'What children need above all is their parent's faith in their interest, if we give them that it is enough.'

Sarah Delano Roosevelt was confident from the beginning that her child Franklin D Rossevelt would be a great man. So much so that she saved every scarp of paper upon which he wrote school exercises, and she bundled and labeled his baby clothes for the reference of future historians. His indifferent career in Groton and at Harvard did not shake her aplomb as to Franklin's superiority. Even when he failed in Greek or scored C's in major subjects she did not feel deterred.

Give your children opportunities to hone their natural talents

Build on the child's particular skills and areas of enjoyment by enrolling him in a class. Do your homework first.

Is the tutor/coach good?

Is he/she child friendly?

Is the infrastructure appropriate?

Does the class give your child the requisite attention (over-crowded)?

Find out a class based on not only his interest but aptitude too. Match them with your child's energy level — classes with lectures or a lot of quiet time could be a poor match for a restless child. Augment his interest by providing materials that relate to a subject the child is passionate about. A telescope for the lovers of stars and space, art material for the ones with the artistic bent, books for the budding authors and writers, a proper racket for the tennis nut, and books on any topic that interests your child, can all help further her exploration.

Einstein had his own lab in the basement even when his mother lived in perpetual danger that one day he would blow up the house and himself too with it. Have reference materials available to give your child access to the world. Use birthdays and special days to give presents that nourish your child's strengths.

Wilbur and Orville Wright

Wilbur and Orville Wright of Wright brothers had a warm and loving family that encouraged learning, intellectual interests and constructive activities. Their mother Susan, the daughter of a carriage maker, was remarkably mechanically adept, and she taught her children to make all manner of things. Their dad Milton, exposed his children to the wide world beyond their horizon through his library and the letters he sent home when he traveled on church business. In 1878, he brought home a rubber band-powered helicopter, and young Wilbur and Orville immediately began to build copies of it. When caught by his teacher while working on one of these toys when he should have been studying, Orville explained that he and Wilbur planned to build a craft large enough to carry both of them. Looking back on his childhood, Orville once commented that he and his brother had 'special advantages...we were lucky enough to grow up in a home environment where there was always much encouragement to children to pursue intellectual interests; to investigate whatever aroused their curiosity.'

➢ Give them space. Yes, you should take your child's interests seriously but don't take the fun out of the activity by putting pressure on her. Children need a balance of space and nudging. Too little space and they feel suffocated, overwhelmed and stressed and may decide to withdraw altogether, too much space and they might get off-track. Space can mean different things for different children. Children may need space from their passions and interests too. Some may need a drop of a day, or a few classes. Others may require a year and would still be doubtful. Eleven year old Sanjana had shown amazing skill in mastering the chakkars, beats and tukda in kathak but after her third year just announced, 'I do not want to go for the classes anymore.' She dropped out for a year and was back again with even more enthusiasm and spirit.

Golden rule: Encourage, but don't push.

➢ Show appreciation. Set aside an area of the house for displaying creations and awards. Frame their certificates, gold stars, encase their medals and display them. If your home is missing this wall, your child is missing his moment of fame. The day six year old Sanaya did thirty-four lengths of our swimming pool we inscribed it in blue paper and placed it on our wall of 'Wow'. Abhishek hit

his most powerful six in his cricket coaching in which the ball burst open. The ball now sits as the proud momento on the Mehta's family shelf. Kabir, for his science project, designed gloves which had battery operated lights fitted on the forefinger. It has been framed and has signs from every family member, his six year old sister wrote, 'My brother is the best'.

Praise and appreciate not only the achievements but the efforts too. Praise their persistence in trying to master a skill, their enthusiasm for an activity. Praise progress, even if the child still needs to do much more. Praise provides encouragement. It directly affects accomplishments. There is a strong correlation between telling your child she has done well and her repeating that behaviour. Kim Hunt, a second-grade teacher in Des Moines, often praises children to convince others to behave, saying things like, 'Oh, do I like the way Emily has already started solving those math problems. She's using her brain,' Ms. Hunt said. 'Praise is almost a contagious virus in a classroom because if you can catch one child doing something good, and if you can verbally praise that child in front of his or her peers, it's going to spread like wildfire and the rest of the children are going to automatically do exactly what that model student is doing because they want the positive attention,' You cannot spoil a child with words of approval: on the contrary, every little bit of encouragement will help to boost his self-belief and his confidence in his own abilities. Athletic coaches know they need to give seventeen positive comments for every negative one. A word of praise, according to child educator and author, Jan Dargatz, is like a verbal trophy, and a child's psyche has abundant shelf space for such honors. Leave little 'nice work' notes on pillows, yellow 'post-its' on homework, messages that convey that you noticed and that you are pleased.

Dad – The Superhero

....

'I cannot think of any need in childhood as strong as the need for a father's protection.' – SIGMUND FREUD

I was seated opposite Mrinal Sen, ready with my volley of questions. Intrigued by the kind of father he has been to his son I wanted to know whether he had passed down any of his famous restlessness. His son works with Encyclopedia Britannica. But before I could shoot even one question, Mrinalda smiled and said, 'Do you know, my son never calls me "baba" or "papa". He always calls me "Bandhu". And that is what I have tried to be to him above all else.' Bandhu means friend in Bengali...

A father can truly be a friend, mentor and confidante to his children as it comes so naturally...

Sanjeev and my younger daughter Sanaya were partners in Monopoly where I had paired up with my older one. After an hour of a nail-biting session where the game could have ended in favour of any team, luck favoured them and they won. We went bankrupt and the triumphant duo began their celebrations. The two hi-fived, did bum to bum, shoulder rub, the thumbs up and the 'v' for victory. Young children respond positively to such display of bonhomie. Had I won, I would have just exchanged a smile with my partner...

Cola was not allowed into the Gupta household, by order of the Supreme Court (mommy of course). seven year old Aryaman got onto

the mission called 'cola smuggle'. He called his dad up at work and whispered the 'black cats' mission. Dad returned home with a bloated tummy. Must be gas, mum thought. Mummy went into the kitchen to organise dinner and out came the bottled gas from underneath dad's shirt. They ran up to the attic, guzzling cola all the way. 'Black cats' came down in time for dinner with satisfied looks of mission accomplished!

Abhishek goofed up the most important paper in the board exam. He called up his dad and said, 'I studied very hard but somehow lost my confidence and did not do well.' His dad replied, 'Genetic lottery my son. I too blew up my maths paper in sheer nervousness. I will be home early and we will discuss our mind-calming strategies for the next paper. For now, forget what happened today and prepare for tomorrow.' Abhishek needed no more consolation. He could let go of his anxiety; after all his father had goofed up too in the same manner!

Tanishka called out to her dad before hitting the bed, 'Hey Dad, do I need to brush my teeth?' He answered, 'Well, just rinse with soda!' 'I love you dad,' she called back.

Kanha excused himself from the evening play session as it was time for his father to be home. Once home he got about setting up the rink for the day's WWF match. Sofas were pushed back, soft mattresses were placed on the floor and the make-shift fencing was done. Kanha then awaited his dad's arrival. He was the 'Black Cobra' and his father had settled on 'Undertaker'.

Saarang's choice for the adult supervision for his play-ground hours was clearly dad. With mom it was an instruction every few minutes, 'not so fast you will fall, not so high, look ahead, you will trip', whereas with dad it was, 'come on, you can go faster, give a little more push to your swing, champ'. Besides most of the time dad anyways stuck to his phone, attending business, leaving Saarang to work out his safety himself. He felt like a grown up and how he loved it.

Three-year-old Kareena's favourite past-time is pretending to be a princess while her knight (Dad) lunges on the dragon (her teddy bear) and saves the kingdom.

Daddies and Mommies parent differently

There are intrinsic differences in the way men and women parent. Their inclinations and methods of operating, their natural skills and even their ways of perceiving are different. *Whereas the moms fuss over their children, dads challenge them to stretch; moms care, dads play; moms hug, dads wrestle;* moms protect, dads encourage; moms support equity, dads cheer competition; moms encourage security, dads independence; moms teach mercy, dads justice; moms cushion their children against irritating stimulation, dads heap them on.

7.1 Fathers do not 'mother'!

Dr. Kyle Pruett of Yale Medical School in his book, *Fatherneed: Why Father Care is as Essential as Mother Care for Your Child*, says, dads matter simply because "fathers do not mother."

Study after study shows children with highly involved fathers benefit in many ways. While each father is a unique person who parents in his own style, there are some characteristics that good fathers have in common.

Fathers have a hands-off approach which helps build the child's self confidence and self esteem. They are more likely to encourage children to explore the outer levels of their competence and try new experiences. A study at the University of Maryland School of Medicine, in Baltimore, concluded that children who have active fathers learn better, have higher self esteem, and are less prone to depression than those who don't.

Fathers tend to withhold giving immediate help to a frustrated child. They allow the child time and space to work out situations by themselves, thus promoting problem-solving skills. Children of involved fathers tend to have a greater tolerance for stress and frustration.

Children with consistently involved fathers tend to be braver! With dads around children learn just how to hit the ball harder, fly the kites higher, jump from the top level at the club's swimming pool or brush up the dust after a fall with 'its nothing'.

Children develop internal limits and control during their interaction with their dads. Dads naturally tend to rough-house and tease children. Says Michael E. Lamb, head of the Section on Social and Emotional Development in the US National Institute of Child Health and Human Development: 'In nearly all instances fathers are much more likely "to get children worked up, negatively or positively, with fear as well as delight, forcing them to learn to regulate their feelings.' This helps them in social skills and teaches them to manage their emotions better.

Dads prepare their children for the real world. Where mothers tend to see the rest of the world in relation to their children, dads tend to see their children in relation to the rest of the world. For instance, it is the dads who are more likely to encourage the child to defend himself from a bully or stand up for his rights with 'Learn to fight your own way out in this world. I will not always be around'. Dads help children see that particular attitudes and behaviours have certain consequences. They are the ones who will say with a matter-of-fact attitude that, 'if you do not study hard you are not going to get into a good college'. They spell the reality out there in black and white.

Researchers like Jay Belsky, Ph.D., at Pennsylvania State University, and Ross Parke, Ph.D., of the University of California/Riverside Center for Family Studies say, 'The classical psychological view held that a father's 'job' was to expand his children's horizon beyond the bosom of the family and the mother-child relationship,' Belsky observes. 'Mothers preserved and protected children from discomfort. But fathers imposed a realistic, the-world-is-tough perspective.'

Fathers discipline in a systematic and consistent manner. They spell out the rules and then stick to them. With dad children know that rules are not pliable. No grace is allowed. If the children cop it they follow the consequence. A dad's discipline is not situational (does not depend on his or the child's moods). Where moms tend to adjust the discipline to the child's current state of mind, dads tend to observe and enforce rules systematically and sternly. This teaches children objectivity and consequences of right and wrong.

According to research, children of involved fathers do better in academics. The June 2000 report from the U.S. Department of Education and the U.S. Department of Health and Human Services showed that in two-parent families where fathers are highly involved, children are more likely to get top grades, more likely to enjoy school and less likely to get into trouble. Noted fatherhood researcher, Henry Biller found that father-involved children are more confident and successful in solving complex mathematical and logical puzzles. This may be because fathers tend to be more specialised in and have a higher interest in analytical problems. Poulter, author of *Father Your Son: How to Become the Father You've Always Wanted to Be* (McGraw-Hill), says there are tangible benefits to fathers becoming deeply entrenched in their children's academic lives. 'First, it shows them you care,' he says. 'Your involvement in such a major part of their lives builds their self-esteem and thus their success in school and, ultimately, adulthood. Second, it shows them that education matters to you. And when it matters to Dad, it usually matters to the kids, too.'

Research shows that the masculinity of sons and the femininity of daughters are the greatest when fathers are active in family life. Also when fathers are involved in day-to-day care, children grow up with more flexible and less stereotypical/traditional gender roles. Children of involved fathers are also more likely to care well for their own children too.

The Review of General Psychology concludes:

'Many studies conclude that children with highly involved fathers, in relation to children with less involved fathers, tend to be more cognitively and socially competent, less inclined toward gender stereotyping, more empathetic, and psychologically better adjusted.'

BUT THIS IDEA OF FATHERS IS STILL FARTHER OFF

Father's time, involvement and everyday care is still a luxury which very few children are blessed with. The west is plagued by physically absentee fathers due to wedlocks and high divorce rates which has created such an alarming situation that their governments have had to step in.

Fortunately, back home though, our homes are relatively more stable, the malaise of absentee fathers, nonetheless, is as pronounced. Fathers here are physically present but functionally absent. *Parenting to a great extent is essentially mothering.* Yes, there are some truly liberated men who are sincerely involved in the child-rearing process, but the question is, what percentage? How many children actually go to their daddies with their stories, problems, chores, wounds and dilemmas? The fact is, very few.

7.2 Common excuses and barriers to father's involvement

Mindset

Traditional beliefs – beliefs about gender roles and men's incapacity to 'mother', influence men's willingness to take on childcare. They believe parenting to be a woman's responsibility for the simple fact that they have an innate tendency to do so. After all who has ever heard of the paternal instinct? They conclude, men can't nurture, shouldn't nurture and women are the natural nurturers. Case closed.

Upbringing – They have been brought up single-handedly by their mothers and do not see any reason/benefit in changing the tradition. In their childhood, dads stepped in only when something was beyond the mom to handle. For instance when the kid got bad grades, did something really naughty, or categorically refused to obey mom. At times, just the threat referring to dad, 'wait till your dad comes home' was enough and no actual confrontation was required. These mom-parented boys have grown up to be fine and capable young men with very little paternal intervention and so the pattern of the lack of paternal involvement is transmitted from one generation to another.

Division of labour – Dads justify their stance by the, 'fair division of labour' theory. They argue that they have not forfeited their duties, but simply divided the responsibility. Through their financer-provider role they have demonstrated their love and care for the family and have thus fulfilled their responsibilities.

Taken for granted – Many men believe that the home will always be around and so can be taken for granted. The child has only one dad; what option does the child have but to love him (if need be dad can even subtly remind of the source of the toys and the goodies to his child). But the boss at work, the deadlines are all real where he has to prove himself every day. It is better to concentrate their time and energies in other 'more important things'.

'Not-my-cup-of-tea' philosophy – For many men their escape is in this non-arguable statement, I am not the type who can sit and read or play with children. It is not in my constitution and no one can change me'.

The Rock – Some men believe that a good father remains emotionally distant from his children. Signs of tenderness have anyways been squelched since an early age as they were taught to be tough. All they are left with is the macho image and they live up to it.

The Rock.

The scenario has changed

Science has shown that men and women parent differently and one can't really make up for the other. However devoted and committed one may be, if the other is absent, children suffer. Besides, there have been big shifts in work and family patterns. Maternal employment has increased and family sizes and structures have changed. Joint family system has disintegrated and mothers are robbed of their valuable support system in this age of nuclear families.

For the ones for whom 'fathering' does not come easily the answer lies, not in making that line the defining statement of their persons, but investing genuine time and effort and work towards the 'role'. According to Pickard (1998), 'Good fathering is hard work, but the most important kind of work men can do'.

If fathers do decide to get involved, interest and constitution will fall into place automatically. Mothers do not magically know more than fathers do, they have learnt so by doing. If men get involved they will get better too.

Besides, kids grow up quickly. Missed opportunities are forever lost. Once children hit their teens their preference slot will anyways be filled with friends. It will be much harder to open lines of communication or develop emotional connections, especially when there is no prior foundation or involvement on which the relationship rests. How long do you think it will take the children to say, 'But dad I have already fixed up this evening with my friend...?' Don't postpone your fatherhood. As one father put it: 'I know my daughter won't have time for me when she's 16. I want her to remember that I took her to the zoo and the book fair and that we used to go cycling together.'

Work and career-the wallet

Even today, by and large, men are the bread earners. In their masculine role as 'breadwinners' or financial providers, fathers feel more strongly tied to their jobs. Their job places much demand on their efforts, time and energies and they have very little left once they are back. Yes, they may have a genuine intention to be with the 'apple-of-their-eye', but the daily grind is a killer and they need their unwinding time to recharge their batteries for the next gruelling day. Mismanagement of time is also one of the set-backs of a man-child relationship.

Be honest with yourself

Remember, no one ever lay on his deathbed and wished he had worked longer hours. Men should ask themselves whether it really is a survival issue, as most of them gravely claim or is it their ambition which is responsible for them hitting home long after the children have gone to bed. Give your child a choice. Ask whether they would like that fancy play station, the new flying Barbie or more hours of their dad's time. Remember the story of the young boy who asks his father how much he earns in an hour? Father, irritated at his son's obsession of the green still does his mathematics and comes to a figure of twenty pounds an hour. The child begs his father for ten pounds. Exasperated, the father throws the ten pound note at his son with the contemptuous look of, 'Is this all that you can think of?'. The child runs to his piggy bank, extracts another ten pounds in small change, extends the twenty pounds to his father and asks, 'Can I buy an hour of your time?'

Children need their dads and not the dad's bank balance! Daniel Petre, head of Microsoft's Asia-Pacific division resigned from his job to spend more time with his kids, and to work on a Ph.D. on work-family balance. In his book *Father Time*, he says: 'Long hours are wrong hours. After a point at work, there is a diminishing law of return.' Time is equity, give some to your kids.

And if the issue is about unwinding, handled well, children can be great de-stressors. It is all in the perspective. When fathers view their children as a burden, or see playtime with them as another thing that they have to do, parenting loses its joy...what remains is just a chore. But if men keep away their worries and tensions of workplace and allow the children to reach them, their presence can actually be very soothing. Says Sajal Agarwal, 'At times I return home in a fuming mood after losing a contract or a retaliation with my boss, but just one "hi dad" from my five-year old melts my anger and frustration away. My boss and the contract recede into the background as I lose myself in the jibber-jabber of his day at the play ground where he hit his first "four".' Says another dad, Karan, 'Often I return from work a bundle of nerves, but with my daughter's acupressure (when she clutches my big legs with her small arms) I feel my heart rate go down and headache dissipate.'

In-house barriers

In some homes mothers often regard fathers' more boisterous style as too harsh or insensitive. They feel that men can't be caring and responsible enough. Moms have their protocol-kids shouldn't eat ice-cream before dinner, they shouldn't be parked in front of the television set for too long, once back home from playing out all evening they should freshen up before hitting the bed, etc. When men don't insist on the enforcement of the same they get the badge of 'uninterested' or 'incompetent'.

For some women the issue is one of 'control'. They have to retain their supremacy and expertise in the household and childcare domain. They unwittingly and subconsciously create an environment where there is very little space for man's participation. According to Allen & Hawkins, 1999, 'One way mothers restrict paternal involvement in the family work is by "gatekeeping" the domain of home and family'.

Even if mothers do not verbalise their feelings it shows from their actions. Such an attitude can derail a dad's desire for involvement. Says Sanjeev, 'My wife and I both make sure that our five year old gets enough to eat and drink, but let's just say that Krutika looks a lot cleaner and neater when Mom's around. Does that mean I am not good enough?'

Accept their parenting style

Women should ask themselves, 'Am I dampening my partner's parenting spirit with my rigid style?' Women need to know and understand that men parent differently from what they do – not better, not worse, but differently. Besides, if there does seem a need to guide, they can do so gently without playing the 'you are so useless' fiddle. Men won't want to help if their every move is criticised or condemned. Consider, just because he's doing something you wouldn't do, doesn't make it wrong. For a man to be the father he wants to be, perhaps a woman has to be less of the mother she wants to be.

Women should also recognise that they can't do it all. There are limits to their time, energy and spirits too. Having men share the parenting responsibilities will eventually work out beneficial for them, the children, as well as the men themselves.

Social and cultural barriers

We live in a society that sees a father's main role as a breadwinner, not a child-carer. In some cultures, involved dads are actually looked down as 'sissies' and 'henpecked'. At work, fathers often feel stigmatized when they exercise their right to stay home with a sick child or a new baby.

Besides, there are virtually no positive role models, preparatory classes or support groups. They cannot easily fall back on their own childhood experiences for guidance. Women's magazines are filled with articles about parenting, but there are no such magazines which deal with dads and parenting. Most fathers shown in the media too are portrayed as buffoons who rarely perform as competently with their children as the mothers do.

Be 'role creators'

True freedom comes when you break the chains of your upbringing and pass on something different to your child. Says Kanhai, 'My dad worked hard to provide for my family. I learned that from him. But out of the hundreds of games I played, he came to only four. I had to figure out for myself how to be an involved dad. But you bet I did that'.

Says Vivek, another dad, says, 'It is not that I am the best dad but I am surely a more aware dad. I reflected on where I missed having my dad around and tried not to let those gaps develop in my relationship with my child.'

Recall your own father as you remember him through your childhood. What did you most enjoy about him, with him? Conjure up times that you miss. Make a list of some of the best memories you had together. Take time to treasure moments that touch you deeply when you think of him.

Next, make a list of the things about your dad that you wish were different. What irritated you or bothered you—either things that he said or things that he didn't say, things that he did or things that he didn't do. Take some time to jot down negative memories from childhood, experiences with your dad (or perhaps where your dad was absent) that are sad memories. What do you wish had or hadn't happened?

☑ *Reality check*

Dads can ask themselves:
Do I wish that my dad had spent more time with me?
Do I wish that he had asked more about my feelings?
Do I wish that he had told me that he loves me or hugged me more often?
Would present dads too want their children to have the same regrets?

Anil Mulchandani
Here is the story of a father who broke more chains than one.

Author and freelance writer Anil Mulchandani was neither a topper nor showed an aptitude for becoming a street-smart businessman. Though he wrote well, nobody took him seriously because that was considered the domain of school toppers. After his B.Com. Anil joined his father in his textile factory. While Anil did okay on the sales and marketing side he could not really understand the nitty-gritty's of machines and parts. Anil said, 'My release came in the evenings when I sat down with a pen and paper to write features for magazines.' He started writing on nature and history and within a few short years had a huge portfolio covering almost every single large magazine and newspaper group in India. His stories got noticed by foreign publishers and projects began to materialise on that front too.

Anil's father too observed his son's natural flair and interest in the creative line while also noticing his disinterest in factory and office work. His father suggested to Anil to start a travel company, an area which he knew Anil loved, and said that it would give him time to pursue serious writing. His father then shared his childhood dream of wanting to join medical college and be a doctor. But his family wished that he take up engineering, and so it was. After studying engineering he worked in Germany and got a good job while in Germany to handle the company's operations in India. But on his return he realised that his father expected him to join the family's textile mill. He left his job and again went along with his father's wishes. Anil says, 'My father said that he was never a commercial person by nature and would have preferred to be a professional but did what the family expected of him. But he did not want me to go through this grill. I was already nearing thirty and most parents would have thought of stability and security rather than interest, but my father encouraged me to follow my heart while offering me the family work as a back up incase I did not click there. Thanks to him and also the support of my wife I got into the profession of my choice and have reason to be proud of my work being so widely published.'

7.3 Perks of fatherhood

The benefits of an involved dad to the child are well documented, but what's in it for the dad? The payoff is enormous and all-encompassing, just that most men have not discovered it yet. Caring for a child is a transforming experience that often brings immense joy, satisfaction and leads to personal growth. Men grow in awareness of everything around them, discover facets of themselves they didn't know existed, and dream and live anew through their children.

Health benefits

Fatherhood forces dads to be on their toes. Children have a way of moving even the most ardent couch potatoes off their butt. Their demands, requests and needs (can we play ball, hide-n-seek, want a glass of water, am stuck under the sofa) keep dads on-the-go. Children are the mechanisms that lead men to become coaches for society cricketing, swimming and other outdoor activities.

Staying healthy for dads becomes a priority with children around. Says Kenneth Goldberg, M.D., author of *The Men's Health Longevity*

Program, 'Men realize they need to take care of themselves if they want to be around for their children.'

A long-term study by the National Institute of Mental Health, in Bethesda, Maryland, found that men with healthy family relationships are less prone to stress-related health problems. 'Dads who have good relationships with their children are less likely to suffer from chest pain, insomnia, fatigue, indigestion, and dizziness,' says Rosalind C. Barnett, Ph.D., lead author of the study.

Emotional, psychological and social benefits

However convincingly men may defend their stance on being hard on time and energy to be really involved in parenting, in their hearts they do feel the void of having been 'incomplete dads'. Psychologists too, say that very few of the visibly powerful men feel a total success in their heart of hearts. Many grieve roads not taken—such as time spent with their children—and then it's too late. What it says on their business card is just not enough.

When men take up parenting seriously it brings immense emotional satisfaction. Knowing that you can soothe a child in a special way or please him is deeply validating. They feel 'complete'. Psychoanalyst Guy Corneau shows that, for men today, regaining the essential "second birth" into manhood lies in gaining the ability to be a father to themselves—not only as a means of healing psychological pain, but as a necessary step in the process of becoming whole. Fatherhood satisfies their sense of purpose and boosts psychological well-being.

Theory of generativity – Erik Erikson

Erik Erikson's theory of generativity (greater time spent in child care activities and higher levels of psychological involvement in the role of parenting) holds that people reach the peak of maturity when they contribute to the growth of the next generation, whether coaching an athletic team or serving a school board. The researchers found that the more fathers nurtured their children socially and emotionally, the more giving and caring these men were when they reached middle age. Fathers who actively promoted their own children's development, taking them trick-or-treating or advising them on dating problems, for example, assumed responsibilities outside of their families later in life.

Fatherhood brings new meaning and happiness. Through the antics of their children, men automatically relive their own childhood. Says Jay, 'Watching my little Khushi squeal with joy at the unexpected ice-cream cup reminds me of the small pleasures of life which I almost miss while shouldering all my adult responsibilities; her nuzzling close to me transports me to the soft arms of my cuddling days with my mom; her mud-stained dress immediately fills my nostrils with the delicious smell of the earth which I used to brush past during my dives to stop the ball from crossing the boundary. I instinctively relive those resonant moments from my own early years and can't help but smile.'

Kids have a way of making adults slow down and look at things they would normally scurry past (or step on). Children are blessed not only with the instinct of being in the here and now, but also of imparting the utmost profundity to whatever they are doing. One may not get as much done, but he will get far more from everything he does. Says Prakash, father of a seven-year old, 'Want to live forever? Well then, you're going to have to learn to stop time. Luckily, your child can teach you how. When my eight year-old would brush, her mouth would convert into a mint froth manufacturing unit, during her baths she transformed into a mermaid, her morning meals would become the battle ground where the cereal in the breakfast bowl becomes the goblin which her pakman mouth gobbled. The shift from one activity to another always needed the prodding of a 'time's up' from us!!! She did not think of the next thing to do when she was doing something right now.'

Children have a different clock and a different calendar. We can learn timelessness from them.

Tarang says, 'My son mimics me to perfection. One day he gave his mum a pat on the bum exactly the way I do. My wife and I looked at each other and roared into a laugh as we had never done before.'

Fatherhood shows men sides to their personality they don't know they have. It makes a hardened, unsentimental dad cry. Men learn things about their inner self, that they can be both tough and tender, playful and compassionate, assertive and openly loving of their family—and themselves.

Fatherhood makes 'better men' out of them. Since they are their children's heroes, and 'role models' they have an image to uphold and protect. This ennobles them. Confronted with the task of teaching values to children they better themselves. With children around dads swear and lie less, respect authority, zealously guarding their morality for fear of what the children will learn otherwise. It also makes them more positive and optimistic. Fatherhood makes dads constantly challenge and reassess their values in life.

Marital benefits

One key benefit to being an involved hands-on dad is that one can rack up an incredible amount of points with one's partner. When dads

share parenting responsibilities moms get their much needed breathing space and that too without the all-pricking guilt feeling of pushing their children off themselves and onto some 'others' who may/may not be as good. With dads, women know that their little ones are in, though inexperienced yet loving hands. Personally speaking I never love my husband more than when he listens to one of their endless tales tirelessly or watches their art creations and even manages to identify the horse as a horse (to me it could be any four-legged creature).

If children need fathers as much as they need mothers; fathers need children even more.

The fortune of fatherhood – Sharath Dravid

Says Mr Sharath Dravid, father of Rahul Dravid, the cricket star, 'When I was young, I used to love listening to cricket commentary on the radio. I always cherished the dream of seeing my son do well in cricket one day. Later, when Rahul was playing at Lords in England, I watched him walk away even when the umpire didn't declare him out. He walked because he felt he was out. As he went back to the stands, all the members stood up and applauded in great respect. That was a dream come true for the cricket lover in me.' Mr Sharath said that he never forced his dreams on his children and when Rahul showed interest and potential in cricket he was more than happy. He says, 'Today, I can proudly say that Rahul's performance has fulfilled my dream'.

How my daughter taught me 'The sense of no commerce'

Raina insisted on giving the Rs 600 Barbie doll to her school friend Gayatri, who came from the municipal quota section and belonged to a much lower income group. Shrey, Raina's dad argued that Gayatri would be happy with something far cheaper and they do not really need to spend that kind of money. Raina in a puzzled tone said, 'But to my other friends, we do give those very Barbie dolls as gifts.' A little embarrassed now, Shrey said, 'Yes, but how can we give them something cheap? What will they think of us?' Raina shot out, 'Do the gifts that we give depend upon who they are or what we are?'

Children have an inherent sense of fairness and a sense of no commerce and Shrey took life lessons from his nine year old. 'I will forever be indebted to her for reminding me of the basics,' he said.

HOW GOOD A FATHER ARE YOU?

☑ *Reality check*

To know how well you know your child answer the following questions:

What is your child's class teacher's name?

Who is your child's best friend?

What does your child fear the most?

Which is your child's favourite T.V show?

What is your child's current favourite possession?

What is your child's favourite playtime activity?

What are your child's three most favourite food items?

What is your child's favourite subject?

How involved are you:

How much time do you spend with your child on an everyday basis?

How often do you go to parent-teachers meets?

How often do you keep promises made to your child?

Write down:

I knew I was a good dad when...

Years from now I want to be remembered as a dad who was...

The most important contribution that I have made in my child's life is...

Ask your child to answer:

What are the two things that your child really wants from you?

What is your child most happy about in your relationship with her/him?

Ask yourself:

Do I judge myself and other men by the size of their paychecks?

Do I define success in terms of big house, car, bank balance, nice vacation?

7.4 Take charge! Mission: possible!

Bill Cosby once wrote, 'If God had trouble handling children, what makes you think it would be a piece of cake for you?' (Cosby was referring to Adam and Eve and their disobedience in the garden.)

Owen Wister, an old college friend of Theodore Roosevelt, was visiting him at White House. Roosevelt's daughter, Alice, kept running in and out of the room until Wister finally asked if there was something Roosevelt could do to control her.

'Well,' said the President, 'I can do one of two things. I can be P\president of the United States or I can control Alice. I cannot possibly do both.'

Creating fatherhood means creating a major psychological shift. Learning to be an involved dad is not easy, it takes time, energy, interest, and most importantly, commitment. But the good part is that when done with sincerity and consistency it brings results. Walls of years of neglect can be torn down with a kiss or an embrace.

Do not be a 'spare' in your child's life

Commit to being a major player.

Given below are tips and ways for dads to get involved. Pick the ones that appeal to you and your children. However, there are two universal principles which apply to all dads which transcend beyond culture, age, interest and boundaries.

1. *The time factor! Quantity*

Children need dad-time, period! And the type of time they need is not all thrown into a once-a-week or month block or some exotic holiday once a year. They need 'everyday' time. Dads may say their children are a priority but if they are not willing to spend any time with their 'priorities', children do their equation fast. Child psychologist, Lee Salk says, 'Children can tell fairly young what their parents consider important. If they see everything comes ahead of them, there is likely to be trouble ahead.'

Children simply expect their fair share of your available time. Be fair to them and give them their share. A young boy received an unusual birthday gift from his dad. The boy peeled back layers of wrapping paper from a tiny box. Inside he found a small, handwritten note from his father. 'Son,' it read, 'this year I will give you 365 hours—an hour every day after dinner.' 'This simple present became the greatest gift I ever had in my life,' explained the boy as an adult. 'My dad not only kept his promise, but every year he renewed it. I am the result of his time.'

> Ask yourself: Am I just a 'Sunday Dad' to my Children

Time cracker for daddies

It is possible, by 'changing the shape of your time' to create extra time for the children without necessarily losing any work time.

➢ Sacrifice one leisure activity a week.

➢ Trade one solitary activity for a family activity. Your golf could turn into family walks.

➢ Your watching ten channels together could be traded for a nice family movie. Instead of going to the gym, go to the playground.

➢ Use the time on-the-run. Take your children on the errands you can. Don't just turn on the news and forget your children when they are in the car with you. Talk or joke with them.

➢ Start work later once or twice a week, and do things with the children instead.

➢ Schedule one television-free night per week with your children.

➢ Wake up a little early and spend that extra time with your child.

➢ Combine exercise time with quality time. Ask your children to ride their bikes around the block while you jog. Ask them to walk with you, or for the little ones, push them in a stroller. A father reports that his child doesn't even mind getting up early to be able to exercise with Daddy.

2. Complete attention! Quality

Quantity of time cannot stand alone – hours spent at home can be wasted. When you are with your child, be with the child mind, body and soul. When you come home do not bring stress along with you. According to Ann Crouter, Ph.D., professor of human development at Penn State University, 'Parents who experience more pressure at work feel more overloaded in general and are more prone to arguing with their children. In turn, their kids feel less good about themselves, becoming depressed or developing feelings of low self-worth.'

Take your 'Time out' and unwind before you walk in through the door in the evenings. Says Chintan, 'I always stop in for a juice break before hitting home and use those minutes to make my transition from the banker to the dad.' Ketan, another newage dad, heads straight for a shower and listens to music for about fifteen minutes before emerging as the 'yes children' daddy.

But do remember that most often 'quality' time happens after sufficient 'quantity' time.

✓ *Checklist*

Are you spending quality time with your children? Ask yourself:

Is my child the centre of my attention when I am with him or do I just try to keep him busy while I do other things?

During our time together are we doing things that both of us enjoy?

Am I happy just spending ordinary time with my child with no particular purpose or goal in mind?

Harsh Neotia on quality time

Entrepreneur, art connoisseur, Harsh Neotia was sipping his morning cup of tea in the library when he heard a big pandemonium going on below. His son, then about nine, had brought a book to be taken to school, which the servant by mistake had taken up to his room. His son asked the servant to fetch the book quickly. She got the wrong one. Since it was minutes before their school gates would close, the boy now screamed at the maid asking her to hurry up and get the right one this time. The poor lady rushed up once again and still came down with the wrong book. Finally he himself went up, grumbling and abusing the maid and got the book himself. That day they reached school late; back home the ayah was in tears for the rest of the day. Harsh Neotia said, I wanted to talk to my son, but only when both of us could have had an undisturbed one hour together. I did not want to tell him when he was rushing to play or I had some business deal on my mind.

The opportunity rose after three days, we sat down together and I broached the incident. I asked, 'Beta, the other day why were you screaming at the aayah?' He immediately began his explanation. I heard it patiently and then said, 'But she doesn't know which book you are talking about, because she can't read. She could have possibly forgotten where she placed the book and then did not know which one it was'. Harsh said, My son did try and tell me that he had explained what the cover looked like and yet she couldn't get the right one. To which I said very calmly that, 'Unfortunately she has not had the opportunity for education like you have had. Besides, she must have tried her best to locate the book but couldn't.' I even said that the maid was upset for the rest of the day perhaps because she thought that he was making fun of the fact that she can't read.' His son was very fond of that aayah and had a deep emotional bond with her. Harsh said, 'I could see him moved and I knew he felt sorry.' Harsh Neotia, though he has a hectic schedule, candidly confesses that he is not happy with the quantity of time that he spends, but nevertheless he is satisfied with the quality.

7.5 Be an 'everyday dad'

Prarit held his one-day-old baby in his arms and after the initial euphoria, doubts assailed him. Would he be a good dad? Would he be able to help his son find his calling? Make him mentally tough but tender-hearted, socially skilled yet intense and passionate? The questions that hounded him were so DEEEEEPPPP and he had not the know-how.

Today, Prarit knows the answer, 'You start with the small stuff'.

Be a part of your child's everyday (routine, activities, chores) life. You will understand the 'big picture' once you focus on the small, everyday details. Says, Muriltharan an engineer dad, 'I was supervising my five year-old's bath one day, when suddenly out of nowhere he said that his teacher hates him and that he can feel so in her eyes.' His son had lost his exuberance since the beginning of that academic session and no amount of coaxing induced him to spell out his problems.

But a regular bath time did. For some reason he felt comfortable and close enough to bare his heart.

Dads can make it a point to have meals (at least one) together on an everyday basis. Meal times can be great for conversations. In the Gupta household, every evening one member got a chance to pick the topic of one's choice. They discussed anything under the sun– current events, their interests, popular music, fashion, or school.

Dads can drive or walk their children to school/bus stops. Research has shown that some of the most important connections between children and their fathers are in the car when he's driving them somewhere!

Dads can either take the responsibility of waking the children up in the mornings and getting them ready for school or tuck them up in bed with a good night kiss and a story or a prayer. Applying lotion to a child's hands and feet can also be part of a bedtime routine. For Shashank bedtime was the occasion where the dad-daughter duo updated each other on the happenings of the day.

Dads can read (even for ten minutes) to their children everyday.

Dads can take up a subject that they enjoy and get involved in its tutoring. For Aman those percentage sums became so easy when dad explained them to him.

Dads and children can take the pet out for a walk together.

Dads can get involved in the day-to-day decisions that affect their kids' lives, however small.

Anup Jalota's newspaper reading sessions
Anup Jalota followed the ritual of 'newspaper reading sessions' to his son religiously every single day. He says, 'I remember showing the newspaper cartoons in the entertainment section to my son when he was just about three or four.' As the son grew, Anupji started reading him bits of news which he thought would interest him and they would often get into discussions and debates over the information. Says Anupji, 'This small habit which took barely fifteen minutes of my time is paying huge dividends everyday.' Anupji reminisces of the time when his son was only about nine and read in the paper that the national award winner film 'Shwas' has been chosen to represent

India at the Oscars but the makers did not have the funds to be there. Anupji says, 'My son came to me and asked me to send them Rs. 50, 000. I sent the money that very day and stuck the receipt on his soft board. When he came back from school and saw the receipt he thanked me and I could see the gratefulness and the pleasure in his eyes. I knew that somewhere I had done something right for my son to be who he is.'

Darshana Zhaveri

Manipuri danseuse, Darshana Zhaveri, spoke about the daily thirty-minute morning ritual where she would lie on her father's lap and they would listen to classical music on the Vividh Bharti together. She said, 'It was my special time with him. I loved the feel of his warm lap and the melodious music on the radio. With that half hour of radio everyday he imparted many values. I learnt consistency as we listened to music everyday without fail; I trained for higher things as I receded to the depths of the beautiful ragas, and most important I learnt the art of going deep into what one does.'

Aparna Sen

Aparna Sen reminisced of the evenings when her father would read aloud poetry to her. She said, 'I was no more than five and couldn't understand much of the words, but I could feel the rhythm, beauty and the eloquence of his voice. Even today I can just close my eyes and picture his beautiful narration of the countless poems.'

Given below are some activities that dad and children love doing together. Pick and incorporate those which seem most 'you' to you and your child.

- Hobbies: Cooking, crafts (making airplanes and boats), fishing, swimming, biking, making collections of coins, stamps, feathers, make great hobbies that can open doors to exciting family time.
- Fixing things around the house: a broken cycle chain, that leaking faucet, resetting furniture, shifting artifacts to give that fresh new

look. When children and dads do chores together they are not only teaching their children about team work but responsibility and accountability too.

- Sharing talent: Dads can pass on their special talents by giving coaching classes in guitar, painting, drumming, cricket, pottery etc.
- Learning together: How to carve a whistle, how to pitch a tent, which properties to buy in Monopoly, how to send a fax. Ajit saved a refrigerator box and turned it into a fort for his young son. 'With a few cuts and a blanket or old pillow, we created a whole fantasy world that was large enough for the both of us,' he says. The fact that it could be dismantled and stored under the couch when not in use, was another bonus.
- Camping trips: Catching frogs, collecting stones, pond dipping, climbing trees and bug collecting could all make for fun-to-do things. If real hiking or camping isn't possible, Dad and the kids can camp out even in the living room. Location isn't important, but the time spent together can create unforgettable lifetime bonds.
- Plant a garden together.
- Sporting events: Kids and dads can go for matches and sporting events like cricket, football.

- Visiting places: Dads can visit places like concerts, theaters, museums, library and book stores, banks, post office, hardware stores. Ketan took his son to the bank and let him help him with dates on forms. They also looked up the ATM together.
- Restaurants and movies: Anahita and her dad regularly go for their 'daddy dates'. This is her special one-to-one time with her dad. She gets to pick an activity of her choice and they have a fun evening which usually extends for about two hours. At times they opt to go out dining or visit book stores, or just go near the shore to watch passers-by and munch on corn.
- Playing games together: Board games, pillow fights, WWF fights, field games like cricket, throw ball etc. I remember the house I grew up in. We were three sisters and a brother. Wild horses could not keep us away at the stroke of 7 p.m. It was dad's time to return home. He would take precisely ten minutes to freshen up and we would spread the battleground on the bed. We had tournaments and kept scores for months. We played many games like Monopoly, Conquest, Stock Market, Scrabble, card games like Pinnicle and the kodi game Chaupad (an Indian version of Ludo). One game dominated for months before we got bored of it and switched onto another. There were always two teams. Dad and mom were captains and the four of us divided ourselves between them. We were loyalists and somehow sided with our team captain even beyond the battle field. But we shuffled our teams every six months and learned to relate to each family member at some point or other. We were always equals. No grace winning was allowed, every mistake had to be paid through blood and how we enjoyed those sessions every single evening.
- Solving puzzles: Dads and children can do crosswords, jigsaw puzzles, Sudoku and Anagrams together.

A hug a day!

Men are notoriously stereotyped as undemonstrative. That's generally correct. Do not reserve pats, hugs and kisses for the weekend.

Communicate your deep love for your children, no matter how old they are. Show your tender side.

There are many ways in which men can express their affection. Children sometimes need to hear their father say 'I love you' to fully appreciate what he does for them.

Use expressions like:

'I love you.'

'You're really special'

'You add so much joy to my life.'

Dads can even use other means such as greeting cards, notes taped on a bedroom door, e-mail, voice-mail messages, a handwritten letter—even a small ad in the local newspaper. Be creative, but be sincere.

Says nine-year-old Kareena, 'My father has never saved me from a burning castle or an avalanche, but he does hug me and tells me to have a good day.'

Says six-year-old Arjun says, 'My father doesn't buy me expensive or fancy toys, but he does whisper to me that I'm his special treasure.'

Reminisces ten-year-old Rashi who is plump, 'My dad came home and gave an air twirl to my four year old brother. They both giggled and then he came to me. Unconsciously I stepped back. How could he have lifted me up, I was far too heavy. Suddenly I saw my dad extend his hand and ask, "Can I have a dance with my princess?" We ball danced for what seemed to me an eternity. I love no one more than my dad in my life.'

7.6 Offer them a glimpse of your work world

Children want to know what life is like outside the home and what their parents do at work. Sure, the kids may know the name of the company or organisation that their dads work for or head. But, what do they really do there? What is the nature of their work? Dad can use a quiet Friday afternoon to show a child around his work place, give him a highlighter and some paper and have him 'help' out. Children can even take their own materials (art supplies, books) and prop up in a corner. They will be on their own yet have daddy around. Best, they will get the feel of what daddy does for eight hours everyday.

Sameer, who runs his own office which deals with computer software says, 'I don't want my son to associate me not being around the home with my office. He should not have a dislike for my office or what I call work because 'office' takes papa way from him. So whenever I am in town (Sameer travels about six-seven days every month) he has complete accessibility to me. He can call me up and I make it a point to take all his calls. If I am in a meeting with the phone on the answering mode, I call him as soon as I finish. Yes, it is time consuming, even gets on my nerves at times, but at the end of the day I know that I have given something invaluable to my son, the faith that I am truly just a phone call away.'

Says another dad high on the corporate ladder, 'My daughter drops in by my office once in a while. I have her photograph on my desktop, her drawings are pinned on my soft board, and one or two of her little craftworks are proudly displayed on my shelf. She chatters with me for a while and decides on the refurnishing regarding her stuff and then sits with my secretary and helps herself to chocolates, biscuits and Pepsi. Yes, she does monkey around but she is six and can get away with it, so why not.'

Karan, a software engineer, says, 'It's a good thing to share your hopes and dreams with your kids because it helps them develop their own.'

Jatin Das

Jatin Das, the famous painter, told me, 'One day I carried my two and a half year old son to my studio. All the time that I was painting he sat there quietly observing me. When I stopped for a break, he came up to my palette, picked the same brush that I had been working with amongst at least ten others, dipped it in the water tumbler with the same delicate force that I use and very gently edged it on the side exactly as I had been doing.'

Radhika Kathpalia

Says architect Radhika Kathpalia, winner of a national prize in architecture and daughter of the architect B. Doshi, 'As a young child there was no where we could not go with our dad. No table, no office, no hours were off-limits because it was work.'

7.7 Communication

Communication is often left to the mothers, while the fathers dispense advice as and when needed. According to the National Fatherhood initiative, by the time the typical American child is six years old, he or she will have spent more time watching television than talking with his or her father over their entire lifetime! Are we really any different?

Get a Masters degree on your child, majoring in your kids.

- Know Your Children's World! Know about their friends, teachers, school

Ask them:-
- Who are their heroes and why?
- What are their dreams and desires?
- What are their fears?
- Which is their favourite game and why?
- About their difficult days at school, with friends at home etc.
- What upsets them the most and why?
- What motivates them?
- What embarrasses them and why?

Dads can also use these 'Thought starters':

I had a dream...

This funny thing that happened...

By showing interest in the child's life, dads are showing that they are important to them. Also, the toughest things for dads is to really listen and control their impulse to advice, problem-solve or suggest. Yes, you may know all the answers but children need to know that you care. It is only when the dads hear that the children will conclude 'you care'. Do not try to be Mr. Fix it. Just extend a loving and a listening ear.

MR. Fix iT!

Says Computer software engineer Priya, 'Digital circuits, C/ Unix were not my dad's subjects, but he listened whenever I talked about them'. And I knew he cared.'

Says AbhIshek, 'My papa is someone I have long conversations with and one who shares my silences too.'

No conversation can be one-sided. For children to open up to their dads, dads too need to open up to them. Men can talk about their lives, dreams and passions, struggles and achievements. They can talk about their family history, childhood stories, and how mom met dad stories. Kids love to hear stories about themselves from their dads too. Take out baby pictures of your children and tell them the story behind those pictures. Dads can even discuss issues, hobbies, similar interests and current events too.

Johnny Lever

Johnny Lever, has everything today; money, fame and respect, he sighed and said, 'But it has not always been so.' He has spent most of his childhood and part of his adult life in the slums. He said, 'Living there defied the very essence of humanity. Jungle Raj prevailed and 'might was right'.' He then looked at me with a small tear in his eye and said, 'I will never forget my roots, nor will I allow my children to forget where their dad has come from.' Johnny said that a man may not have money and resources but he has dreams and hopes and he is worthy of love and respect. What one doesn't have should never become the defining stance of what he is. He said, 'This is one lesson that I want my children to internalise for life. Even today I take both my children every once in a while to my childhood home where they see the other, not so pretty side of life. If there is one thing which I want to give them above all it is the value of compassion and humility.'

Rajeev Kathpalia

Rajeev Kathpalia, winner of the President's award in architecture, and his sons formed a cartel and they regularly watched war movies on The History Channel and then spent hours discussing over the 'why', 'what' and 'what if' of it.

My husband, Sanjeev, can easily talk to my daughter about 'boys' a topic which I am not very comfortable with.

Dads should grab small pockets of time to maintain the rhythm in communication. They can call their kids in between appointments just to say 'hi'. They can send them an e-mail from work. One dad made it a point to tuck in a message or a quote in the lunch box. His child connected with him at 12 every noon even though they were kilometers away.

Aparna Sen

Aparna Sen said she went through a paralysing shyness in her early teens. She said, 'There were many parties which we were expected to attend. Before one such party I went up to my dad and confessed my malaise. I said that I felt very tongue-tied and really had nothing to contribute to in the conversation. My father then disclosed a secret. He said that most people love to talk about themselves and so I must just lead them to themselves and pick up cues from their conversation and start asking questions. I never felt socially unequipped after that,' Aparna she said, 'But even more important than his advice was his approach to the matter. He did not dismiss my fear by calling it silly but could see it from my perspective and that is what gave me the confidence to go to him with my troubles.'

7.8 Take an interest in the child's school

In *The Educated Child*, author William Bennett tells the story about a professor who overheard a conversation that his son was having at school. They were talking about their parents and their occupations. One child boasted that his daddy was a doctor and made a lot of money. Another boy bragged that his dad flew to Washington and talked to the president. Then the professor's child exclaimed, as if there was nothing greater, 'My daddy is here!' with a proud look in his father's direction.

Kumar Mangalam Birla attends most of the PTAs in both his children's schools.

School and its related activities form a big part of a child's life. Consider this, men spend eight hours at work everyday and think about it for the rest of the waking hours. For children too, school is a place where they not only spend six hours, five days a week but come back with school related work which stretches for another two hours or more per day.

Discussing school- teachers, friends, academics and activities can be an easy bridge over which dads can connect and communicate with their children.

Tips for dads:
Don't leave sports, science fairs, school plays and other events in school just to Mom. Faces shine twice as brightly when they see both parents in the audience.
Fathers should make a point of meeting teachers and knowing what each child is studying in school.

According to Ladson-Billings, a professor in the department of curriculum and instruction at the University of Wisconsin in Madison, it's critical for parents to share as much information about their child as possible with a teacher. She says, 'Parents begin to see early on what things are most helpful for their children and how a child learns best. Parents assume teacher expertise, but teachers are dealing with twenty or twenty-five kids at a time and it's difficult to be specific and focused enough. Parents need to tell teachers about their child's strengths. Otherwise, they may get lost in the shuffle and not reach their potential.'

She suggests, parents ask these three questions:
1. What does my child know and what is he able to do?
2. What does my child still need to know and be able to do to be successful?
3. How can I help?

Dads can also show that they are truly interested in their children's education by asking them what they did at school and looking at their books, projects, and assignments with them. They can read their essays and offer praise and constructive suggestions. They can help them with homework and project work.

Fathers can share their talents with the school. Schools today encourage positive parental support and interaction. Dads can contribute in a myriad ways. Dads who are knowledgeable about a subject that children find interesting, can deliver lectures as guest speakers. Fathers with technical skills can set up the class e-mail list or help with the school web site. Nikhil, a guitarist helped out with the school's annual musical programme. Vijay Bhardawaj, who works for AEC (Ahmedabad Electric Company) organised a visit for the school children where they saw the entire process of power generation. Rajeev Kathpalia helped the school with its architectural expansion. Shashank Chokhani, the owner of Kalory bread organised a tour to his factory and the children saw flour turning into bread.

Whatever the expertise, dads can offer their services to school. Not only will the schools benefit but the children will see their schools too in a more serious light. By being involved at their child's school, fathers emphasise that school is important and that they are willing to spend their time with the child there.

CONCLUSION

You will find that some of the resources and strategies mentioned here may work better for you than others. That's fine. There's no one way to learn to be a better father. In the end, don't put pressure on yourself to be the 'perfect father.' The fact is, he doesn't exist. All a child needs from you is you-completely.

In the course of parenting, many times you may find yourself at the end of your wits, energy, patience and understanding. It is alright. As Bill Cosby famously said, 'No matter how calmly you try to referee, parenting will eventually produce bizarre behaviour, and I'm not talking about the kids. Their behaviour is always normal.'

Tide through the lows. Consistency is the key to involved parenting. Because at the end of your life, you won't be thinking about the hours spent in front of T.V. flicking channels, the innumerable drink parties you hosted or attended, your career accomplishments or even your stock portfolio. You'll be wondering what you should have done different with your kids.

What my dad taught me

My dad taught me to face the world even if it scared us both.

My dad did not really guide me into making the right career choices, but he did teach me to finish what I took up and to love a job well done.

My dad did not teach me how to choose a spouse wisely, but I knew that I have an intrinsic worth with or without Mr. or Mrs. Right.

My dad was someone who knew when to leave me alone, but was always there when I looked behind my shoulder.

Thank you papa for being there, always!

Trial and Error

···

I think, therefore I err...

German psychologist, social researcher and author Gerd Gigerenzer, in the magazine *Spring 2005*, says, 'In an uncertain world, thinking as well as elementary perception involve making bets and taking risks. To err is not only human but is a necessary consequence of this kind of intelligence. I hope Descartes will not mind a modification of his dictum accordingly: I think, therefore I err. Whenever I err, I know intuitively that I am.'

Trial and error is a method of reaching a correct solution or satisfactory result by trying out various means or theories until error is sufficiently reduced or eliminated. Making no errors would destroy the intelligence of the system. There is a close parallel to the Darwinian theory, where random variability and mutation–copying errors–are essential for evolution by natural selection. Not making these errors would eliminate evolution.

Trial and error

The British, who ruled India, constantly warned the Indian freedom seekers about the awful mistakes the inexperienced Indian leaders would make if they were given the power to rule. Gandhi, the chief architect of the freedom movement and father of the nation, countered, 'But those will be *our* mistakes.'

During one of his famous 10,000 experiments to light the electric bulb, Edison actually tried to pass current through wood. It was only after the experiment failed that he ticked wood off his list. Today all of us confidently say, 'Wood is a bad conductor of electricity'.

Even as a young girl, beauty tycoon Estee Lauder occupied her time experimenting with new formulae and ingredients for skin-care products. Before she even had a company office or a laboratory, Lauder would spend her days in her kitchen, creating beauty recipes over the burners of her own stove. She found that it was only in doing things that had never been done before that she was able to find success. It wasn't just in the area of production that Lauder ventured out with untested strategies through trial and error. She became a marketing queen, whose unique tactics would later become standards not only in the beauty industry, but also in industries market-wide. The only woman on *Time* magazine's 1998 list of the twenty most influential business geniuses of the century, Estee, said in her autobiography, 'Don't be afraid of the trial-and-error approach...Trust your instincts...create your own style.'

8.1 Learning happens best when it comes through trial and error

Wrong answers lead to right answers. Trial and error offers a direct feedback loop. When children are allowed trial and error to draw their own conclusions following their attempted guesses and experiments, they know what works and what doesn't from what has worked and what hasn't. It is 'learning' which comes from 'being'...there is no better teacher than personal experience.

Research from all over stresses the importance of trial and error, especially in context with student life. Paediatrician and child-care expert T. Berry Brazelton emphasises that children develop self-esteem through the sense of competence and mastery that comes from tackling and triumphing over challenges, even modest ones. Brazelton emphasises the value of leaving a child to work through a problem for herself, trying out different approaches to a task until she succeeds. For a child accustomed to learning by trial and error, frustration can serve as a source of motivation and energy rather than an obstacle.

Michael Liebowitz is a clinical professor of psychiatry at Columbia University and head of the Anxiety Disorders Clinic at New York State Psychiatric Institute. He says that parents who allow their kids to find a way to deal with life's day-to-day stresses by themselves, are helping them develop resilience and coping strategies. He says, 'Children need to be gently encouraged to take risks and learn that nothing terrible happens. Having overprotective parents is a risk factor for anxiety disorders, because children do not have opportunities to master their innate shyness and become more comfortable in the world.'

8.2 Our childhood

During our childhood most of us were left to ourselves to work out the rules ('burners are hot', 'wet floors are not too good for running'), find our way through deadlocks and arguments ('mummy can I gift Sanjay a Cadbury slab as we have had a fight which was essentially my mistake and I want to patch up with him?'; 'you want to play hide and seek and I want to play dog and the bone let us settle for cricket'), manage our school work (homework, examinations and the works) and solve those puzzles and mysteries by ourselves. We fell out of trees, got cuts, broke bones and teeth, ate mud pies *and the worms did not live in us forever. Little League had tryouts and not everyone made the team. Those who didn't, had to learn to deal with disappointment.* Our parents were busy with their chores and by providence the rule of our childhood was:

'Try harder next time'
'Help yourself'
'Find out for yourself'
'Try other ways'

We had freedom, failure, success and responsibility, and we learned how to deal with them. During the course we learnt: problem solving, resilience, patience, risk-taking, exploration and decision-making. In the process we became: confident, independent, daring, persistent, courageous, socially skilled and mentally tough.

8.3 But times have changed

Little Ketan was praying to God with, 'Please God, let mom develop another interest in life besides me.'

Parents today over-parent, over-protect, over-monitor and over-indulge. Parents really can love until it hurts

The reasons are manifold

➤ Families today are smaller. Parents end up paying too much attention to too little kids.
➤ Parents are more aware and geared up for the huge responsibility placed on them for nurturing their 'Einstein babies'.
➤ Parents justify the micromanagement of their child's life under the

pretext that children require every iota of support and guidance to enable their children to carve out their space in this competition-frenzied world.

➤ For some parents it is, 'I did not get enough guidance and direction, I will make sure that my child is equipped with all my knowledge too'.

➤ For some, (especially stay-home moms), the agenda of life is 'parenting', after all they need some identity somewhere. No one can come in between them and their purpose, not even the children themselves!

➤ Some parents have a terrible fear that they won't turn out to be good parents so they overcompensate by trying too hard.

And so parents become selfless martyrs concentrating all their time, energy, material resources and learning, at times even stretching beyond their capacity to hand the 'world' on a platter to their children.

Parents of today believe:

- They must overcome all their children's problems for them.
- They must protect them from the challenges they can.
- They must take all their decisions for them.
- They must save them from disappointments and failures.

- Children should not be inconvenienced and discomforted even a bit.

Children are thus under their parents protective wings for 'their good only'.

Although error and experimentation are the true mothers of success, we take great pains to remove failure from the equation. Some of us invest more in our children's school work than they themselves do. We burn more calories running alongside them to buck them on their skating, or cheering them at tennis sessions, than they themselves have. We hold on to their cycle backs long after we should, because they may fall. We remember their homework assignments, for what if they forget and are ridiculed in the class, which may lead to school aversion. We figure the best and safest ways to climb a tree, play in a jungle gym, etc. If they don't get the lead in the school play we either try to fix it up with the concerned faculty or try and make up to the child in other ways. At the slightest discomfort and challenge we jump in to help our little ones because we believe that they can't help themselves. We lecture them repeatedly over how they can avoid failures, ring warning bells of what works and what does not and hammer them with 'do this-don't do that'. If they still manage to chalk out their independent path and get into a problem due to it, we rush in, take charge and set things straight with a, 'I told you so'. Worst of all, we believe this to be good parenting!!!

8.4 Effects of over parenting

Children who are monitored, examined, guided and coached at the slightest tribulations lose their independence and self confidence to handle their challenges themselves. They become risk-averse, anxiety ridden and psychologically fragile. Besides being examined all the time makes them extremely self-conscious. They get less communicative as scrutiny teaches them to bury their real feelings deeply. An over-protective environment leaves them:

Less confident
Impatient
Risk-averse
Non-perseverant
Dependent
Irresponsible
Indecisive

This has turned out to be the spreading psychic fault line of the twenty-first-century youth.

Shoba Srinath, Head of the Department of Psychiatry at the National Institute of Mental Health and Neuro Sciences (NIMHANS) who also heads the Child and Adolescent Mental Health Unit there, agrees that 'over-involved parenting style' is largely an urban, upper-middle class phenomenon. According to her, 'overzealous parenting can also interfere with a child's ability for decision-making, independent thought, problem-solving and evaluation'. Dr. Marilyn Heins, on the Web site parentkidsright.com said, 'A real downside to overparenting: Children can grow up to be scared adults who have never learned to

master fears or, uncommitted adults who have never learned how to make a decision.'

'A Nation of Wimps,' said, Harvard psychologist Jerome Kagan, 'has shown unequivocally that what creates anxious children is parents hovering and protecting them from stressful experiences.'

According to John Portmann, professor of religious studies at the University of Virginia, the effects of over-parenting are even more pernicious—it weakens the whole fabric of society. He sees young people becoming weaker right before his eyes, more responsive to the herd, too eager to fit in—less assertive in the classroom, unwilling to disagree with their peers, afraid to question authority, more willing to conform to the expectations of those on the next rung of power above them.

Success requires independence, over parenting encourages dependency. Success requires resilience, over parenting fosters apathy. Success requires risk taking, over parenting makes them fearful and thus risk averse. Success requires patience, over parenting makes them impatient and consumed by instant gratification. The more parents' micromanage, the more passive children become. By (over) serving children parents eventually create adults who are incapable of serving themselves. Dr. Maria Montessori said, 'Every useless help to a child is an obstacle to development.'

Besides, this kind of vigilance is enormously taxing and stress inducing. It takes much of the joy out of parenting as well. Besides, parents stuck in the 'martyr' trap neglect their own needs of recreation, companionship and relaxation. This sours marital relations where one or both the partners may be left feeling dissatisfied and resentful. Quality parenting takes place when adults have their own lives in balance.

You are your child's first world – Chamanlalji Gupta

Scientist and academician at Auroville, Pondicherry, Chaman Lal Gupta said, 'Parents are a child's first world. Let your child try her experiments, explore the world of right and wrong with her first world, you. Let her come to her own conclusions on what works and what does not. Where else can your child get a better and safer haven to make mistakes and yet not get shattered by them? Allow your child the natural advantage. Everything that you will tell her about right and wrong is rubbish. It will be of value to her only when it becomes her truth.'

I immediately asked Chaman Lalji, 'How do I allow her a wrong, right in front of my eyes. How do I will myself to look away?' Chaman Lalji said, 'By remembering your childhood. Tell me what has left a deeper understanding, your parents' instructions of the best way to do a thing or your own realisation of the laws following trial and error approach? The struggle that your child will go through will help her gather courage to see a job through by herself.'

And when it boils to the basics isn't that what we want from our children, that they handle their own challenges by themselves? Remember, a good judge remembers what it was like to be a lawyer. A good editor remembers being a writer. A good parent remembers what it was like to be a child. Thinking like a child with the experience of an adult can be a powerful combination.

8.5 Allowing children trial and error

Fight the action, not the emotion

Since we are the devoted benefactors of our children it is very natural to want to extend a helping hand whenever we think they are faced with a new or trying situation. There is nothing wrong with wanting to help, but perhaps with actually rushing to do so. Resist the urge. Look away when the wrong puzzle piece refuses to be pushed in, refrain from analysing how the wrong purchase made your child go bankrupt in Monopoly, control the urge to say the famous, 'I-told-you-so' when your child comes down with a terrible stomach ache caused due to pigging on cashew nuts. Every time you withhold help, your child will grow a little wiser, smarter and stronger. It may seem like a paradox but the truth is that, by helping them less, you will help your child more.

Allow children independence

Remember all children want to learn, but at their own pace without parental pressure. Whether the challenge is psychological, physical, intellectual or emotional, allow your child independence. Develop tolerance to see your child fumble and then find a way out. Wait for the child to figure out the best route/solution/method, however long he might take. Have patience.

Allow them their hands-on experiences, be it in handling equipments, scientific experiments, creating art, pottery or music, planting their own vegetable garden or managing finances through budgeting. Hands-on experiences provide the basis of learning; for the young child-hands are the instrument of his intelligence.

Give children opportunities to evaluate their own accomplishments. Rather than stating that you think they have done a good job, ask them what they think of their work. You'll never go wrong by asking the question, 'What do YOU think?' Ratnesh Mathur of Genie kids says, 'Answer this: Have you ever thought of a question without thinking of possible answers? In which case, if the child asks a question, hasn't the child already thought of some possible answers? Are those thoughts more valuable than your WISE answer?'

Allow children independence by allowing them decision making. Viktor Frankl, a survivor of Auschwitz, best known for his book *Man's Search for Meaning*, writes, 'Research on heredity has shown how high is the degree of human freedom in the face of predisposition. As for environment, we know that it does not make a person, but that everything depends on what he makes of it, on his attitude toward it. But there is another element: decision. We ultimately decide for ourselves! And in the end, education must always be education toward the ability to decide.'

Mayur and Ansuya Adhikari

Educational consultants Mayur and Ansuya Adhikari have given complete independence to both their children. Right from trying to find the arm holes of the shirts, to picking out their own clothes, tying their own shoelaces (in fact, her child tripped more than once as the laces came open), to ordering their own food in the restaurant (eating whatever they ordered), reading themselves (the three-year old daughter was given the Early World of Learning set of books, maintenance and upkeep was her responsibility from then on), struggling with the manuals of a new toy or play station, to working out their own schedules of study for examination, they have been largely on their own. She says, 'Yes, every time that my children were in a jam of one kind or another, every fiber in my body wanted to lend them a hand and help them out but since I am an educational consultant the "success cycle" has been drilled into me. It follows, trying out a new thing, experiencing a setback, getting frustrated and finally, finding a way out'. During such times I always reminded myself that I am the observer and he is the "doer". I have to rise beyond my heartburn and allow him his full "success cycle". Says Mayur, if at all they have to use any threat to make them do something, it is, '...I will do your homework for you'.

Patsy and Shriram's story

Patsy and Shriram had participated in the 'Reading Voyage' organised by the British library. They were to make a presentation on a story picked by them in any manner they chose to. They zeroed down on 'The Deep Sea Diary' and decided on doing a shadow puppet show presentation. They worked for five days after school hours, created paper puppets of the characters, made the tracing paper screen and the sea background with the relevant flora and fauna. Once they finished their prop work, they began working on the narration which took another two days.

They exhibited their presentation in front of their parents before the actual show. Before their parents could even take in the settings and the flow of the puppets, the show was over! Their parents were impressed with the creative ideas but also noticed that the short narration robbed the presentation of its beauty. They didn't utter a word to the children about it though.

Patsy and Shriram began their show amidst enthusiastic cheers the following day. They saw a keen interest and appreciation in the audience's eyes for their novel medium of shadow puppetry and were internally patting themselves for a job well done. But their ending left a 'questioned' expression on the audience which they read as well. They clearly saw the audience's struggle with the realisation that the story was over. Yes, claps came, but after a considerable pause. They knew that the claps were of 'good efforts' and not of 'brilliant'. They knew exactly where their presentation fell weak.

When Patsy came home her dad asked, 'How did it go dear?' She said, 'Our artwork was great but somehow we lost on the narration bit. It was too short. But next time we will get everything right.' Dad said, 'I do not doubt that one bit.'

Why didn't Patsy's father point out her mistake? It could have helped them be 'brilliant'. Yes. Perhaps they would have been 'brilliant', but would they have also completely owned the 'brilliance'?

Now, would it not be robbing them of a precious learning experience? They understood that their narration was short because it was left short. If the parent had insisted on them lengthening it, the reality would have been different and they would never have known where they had erred. In all probability the next project too would have had elaborate artwork with inadequate narration. This could have spilled over onto other projects and assignments too. But they were allowed their error and they learnt from it.

What we understand from direct experience is never lost upon us. The short narration and the effect it elicited drove the point home loud and clear.

Besides what was the cost of that experience? It was a Reading voyage, the purpose of which was to give children exposure. Their careers did not depend upon it, their University admissions did not rest on them. If they goofed they could have very well afforded to goof!

Let us now suppose that Patsy's parents had mentioned their error and the children would have rectified it. Would they have not been left feeling any or all of the following:

I could never have done it without my dad's help.

Why don't my parents let me manage things on my own?

May be my parents know best.

Let us now suppose that even after their parents' suggestion they would have decided to stick to their original narration in the spirit of, 'I am supposed to do it completely on my own' and then gone ahead and earned this realisation from the audience, they would be left seething with:

'They had told me so'

'I should always seek their opinion and act upon it'

Or 'I worked so hard and it was all in vain'.

But they were allowed their trial and error and they learnt their lesson in the healthiest way possible. They were the proud owners

of their superior artwork and also the wise learners from their too-short-a-narration. They completely owned their success as well as their goof-up.

Perhaps the best thing to do is to pause and ask ourselves, 'What is at stake here'? If life and limb are at stake, it is better to help the child out. If not, allow them their errors, experiments and their explorations. You can, however, provide an emotional safety net when trial and error results in more error than immediate success.

Allow children the pain of wrong choice

Since behaviour is maintained by consequence allow children to face the consequences of their choice. Allow them the pain of their wrong choices, but without an, 'I told you so'.

It was still early February and Suman knew that the water still had that chill and so it was advisable not to swim. But her eleven-year-old daughter Juhi did not think so. She tried explaining but Juhi thought otherwise. On the 5th day she contracted a bad cold. She came up to her mother and said, 'I think it was the early morning swimming.' She missed two days of school, had loads of homework and a bad running nose which kept interrupting her work. Lesson learnt: Biology.

Prarit's school magazine carried his name in the list of accomplishments as 'stood second in the diving competition' held at the local club. When Prarit's mother read the news she was appalled because Prarit didn't even know how to keep afloat let alone perform complex skills in the pool. She asked him, 'Why'. He said, 'Since my best friend spoke about his black belt in Karate I wanted to boast about something too.' She quoted Nitezche's quote, 'What matters is not that you lied to me. What matters is that now I can no longer believe anything you say.' She then asked Prarit to think of ways to set the facts right. He decided to approach his class teacher and confess in front of the entire class. Lesson learnt: Ethics.

Hemangini Sinha

Hemangini Sinha on the faculty at NID, was having a full-scale battle with her twelve-year-old son every morning. Since she had taken the responsibility of getting him up at the car pool time and he had given her the whole problem. He would either wake up late, or spend extended time in the bathroom with her constant 'hurry-up' at frequent intervals. One fine day she got him an alarm clock and told him that now getting ready for school on time was his problem. Of course he did not take her seriously. The pool car came and left and she refused him a ride to school. She went for her work on time. He missed school. Shaurya loved school and was irritated at the idea of missing a day just because his mother decided to change her attitude. He missed another day. She said, 'Catching up with the work you miss is your responsibility too. You can decide what works best, to allow yourself leisure in the morning and chance missing school or keep it for the evenings when you actually have that kind of time.' Lesson learnt: Responsibility.

Believe in your child

Believe that your child will eventually fend for himself and figure out a way. Trust in the power of his learning and his conscience.

Thomas Edison

Thomas Edison was thrown out of school when he was twelve because he was thought to be dumb. He was noted to be terrible at mathematics, unable to focus, and had difficulty with words and speech. He said, 'I remember that I was never able to get along at school. I was always at the foot of the class.' Edison's mother thought that wasn't right, so she pulled Thomas out of school and taught him at home. Thomas Edison gave his mother's homeschooling credit for his success in later life: 'My mother was the making of me. She was so true, so sure of me; and I felt I had someone to live for, someone whom I must not disappoint.'

Hemant Trivedi

Fashion designer Hemant Trivedi's father was a pilot, but when Hemant expressed his interest in designing, his father, without as much as batting an eyelid, said, 'If you know what you want to do, just go ahead. Only remember to do it really well.' Hemant said, 'My parents not only gave me latitude but believed in me, that reinforced my belief in myself.'

Darshana Zhaveri

Manipuri dance exponent Padmashri Darshana Zaveri said, 'We are four sisters and each was intensely involved with the Manipuri dance form. Though my sisters got married, I chose to remain single and give my life to the form. That was way back in the '60s and '70s. A girl wanting to remain unmarried was almost unheard of. But my parents even till today have not asked me 'why not'. They had faith in what I wanted to do and they gave me the freedom and support. Today it is more than fifty years that I have spent with Manipuri dance and when I sit back and reflect I think, 'where did the years fly'? Can life be more satisfying than this?'

Manali Vengsarkar

Indeed is there a better pleasure than to spend one's life in the way one wants too?

Says Manali, wife of cricketer Dilip Vengsarkar, 'Our son rejected cricket as an option long ago. He took up architecture and is doing well for himself. We are proud of him. After all how many lives do we have to do what we want to do, just one. Why can't we allow our children that and believe in that they would find happiness and satisfaction in it?'

Trust your child to be resourceful

Suman Agarwal

Says nutritionist Suman Agarwal, 'I allow children independence by respecting their resourcefulness. When my children come up to me to ask for help for their project work or to get a sleeping bag for their outdoor camping trip, instead of rushing in with my advice and help I ask where can we get the information or thing from. Do you think the library might have some books on the subject or it would be nice if you can call some shops to find the price range?' In fact Suman's children gathered information by themselves online on the best fare available to fly to Ahmedabad to meet their cousins. They simply told Suman of the alternatives and then picked the best deal and confirmed the bookings with her help online through the credit card. Suman says, 'The print-out of the airline tickets was no less than an award for my then eleven-year old.'

How I learnt through trial and error

Natrani, an art club in Ahmedabad, hosted a drama workshop for children aged four to eight and ten to fifteen and I enrolled my then five-year-old in it. The workshop was to culminate in a stage performance; to this end both the age groups were put together and a play was chalked out. The script was read to them and each child was asked to chose his/her role. Aishwarya opted for the monkey's role as had done most children from her batch. But while dropping her off to one of the classes I caught a small part of the play, and saw that the monkeys besides being far too many, did nothing else except jump and dance and when they did speak it was in a sing-song chorus. I made Aishwarya opt for the 'scientist wolf's' role which had individual dialogues and also substantial time on stage. The drama sir hesitatingly mentioned about how happy the kid was prancing along with others, but as a parent I had to keep the larger picture in mind for my child. My entire family and a few neighbours were to come for the show and Aishwarya should be visible. Was I expected to identify one of the monkeys as my kid to them? And so, Aishwarya became the 'scientist wolf'. I was so convinced about my timely and right decision that poor Aishwarya too began to believe that that was the right thing. On the day of the show all the monkeys were having a great time giggling, dancing and having fun. When they moved the bunch moved together, when they danced the bunch danced together, when they spoke the bunch spoke together. The audience was thoroughly enjoying their pranks and I was keenly awaiting my character's entry. Yes, Aishwarya did take hold of the stage with the bear, she did murmur her precious lines, but it was all so flat. She was performing by rote. The moment the monkeys rushed in I saw her eyes light up. But she had her dialogues to attend to and the flat expression came back once again as she scaled along with her recital...

What we want from our children and what they want for themselves could be different.

I think as parents the healthiest thing we can do is grant ourselves the freedom of a few mistakes along the way. Call them learning experiences.

Cocoon becomes a butterfly

A man found a cocoon. One day a small opening appeared, he sat and watched the butterfly for several hours as it struggled to force its body through the little hole. Then it seemed to stop making any progress. It appeared as if it had gotten as far as it could and could go no farther. Then the man decided to help the butterfly.

He took a pair of scissors and snipped the remaining bit of the cocoon. The butterfly then emerged easily. Something was strange. The butterfly had a swollen body and shrivelled wings. The man continued to watch the butterfly because he expected at any moment, the wings would enlarge and expand to be able to support the body, which would contract in time. Neither happened. In fact, the butterfly spent the rest of its life crawling around with a swollen body and deformed wings. It was never able to fly.

What the man in his kindness and haste did not understand, was that the restricting cocoon and the struggle required for the butterfly to get through the small opening of the cocoon are Nature's way of forcing fluid from the body of the butterfly into its wings so that it would be ready for flight once it achieved its freedom from the cocoon. Sometimes struggles are exactly what we need in our lives.

If Nature allowed us to go through all our life without any obstacles, it would cripple us. We would not be as strong as what we could have been. Not only that, we could never fly.

Author Unknown

8.6 Teach and support safety measures rather than (over)protect

An ounce of prevention

Sohail will not allow her seven-year old son to go on a picnic to a beach for fear that he might drown. Preeti did not allow her daughter to go to a friend's place who had a pet, for fear that she may be bitten. Eleven year old Ankit is still not allowed to step out of the society compound walls for cycling, it is not like the old times when we could trust almost anyone in town...she reasoned. Karen was not allowed to walk to school on her own even when her school was just two blocks away...

Times have changed. Potential dangers today lurk everywhere from the family kitchen to the shopping mall. Children of today must learn skills to be safe. Freedom and independence could prove fatal for our children unless accompanied by safe habits, knowledge and wise decision making skills. These are required to handle threatening situations. Besides, even if we want we can't be with our children every second of the day. Traditionally in India, parents have had the support of relatives and servants to help in supervising the child. However, such resources are no longer available and increasingly un-chaperoned time has become a reality in the urban child's life. Though times have changed children remain children. Their fuzzy judgment, wobbly coordination, and endless curiosity may lead them to situations which could prove injurious to both their bodies and their psyche. Though there are myriad dangers in the world, the greatest risk to a child's safety is not what's 'out there' but their lack of preparation to meet potentially threatening situations.

A parent is the best person to teach the child about personal safety. Children should have clearly spelt out safety rules and boundaries. They should know about 'potential threats' and their best options in case those situations do arise. We have to teach our children to be safe, smart and strong. The lessons we teach today could save our child from a dangerous situation tomorrow.

Christina Elston, author of *Safe and Secure: The Loving Parent's Guide to Child Safety* (1998), Elston concurs: 'A kid with common sense and good judgment is always safer than one who has spent most of his time behind a baby gate.'

Do remember:

Take time to talk about safety thoroughly and often.
You can avoid causing unnecessary fear by discussing safety, often in a matter-of-fact way, starting at an early age. Don't wait until a neighbourhood child has an accident to talk about bus safety, or postpone discussing stranger-danger until a high-profile kidnapping case is in the media.

Frequent talks and safety drills help children understand, that learning about safety is an important step in growing up and taking care of themselves.

When teaching kids about safety, be sure to stress that they have the power they need to protect themselves.

Christina Elston says, she doesn't think children are scared by information, but they are frightened by parents' panicked, emotional displays. She says, 'Give the child skills to handle a world of danger and give them confidence to feel they can handle it.'

I remember the time a seminar called, 'Sexual abuse and its prevention' was held at my children's school. My elder one was in the fifth grade and the younger one in the second. Volunteers from a local NGO went to each class discussing and explaining to children about the same. Most of the children were shocked with the information presented and my daughter actually did not even go to the society park to play for the next two days. She did bombard me with questions and I answered them in a calm, but serious tone stressing on the importance — of internalizing the information. But that was the gestation period. The information sank in, she became comfortable with it and she resumed her daily life but now as a smarter and more aware child.

Basic safety measures:

- Your child should know his home address fully. He should know the (mobile as well as landline) telephone numbers of his parents, neighbours (trustworthy) and at least one relative.
- Your child should know how to dial the local police or emergency number in case of an emergency.
- Your child should be told not to play in deserted areas like parking lots, deserted buildings, construction sites etc. Recently a seven-year-old girl in Ahmedabad while trying to find an unusual hiding place fell into the lift shaft and lost her life.
- Set check-in times and tell the children to be home at the agreed time. At all times the family must be aware of their whereabouts. In case they were to go out with friends and plans change mid-way they must call home and inform.
- Make a list with your children of the neighbourhood boundaries and up to where they can go on their own. Show them where they can play safely and the limits beyond which they cannot go (but for which an adult still must give permission to go).
- Tell them clearly that they must never go off with anyone, not even someone they know, without first asking you or the adult who is looking after them.

- If the child gets separated from you in a mall or store, teach him to go to the help or information desk.
- Tell your children to trust their instincts.
- Point out potential hazards in the home, such as electrical outlets and heating equipment, and explain to kids how to avoid injuries that might result from them.
- Kids should also know what to do in the event of a natural disaster. Practise disaster safety strategies regularly with the entire family.
- Children should also be suspicious of anyone who asks them to keep a secret from their parents.
- Children need to believe that they can talk to you about anything and that you will take them seriously and believe them.
- There is safety in numbers. Being in a group is a safeguard. Tell children to play together, walk to school and other classes together.

Stranger danger

Children must have clearly spelt out 'stranger rules'. Tell them:

Never go anywhere with a stranger (a person he doesn't know), even when that stranger is a child, without first getting permission from the parents.

Never accept rides, candy, gifts from a stranger. Their kindness may have harmful designs. Don't offer to help a stranger; adults don't have to ask children for help.

Never assume that they know someone just because that someone knows their names. Children's belongings carry names which can be easily read and used. Stranger rules apply if they do not recognise a person.

Safeguarding against Sexual Abuse

A research carried out by Sakshi, a New Delhi-based non-governmental organisation, says that 80% of Indian girls and women, belonging to all social classes, experience sexual abuse in their own families and friend circle. Majority of them prefer to remain silent.

According to the State of Child Rights in India, incidences of child abuse are definitely on the rise especially since the nineties.

It is quite shocking to know that

– 66% sexual offenders know their victims.

– 32% paedophiles have abused their own children.

– 49% paedophiles are attracted to unstable children.

The possibility of sexual abuse of your child is something most parents prefer not to think about. But it does happen and often the perpetrator is someone the child knows or trusts...the domestic servant, neighbour, driver, teacher, etc. It is important to give children sex education as early as possible.

Tell them:

- They are the bosses of their bodies. No one has the right to touch, kiss or hug, if they do not want them to.
- When someone touches them in a way that makes them scared, uncomfortable or confused they must say, 'No'.
- When others try and make the children touch them in a way that makes them uncomfortable, confused or scared, they must say 'No'.
- No one should force them to expose their private parts.
- If anyone makes obscene gestures, or shows sexually explicit material, video, pictures etc, they must ask them to stop and say 'No'.
- They should come and tell their parents if any of the above happens. Assure them that you are on their side and will see to it that they are not left alone with such people ever. You will work out the issues in other ways too.
- Teach your children the vulnerable areas of the human body and the best way to use that knowledge to his/her advantage in case of a sexual attack. Teach them where to hit, kick, bite, elbow or knee both male and female attackers. But they must

use these moves only if someone is trying to molest, kidnap or otherwise abuse them.

* As a parent one must be vigilant for any signs of sexual abuse. Sudden shifts in temperament, mood withdrawals, nightmares, bedwetting, bruising or swelling of genitals, fear of a certain individual, loss of interest in academic and social activities are all good indicators of sexual abuse.

Fire safety

Tell them:

➤ Fire is an adult tool. Playing with fire matches, candles, etc. can be very dangerous.

➤ They should not stand close to stoves, grills or fireplaces.

➤ Teach them the life safety skills that can save their lives in a fire:-

➤ If clothes ever catch fire, remember to "Stop, drop and roll"

➤ It's important not to hide, and to get out and stay out.

➤ They must not come back into the house if there's a fire, even for a favourite pet or toy.

➤ Fire drills are very important. Teach your children the quickest route out of the house.

➤ They should not use elevators in case of fire.

➤ Teach children that in a room filled with smoke it's best to get on all fours and crawl through smoke because smoke rises and all the good air will be close to the floor. Model this skill by getting down on your hands and knees and holding your head up.

➤ You can even plan a visit to the local fire department. Seeing what firefighters do for a living, and seeing examples of what fire does to toys, clothes, and other possessions is often an eye-opener for both children and adults.

'Home alone' rules

Your children should have a list of rules that they need to follow when they are home alone.

Tell them:

➢ They must not answer the door unless they see who is out there. If it is someone they don't know they must ask them to come later. They should never allow anyone into their homes without asking the parents' permission first. In this era of mobiles, 'home alone' children can stay connected with their parents at all hours.

➢ They must never tell callers that they are home alone. They can just mention that mom and dad can't come to the phone and that they will pass on their message.

➢ They must not enter the house if things don't look right or normal- a broken window, ripped screen, or open door.

➢ Once inside they must keep the doors locked.

➢ Children below ten years of age are generally not capable of safely handling the stove completely by themselves so they should not try any stove or burner cooking when they are alone at home.

➢ Post 'emergency' phone numbers near all the telephones in the house, and be sure to include contact information for neighbours and other relatives who live nearby.

Put together a First Aid kit with your child, and discuss appropriate measures in the event of an injury.

Animal safety

Tell them that they should not:
- Disturb a sleeping animal
- Tease an animal
- Take away their food, toy or anything that they are playing with.
- Approach a stray dog or cat

- Pull an animal's ears or tail
- Go near or pat a dog that has been trained to be aggressive or to work as guard dog

Safety on the go...walk wise

Traffic education was introduced in 1977 after it was found that 22% of road deaths were of schoolchildren in India.

Teach children road safety

Tell them:

➢ Running on the street is a complete 'No-No'.
➢ No playing on the roads and streets.
➢ Teach children to stay away from the edge of the sidewalk.
➢ They must cross in crosswalks and obey traffic lights.
➢ It is always safer to walk against traffic on the sidewalk. They must walk against the flow of traffic so that they face oncoming cars.
➢ Teach them to get in and out of the car on the curb side.

Water safety

Many parents of today do not know swimming, but it is imperative that our children do so. Learning to keep afloat can be life-saving. Teaching swimming should be one of the basic agenda on the parents list of 'to do' with their children.

We must also teach them what to do when things go wrong in water such as leg cramps, exhaustion or getting caught in a fast-moving current.

Handling dangers in cyberspace

Most children are unaware of how to protect themselves from online dangers. Online relationships develop quickly. Most children are taught not to talk to strangers. After talking to someone online for a while, these people no longer feel like 'strangers'. Child predators are skilled at making a child feel comfortable. They spend time getting the child to open up.

Establish rules for going online.

Tell them:

Never give out your personal information like your home address, telephone number, school name or location, parents' work address/telephone number, or their password. A good many people on the Internet are adults pretending to be children. People often pretend to be someone they are not. Because you can't see or even hear the person, it would be easy for someone to misrepresent him- or herself. Thus, someone indicating that 'she' is a 'twelve-year-old girl' could in reality be a forty-year-old man.

Tell them never to meet with someone from the Internet without checking up with you first.

They should not send a person (they don't know) their picture or anything personal without first checking with you.

They should not download or install software without checking in with you. Spyware allows strangers to track not only where you visit on-line, but also personal information.

Any 'online offer' like they have won an I-pod or a Handy-cam which seems an offer 'too good to be true' probably is. Such offers may require being there for a meeting at the venue picked by them or having someone visit the house. Kids should be taught to recognise online advertisements.

Delete unknown email attachments before opening them. They may contain destructive virus.

Talk to your kids about their internet experiences, the good and the bad. Let them know it's OK to tell you if they come across something that worries them. (It doesn't mean that they're going to get into trouble)

For parents

Put the internet computer in a public area of the home, such as the living room, rather than a child's bedroom. Get to know the services your child uses. Make sure they aren't going to 'inappropriate' websites.

Find out whom they are talking to. Make sure their best friend 'Sahil' isn't teaching them how to build bombs, or 'Chintal' isn't teaching your daughter how to send him pictures over the Internet.

SOME SITUATIONS WHICH CHILDREN MAY FACE

What if the child was at school and a stranger appeared and said his mommy sent him to drive your child home?

Many families are now developing a code word that is known only by them and close friends. This code is used in instances where a child is approached by a family member, or someone else, telling the child to come with them to see their parent or other family members. If that person does not know the code, the child is not to go with him no matter what.

What if he gets lost in a public place?

Children should never leave an area (store, zoo, etc.), even if the person helping asks them to.

When entering crowded areas pre-determine where to meet if you get separated and make sure your child clearly understands. They can go to the checkout counter or, if that doesn't work, look for a woman with children to help them. Establish a secret family code word or phrase. Instruct your child to ask for that code word before going anywhere with an unfamiliar person. If the person doesn't know the code, the child should refuse to go.

What if they get a strange smell which is a gas leak?

Teach them to identify the pungent smell of a gas leak by taking them close to a burner. Tell them what to do if they ever enter a room with that smell hanging in the air.

What if they think that they are being followed?

If you think you are being followed, go into a store or office and ask for help.

Basics

Remember to make the conversation informative, not scary. It is difficult to retain a sense of perspective when the safety of children has become a permanent item of news. It's a fine line between informing a child and giving him the feeling that the word is unsafe. While walking that line is difficult, it is vital to your child's health and safety. Instead, encourage your child to trust his/her 'gut instinct'. Be sure that you are calm yourself when you talk to your daughter. If you sound anxious, she will pick up on that. Tell your daughter in a matter-of-fact way that you believe that most people are GOOD, and that this means that most strangers are good, but that a few people have problems that might cause them to hurt kids.

Make sure that your communication lines are open. You want your children to feel 'safe' in sharing their fears with you at all times.

Practising skills to rehearse how to handle different situations almost always reduces anxiety and builds competence.

You can refer to books

- ¤ Child Quest International—This comprehensive site offers links to information on child safety, statistics and missing kids.
- ¤ By Miriam B. Settle and Susan Price. (Macmillan, 1999, $15.25). This straightforward, humorous publication offers advice on everything from injury prevention to air-bag safety.

¤ National Center for Missing and Exploited Children—This national organisation has safety tips and free downloadable publications and posters in English and Spanish.

¤ By Tova Navarra. (Barron's Educational Series, 1993, $8.95). This acclaimed book helps kids deal with large and small problems that may occur when they're home alone. It's specifically geared toward latchkey kids.

¤ By Gavin de Becker. (Dell Publishing, 2000, $10.75) This new book from America's leading expert at predicting violent behaviour explores myths about danger and safety and helps parents make the best decisions for their children and families. The author focuses on steps to enhance children's safety at every age and offers parents the tools they need to allow their kids freedom and still get some sleep at night.

¤ By Donna Chaiet and Francine Russell. (Morrow, William & Co., 1998, $4.45) Designed for an eight to twelve-year-old audience and their parents and caregivers, The Safe Zone helps families prepare for potential threats of violence without instilling fear. Topics include various self-defence options, setting boundaries, being safe at home and on the street, dealing with strangers and handling bullies.

¤ *A Stranger in the Park* by Stuart Fitts and Donna Day Asay (1999).

¤ *Never Talk to Strangers* by Irma Joyce and S.D. Schindler (2000).

¤ *The Berenstain Bears Learn about Strangers* by Stan and Jan Berenstain (1985).

Understanding Failure, Anger and Fear

....

9.1 Understanding failure

The burning fire razed high as it devoured everything fed to it with a vigour; all stationary, bill books, packet covers and other important documents were thrown in, so that with its end would also end the utter disgrace and pain that came with the failure of the tea packet brand Wagh Bakri. The year was 1953 and Piyush Desai, one of the silent witnesses to the bonfire, was just fifteen then. He said, 'I still remember watching my family's dream of making Wagh Bakri a household name in tea, crumble and burn to cinders right before the entire family's eyes.' The abject loss filled him with a burning challenge. He said to me, 'There is something about failure which moves you at the most profound level. It makes you think, "Why" and then it makes you think, "Why not".' He promised himself that one day he would revive the packet under the very name Wagh Bakri and make the family dream a reality. Revive he did but only after a thorough and careful analysis of the past. He studied what was not right and structured his strategies accordingly. Everyone around him dissuaded the move, but Piyush bhai knew that he could give the consumers exactly what they wanted...a blend not only delicious to the tongue but hygienically packed under the most stringent regulations. Brave and uncompromising, he stuck to the same name. Today, Wagh Bakri Tea Group exceeds an annual turnover of Rs. 250 crores while blending and packing more than 15 million kilograms of tea annually.

We all make mistakes and we all fail. That is how we succeed.

Ana lost the race, Nikki forgot her lines on stage, Rohan failed his spelling test. Harsh did not get selected for the school cricket team, Samiksha could not finish her drawing in the stipulated time...

> 'It is on our failures that we base a new and different and better success.'
>
> — HAVELOCK ELLIS

No one knows errors and setbacks as children do. Childhood is the phase where learning and growth is at its optimum. Practically every moment in a child's life is a challenge as he struggles with the learning process, vis-à-vis himself and the world. As children learn new skills, develop different faculties, venture into hitherto unknown territories, they go through endless cycles of learning, experimenting, trying out and testing. Mishaps, blocks, errors, goof-ups are bound to happen. But it is through this process that they understand not only what the world expects of them but also what their interests are and what they are capable of giving to the world.

We, as adults today, look back and philosophise about how each block made us more enterprising or how a failed attempt made us stronger and wiser. We know from our childhood experiences that stumbling, missing and goofing is a part of life and the learning process. Yet, when it comes to applying the same wisdom in respect to our children's falls, we inevitably lose perspective. We would rather that they do not face any tribulations, losses, failures, blocks, mishaps, for we can't bear to see them in pain. We know what makes the foundation of growth and learning, yet are unable to support its natural cycle when it comes to our own children. This is sad and disturbing but true to the core.

Recall a time that your child crashed into your arms sobbing after losing 'xyz'. What was the first thing that you said:-

It is alright

It is no big deal

There is always a second time
I think you deserved to win
You were great whatever others might think

9.2 Failures, mishaps, errors, setbacks are painful

Failure is tough to deal with, and we want to do our best to soften its blow on our children. We rush in with our comforters—impassioned statements of their goodness, a 'foul-cry' over the unfairness of the coach/teacher/coordinator involved, or promises of a better future. We want to take away the pain of failure and mend their splintered soul as fast as possible.

Besides, deep down, we hurt for ourselves too. When our children fail, in a sense we fail too. Their losses are not just their losses...we see them as a let down of our effort, time and expectations. We spend hours listening to and correcting our children's elocution and they forget their lines on stage, we accompany them for hours to their practice sessions and they lose heart with the fall of the first wicket. As Preeti, the mother of a nine year old boy said, 'When Tarang came ninth in his class, I could not believe it. He had never gone beyond the 3rd rank and this was like a slap on my face. All these years I have taken the pain of teaching him myself when I could have easily kept tutors and I certainly do not deserve this'.

Even though we go through exasperation, frustration and anger on their account, we rise above ourselves and concentrate our energies into putting them into the positive attitude frame once again. After all if we do not, who will? We reason that as parents, it is our duty to help our children navigate their fragile world of learning and failing with our positive intervention. We must use our experience, knowledge and wisdom to guide them through their developmental stages.

But our children need to experience their failures, suffer from them, learn from them and eventually rise above them. The process has to take its rightful, but more importantly the 'FULL' course. Children have to own up to their failures, we can't take responsibility for them. They have to derive their own learning from what went wrong, they can't learn from our experiences. They have to have the courage and determination to get up every time they fall, we can't walk their paths for them. But through all this, we can be their Rock of Gibraltar with our unconditional love, support and faith in them. We have to teach our children to both—welcome and learn—from the mistakes they will surely make during their lives instead of being shattered by them. Only then will they strive for personal excellence, which is what we really want for them. In doing so, we will be helping them not only deal with their present but set a winner's attitude for their future too.

9.3 Helping them through tough times

Step 1

Let them grieve

Failures are natural but painful

Yes. Failures are natural but each one is every bit as painful, frustrating and disparaging for our children as it was for us. Failures shatter their immediate world-self esteem goes topsy-turvy. Feelings of frustration and helplessness envelope the psyche and the thought of letting down their parents gnaws them. As eleven year old Manan says, 'Failure to me means I am not good enough.'

Sneh sobbed and said, 'Papa, I played well, yet I was not selected. It hurts so much'. Her father just held her in an embrace and said, 'Yes. It hurts a lot.'

Allow the child catharsis. Do not try to underplay the pain as yet. Let the pain surface and thereby be released. The child needs to go through his pain. Give him the latitude of expression. Encourage him to vent his emotions.

Recall an incident of your own failure. Did you not go through the 'I-am-miserable' stage before you were ready to think on 'how-to-be-better next-time'? Why rob your child of this natural cycle? Yes, there are some children who ruminate excessively on a loss. Then one does need to intervene and redirect the sense of loss of hope, but in normal course, grief is best left undisturbed.

'Kids need to feel badly sometimes,' says child psychologist David Elkind, professor at Tufts University. 'We learn through experience and we learn through bad experiences. Through failure we learn how to cope.'

The value placed on self-esteem by the mental health profession over the past thirty years has been critiqued by psychologist Martin Seligman. Seligman claims in order for children to feel good about themselves, they must feel that they are able to do things well. He claims that trying to shield children from feelings of sadness, frustration, and anxiety when they fail robs them of the motivation to persist in difficult tasks until they succeed. It is precisely such success in the face of difficulties that can truly make them feel good about themselves. Seligman believes that this attempt to cushion children against unpleasant emotions is in large parts responsible for an increase in the prevalence of depression since the 1950s, an increase that he associates with a conditioned sense of helplessness.

Besides children need to know that we understand their pain and it is not 'nothing'.

Remember the time that you were upset and the person you were pouring your heart out to tried to undermine the pain or guide you to a positive direction? Did you not feel that he/she really does not understand your feelings at all?

The broken glass toffee...

It was Aishwarya's eighth birthday and her grandmother presented her a Murano glass toffee. Its vibrant colours held Aishwarya captive and she played with it all morning. Whenever she tired of it, it was safely tucked away in her cupboard until she was ready to play with it again. In the evening her five year old sister Sanaya asked if she could just hold the glass toffee for a few seconds. Aishwarya placed her treasure very delicately onto Sanaya's tiny palm. As fate would have it (after all how stable can a fiver-year-old's palms be) Sanaya dropped the glass toffee. It shattered into a hundred pieces. The sound brought me into the room.

I saw both Sanaya and Aishwarya in a state of shock. Aishwarya's eyes said 'how-could-you-be-so-careless', and Sanaya's guilt ridden expression was 'how-could-I-be-so-careless'. Both, however did not utter a word to each other. I wanted to help them both but didn't know how to begin. I wanted to reprimand Sanaya for not being careful, but more than that I wanted to console Aishwarya at her loss. I also wanted to pacify her by explaining that these things happen and that Sanaya had not done it on purpose. But I held back, saying nothing, doing nothing. I allowed both of them their grief. Aishwarya sobbed unable to draw her eyes away from those fragments, Sanaya sobbed too alternating between looking at her sister and those glass pieces. In about five minutes flat they were both done with their catharsis. Sanaya tried to lisp the words 'sorry' but another wail escaped from her instead. Instantly Aishwarya took her in her arms and they both cried some more for the broken glass toffee.

Step 2

Reinstate their confidence in themselves

When Manjari lost her state level chess match with an opponent who she thought would be an easy win, she was shocked. She came out of the competition room and said, 'I knew I was better, still I lost. I am not good anymore.'

Manjari's plummeting self esteem needed an upward pull. Bhairavi, her mother, allowed Manjari her sulk time and then got onto stage two.

She made Manjari recall her past victories, the distance that she has already covered and the progress that she has already made. Manjari was there in that room playing at the state level because she had fought her way up. Bhairavi then concentrated on what Manjari had achieved, even though she lost that particular match. Manjari took lessons throughout the year and even practiced regularly at home. Her coach too had great faith in her potential. She reminded Manjari the words of her coach, 'One defeat, even though a crucial one, still does not define your future.' She asked Manjari to think of all those times that she was proud of herself.

She reminded her of all the other things that she was good at. She had a keen ear for music and could play the piano well. Her academic performance was more than satisfactory and she was well loved by her peers and teachers.

Bhairavi shared her own failures too and told her about the time she lost the school elections for the post of her house captain. At that time she felt completely dejected. She said, 'Failure hurts terribly. But it is a heavier burden to feel that you can never fail.' She taught Manjari to separate her sense of self from her loss, with the words, 'You are more than your defeat.'

Bhairavi told her stories of people who have emerged victorious after a series of let-downs. Walt Disney's first cartoon company went bankrupt. Abraham Lincoln lost eight elections before he became president of America. Edison tried 10,000 different ways before he succeeded in lighting the electric bulb. Mr. Goodyear tried to make rubber hundreds of times before he got it right. She taught her child that there was no quota of failures!

She gave Manjari hope for the future. There is always another time, another tomorrow, another trophy and generally, another chance.

Finally, Bhairavi ended with her trump card, 'Your dad and I love you for what you are, not for how well you play. We will be there for you always.'

She then asked Manjari, 'Do you really think that it is beyond your potential?'

When our children fail, it is important to:
- Not let them focus so much on their failures that they completely overlook what they have achieved.
- Not let them beat themselves up emotionally over their failure, over and over again.
- Give them unconditional love and support
- Offer them hope for the future, and optimism
- Perhaps share an episode from our past of, 'from hopelessness-to-hope'

But all this must be done after stage 1, not before it.

Life is beautiful! Johnny Lever

Johnny Lever reminisces of the time when he set off for the railway tracks to end his life. About twelve years old, he was already tired, depressed, frustrated of the violence, poverty and hopelessness which he witnessed every single day of his life in the slums. His father as always, had come home drunk and was abusing his mother. Johnny said, 'Even today I remember vividly the stoic walk on the cold metallic track. I saw the train approaching with a rage, but within me everything was dead. I said to myself, 'Even death can't be worse than the life I am living' and so I kept walking undeterred towards it." As the train was just a few seconds away the image of his sisters and his mother flashed before his eyes. He thought about what would happen to them once he was gone. What if they too, took the same path? Johnny said, 'I jumped off the tracks. Though I had got over the impulse of the moment, I was still very sad and hurting within. I went and sat behind a makeshift box-type salon so typical a sight in any slum, with my head in my hands, thinking, "what now?" It was then that I heard a beautiful piece of music which was playing on the radio in the salon. It was a song from Lataji. Her melodious voice engulfed all my pain and for some time I was aware of nothing but just the beauty of the lyrics, and the voice of the singer. The voice was healing me, soothing me, comforting me.' Johnny Lever sat there for more than two hours enjoying the beauty of the melody and realised that if there is pain in this life there is healing too. If there is hopelessness, there is hope too. If there is ugliness, there is beauty too. That day Johnny knew that he would never ever give up on this gift called 'Life'.

Step 3

Make them analyse their failure – What really went wrong

Success and failure are the result of the interplay between ability, effort and a host of other circumstances. We should all learn from failure—but it's difficult to do so objectively. In the excerpt from 'Failing to Learn and Learning to Fail (Intelligently)' in Long Range Planning Journal, HBS professor Amy Edmondson and coauthor Mark Cannon says, 'Social systems tend to discourage this kind of analysis. First, individuals experience negative emotions when examining their own failures, and this can chip away at self-confidence and self-esteem. Most people prefer to put past mistakes behind them rather than revisit and unpack them for greater understanding. Second, conducting an analysis of a failure requires a spirit of inquiry and openness, patience, and a tolerance for ambiguity. However, most managers admire and are rewarded for decisiveness, efficiency, and action rather than for deep reflection and painstaking analysis.'

The scenario is not very different for our children too. It is not easy for them either, to open a painful episode and scrutinise it in order to understand and ascribe the correct reasons for the failure. But with our support and guidance we can teach them to take responsibility for past action, develop the faculty of reasoning and logic by understanding the 'why' behind not getting the desired result and develop the progressive attitude of planning steps which can be implemented to improve performance for the future.

Give the child the tools for analysis. Once the child is calm and can think rationally ask:-
- Were you under prepared?

- Were you over confident?
- Were you nervous, anxious or overwhelmed?
- Were you not fresh (tired, burnt-out)?
- Did your self confidence flounder?
- Do you feel that you have not used your potential to the maximum?
- Did you give it your best shot?

Blame game

The child may try and put the blame on others. The tutor did not pay attention. It was my unlucky day. The judges were partial. The ambience was poor (hence I could not concentrate). Let the child run his course of the blame-game. In the end ask, 'How much truth do you think is there in it?'

When Kshitij lost the football game, he gave a host of reasons to which his father listened patiently. In the end Kshitij himself said, 'Dad, I think the better team won.' His father then asked, 'So what do you think you have to work on individually and as a team, to beat them?' Kshitij gave deep thought to this question and began thinking of his own shortcomings.

Teach your child the art of developing inner responsibility.

Step 4

Teach your children that failures/mistakes/goof ups can be great learning experiences

Cognitive psychologists have shown how central failure is to learning. For example, Collins and Brown have found that errors are essential to the creation of mental strategies in problem solving. Van Lehn has shown that real learning only occurs at an impasse during a problem-solving episode. Research by Foss has shown that not only do students learn when they encounter errors, but they also improve their ability to 'detect errant solution strategies'. In other words, when faced with errors, students learn not only about the subject at hand but also more generally how to plan solutions to similar problems.

Lines you can use with your child to see failures as learning opportunities:

Failures:
- Show you that you have work to do
- Tell you that they have something in them for you to learn.
- Ask you to identify them—Do you need to change tactics, look in another direction?
- Tell you—Get over your, 'I am not (will never be) good enough' so that we can move ahead.
- Say—Overcoming me takes time, effort and perseverance. I specially fear perseverance... if you give up I win, but if you persevere, I give up.

Kumar Mangalam Birla

Kumar Mangalam Birla sat for his CA entrance within three weeks after the completion of his twelfth board exams. He confessed candidly, 'I had not put in the requisite work and I flunked. I could have put the blame on a hundred things and excused myself in others as well as my own eyes. But whatever the reasons were, the fact was that I knew fully well the schedule of the CA entrance and yet I did not give it my all. Naturally I didn't make it. But this one mistake taught me that education was something I could not take lightly. I appeared again, planned my study hours worked diligently and got a national ranking in the same exam at the second attempt. The experience has stayed with me. Failures are good because when you see one bang on to your face you don't want to go through it again.'

Kumar believes that there is an almost indelible stigma attached to failure in our country much more than in the West. He says, 'The family, the peer group, the society—all still frown on failure—of any sort, no matter how heroic and daring the effort that preceded it. This attitude thwarts experimentation and stifles innovation.' He says, 'I have often wondered whether we should expel the word 'failure' from our lexicon and instead talk of 'failed attempts.'

In the same vein he continues with, 'Take the example of the space shuttle Columbia. Shuttles have been America's space workhorses for well over twenty years. Even as space shuttle Columbia crashed, America will be embarking on the mission again, but only after thoroughly scrutinising its failure and factoring the lessons learnt.'

He ended our conversation with a quote from Alvin Toffler, futurist and author of the path-breaking work, *The Third Wave*, who wrote, 'The illiterate of the 21st century will not be those who cannot read and write, but those who cannot learn, unlearn, and relearn.'

Johnny Lever

Johnny Lever has taught his children to learn their life lessons from every situation which comes up on them. He said to me, 'There is something one can learn from every situation, however dismal, humiliating or abject it may seem.' He gives his own life as an example to support this claim. Johnny spent most of his childhood and even part of his adult life at the Dharavi slums. He said, 'Dharavi is a little India by itself with people from every province and state who migrated to this dream city to make it big and ended up in the most violent, difficult, filthy and largest slum of Asia. Living there defied the very essence of humanity. Jungle Raj prevailed and "might was right".'

Johnny remembers not only the violence, frustration and complete hopelessness of the lives of people around, but also days of abject poverty where many nights sleep did not come easily because of the gnawing hunger in his stomach. He said, 'But there was a good side to it too. Dharavi made us at once unique as well as universal. We were all one in the sense that though we had nothing in our pockets, we still had dreams in our hearts. We were all unique as we came not only in every hue of brown, but each also had a different language, eating habits and dressing up style. Since there were people from every state and culture, consciously or subconsciously my expertise of mimicry took root in the daily interactions with them. I owe my style to the uniqueness of the Madrasi chacha's spat with his wife, to the Kashmiri mama's talks with his children, to the Gujarati's bhai's obsession for America and the Bengali dada's love of Chingri mach. I got firsthand knowledge of every community from every corner of the country sitting day in and day out in the dirty chowks of Dhaaravi.' In fact the different languages and habits of the myriad residents of the slum fascinated Johnny so much that he too adorned a new persona every day. He said, 'I internalised the nuances of their diction, walking style, likes/dislikes, moods and interests and out of it emerged my own theatrical pieces'. He said, 'I don't remember exactly how and when this hobby of mimicking others became my profession, but today I can proudly say that my Little India of Dharavi has made me a player of big India'.

Step 5

Planning action

Make them charter their course of action for future, based on their learning from the past. The best way to treat a child as if he/she is responsible, capable and intelligent in handling his/her own mistakes is by introducing him to the tools of goal setting! Teaching these skills

says, 'You are capable and responsible, so here are the tools to run your own life and make your own decisions'.

A great opportunity to introduce your child to the magic of goal setting is by tapping into what your child most desires at the moment. Use the immediate failure, mistake or goof up as the bait. Tell your child that a written goal followed up with clear, organised steps to achieve it, works magic. Goals work like a wand in turning around past failures into future successes!

Show your child how to define a challenge and put it in the form of a goal. Give him a notebook and let him pen down his goals, minor as well as major. Besides using the past mishaps and errors as goal destinations, you can even tap into other student pertinent areas.

Ask your child:
- What are the things you want to accomplish in:-
  - Academic (grades, reading, math, spelling)
  - Relationships (peer, parents, teachers)
  - Sports (stamina, skill)
  - Self (values, habits, attitudes)

Make goals manageable

Once the analysis stage is over, encourage the child to charter his own growth process by creating a scheme, a design, or proposed or intended course of action. Teach children to set long term as well as short term goals. The long term goal can itself be broken into small short term daily goals. This will help them measure progress and thus keep motivation high.

Define small steps

The child needs to ask himself 'What do I need to do?' (Practice more, try different techniques) 'When?' (Half an hour daily, an hour every alternate day, mornings before school etc)

'What resources can I pool in?' (Coach, friend, books)

Saikat messed up his UC Mass paper and realised that he was not good at mental sums. His long term goal was to clear the exam with an aggregate of 80% or above. His short term goal was to practice twenty mental sums everyday in the morning hours.

Rahana's long term goal was to be selected from her class section to participate in the elocution contest. Her short term goal was to read a new passage everyday and work on her enunciation before the class got the script of the same.

Shubha's long term goal was to swim the 400 meter race. For this she had to work on her stamina as well as her speed. She set the short term goal to do pranayama to enable better use of her energy, as well as increase the laps of her club pool by two every week.

Says Jim Wiltens, a leadership-training instructor in the San Francisco-area schools, 'Little goals are the best way to get kids moving towards big goals. Meeting a goal gives kids an incredible surge of energy.'

Jogenda

Master artist of the unbroken line—Jogenda, said to me, 'When one starts an activity, problems are bound to come up. One gets knotted, confused and overwhelmed with all that has to be done. It happens with me all the time. It is then that I take out my note pad and pen and write down all that is confusing me or all that I need to do. The written words clarify things and guide me. I can sort the important from the unimportant, I can see through the haze and I know what to do. The preferable solution emerges on its own via the written words.' He said, 'I tell my son the same. Write down all that you want to do and you will be able to do them'.

Review

Teach your child the art of review. Teach him to ask himself at regular intervals:

➤ Am I more-or-less keeping up with my schedule?
➤ If yes, have I made progress?
➤ If yes, what else can I fit in?

> If no, what do I need to change?
> If I am not keeping up with the schedule, 'Why not'? Is it unrealistic?

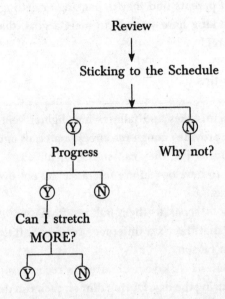

Frequent check-ins of how your child stands against his goals is a great way to keep the momentum moving forward. Teach him to monitor success and judge honestly whether steps are being taken in the right direction. Goals are destinations and the planned steps to achieving it is like a map leading the way to that destination. Children need to check their maps every now and then to ensure that they are on the right path. If the pre-chalked out path is not leading to the destination, children can try a different route too- that's the great thing about maps, there are many different roads that can be taken in order to reach the same destination! Review enables a detection and analysis of the path taken.

Discuss the possibility that some goals will not be reached at the first attempt, but that it is important not to give up. The effort that a person puts into the process of achieving a goal is just as important as reaching the goal itself.

Remember you are there to aid the child in setting and achieving goals. Allow the child latitude to decide on the 'what', and 'how' of it. Warns Edward L. Coyle, Ph.D., a clinical psychologist in Oklahoma City, Oklahoma, 'If parents find they're nagging or getting angry that their child isn't working hard enough to meet a goal, that's a signal they need to back off.'

9.4 Miscellaneous tips

- Take your own mistakes and failures in a lighter vein.
- Where possible provide enough resources (materials and supplies) so that the children feel they can start over afresh.
- Teach children to develop 'failure tolerance' by not over-reacting to their mistakes.
- Teach children to separate their failures from their self-worth. Help them see that there's a difference between failing at a task and failing as a person.
- Use mistake contests. Ask your children to record every mistake they've made during the day. During dinner, each can describe the mistake from which they've learned the most. The entire family can then decide which one was the best and why. Because this unmasks the advantages that each failure offers, children become more accepting of their shortcomings and mistakes.

Mr. B. Doshi

Architect, academician and builder Mr. B. Doshi who has been a senior faculty member with School of Architecture, CEPT, Ahmedabad said, 'One day during one of my lectures I failed about twenty students saying that their work was not good. Next morning very few students appeared for the lecture. I realised my mistake and since then my rule has been "'There is nothing like failure, it is a success, maybe of a lesser degree". I also understood that no one fails, it is just that he'/she requires a little more time to grasp.'

9.5 Anger management

Lynzzie Stirling, who provides anger management treatments at Edinburgh-based Stress Management Scotland, believes that as a society, we are becoming angrier—and there's a good chance that our children will be even worse.

Are we handling anger in children the right way?

By the time Hema heard the screams from her children's room and rushed towards it both her children were in the tear-you-apart mode. She separated them, gave them both a scolding and sent them to separate rooms. They were not to come out till they learnt how to behave. Further, they were forbidden to watch T.V. for the entire week. 'That will teach them not to get into fist fights,' Hema told herself.

Hema told her children what not to do but did she help them understand what should they have done in the first place? Did she go into the metaphysics of the conflict which enraged the two to understand what essentially perpetuated the rage? How could they have handled it differently? No. She perhaps did what most of us as parents do in our regular course. She concentrated on treating the symptoms without delving into the root of it.

When our children strike out in anger whether through words, their hands, by bawling, lying flat on the floor (every kid's most effective anger expression tool) or sulking, we do either of the following:

Scream or shout at them at a volume higher.

Give them a whack to stop the anger expression.

Send them into solitary confinement till they can behave more acceptably or punish them in any other way which we deem appropriate.

Wait till the anger outburst is over and then give them a thorough scolding.

Use the guilt induced emotional blackmail approach by telling them, 'I was always so proud of you and told all my friends as to what a well behaved, sweet and calm little angel you are. Now look you have spoiled everything.'

In essence the message that we flash is, 'Anger is unacceptable'. When, what we really want to say is, 'The way you are expressing anger is not right'.

Most of us regard anger as negative. It's all right for our children to feel and express sadness, anxiety or other emotions, but feeling or expressing 'anger' is a complete no-no. Unknowingly we flash messages like:

'You should not be feeling like this.'

'If you feel it, bottle it.'

'Push the ogre down with all your force-it is evil.'

'Be a nice kid, for anger is not nice.'

After all we have handled our own anger issues probably in the same manner. We have suppressed, ignored and ridiculed the emotion itself. After all our parents too did the same with us and perhaps their parents too and so like a precious family tradition we pass it on and on and on. This vicious chain must be stopped.

Is anger abnormal and unnatural?

At its purest, anger is an emotion as natural and as acceptable as joy or love. According to Lloyd J. Thomas, Ph.D. 'The emotion we call "anger" is a natural response to frustration, pain, loss or neediness. It may also occur out of "old habit" or imitation of an angry parent.' According to research, a person can feel angry from the moment his nervous system is in place and functioning. Even in the womb the fully-formed fetus can experience feelings of displeasure and frustration, for example from physical trauma. Therefore it is possible that the baby is born already experiencing feelings of anger.

According to the U.S. Department of Health and Human Services, 'Anger may be a defense to avoid painful feelings; it may be associated with failure, low self-esteem, and feelings of isolation; or it may be related to anxiety about situations over which the child has no control. Angry defiance may also be associated with feelings of dependency, and anger may be associated with sadness and depression. In childhood, anger and sadness are very close to one another, and it is important to remember that much of what an adult experiences as sadness is expressed by a child as anger.'

Children who are made to feel that their anger is not O.K. – that it is wrong to express it, and in fact, that they shouldn't even experience it, do not learn acceptable and suitable ways to deal with this emotion. Anger, whether released inappropriately through explosive behaviour (violence, aggression) or suppressed by ignoring, denying or bottling the emotion itself, can lead to harmful physical, psychological, emotional and social consequences. Says Dr. Yeva Rubinstein, MD, Virtua psychiatrist, 'Usually violence from a teenager is not the beginning of a problem, it's the end product of what has happened to them throughout childhood.' Persistent feelings of anger can lead to hostility, hatred, and patterns of aggressive behaviour. If we don't help children figure out how to manage their burgeoning anger, we will see more road rage, workplace violence, domestic abuse and hostile social behaviour when they're adults, experts predict. Psychologist Tiffany Field, Ph.D., of the University of Miami School of Medicine noted a major difference in the behaviour of French and American preschoolers: On playgrounds, French youngsters were aggressive toward their playmates only 1% of the time; American preschoolers, by contrast, were aggressive 29% of the time. It is probably not a coincidence that France has the lowest murder rate in the industrialised world, and the United States has the highest. Because chronic anger is a health risk too, angry people experience heart attacks and strokes at earlier ages, medical researchers say.

Anger is not only normal and natural but has a 'positive' value too. It gives us a signal that something isn't right. It tells us that something is bothering us. Anger is in reality a great motivator for change. It can be turned into a source of strength, the way we handle it is what determines its fate. When something needs to change dramatically, anger not only lets you know but it gives you the power to do something about it.

Mahatma Gandhi
Mohandas Karamchand Gandhi, a twenty-two-year-old young barrister, fresh from the Inner temple in London, was thrown out of a first-class compartment in Pietermaritzburg, South Africa, while holding a

valid first class ticket and pushed to third class and later beaten by a stagecoach driver because his fellow passenger, a white, did not want to share the compartment with a coloured man. His offence in both cases had been to occupy a seat normally reserved for Europeans. Gandhi ji spent the night in a dark, dank waiting room. He wrote: 'It was winter... the cold was extremely bitter, my overcoat was in the luggage but I did not dare to ask for it lest I be insulted again, so I sat and shivered. There was no light in the room....' The anger in him led to introspection and deep thought. It changed not only his consciousness but also the future course of humanity. Gandhiji decided to stay back and fight the 'colour prejudice'. In his words 'I began to think of my duty. Should I fight for my rights or go back to India, or should I go on to Pretoria without minding the insults and return to India, after finishing the case? It would be cowardice to run back to India without fulfilling my obligation.' Subsequent Satyagrahas in South Africa are very well known.

9.6 Dealing with anger in the child

What's O.K., what's not!
Tell your child, anger is 'O.K.'. Sometimes life hurts, sometimes life is not fair and we feel angry. Anger is a natural feeling in response to displeasure and frustrations; and feelings are meant to be felt, understood, explored and then dealt with. The important thing is to understand what the 'feeling' is trying to tell us.

What is not 'O.K.' is expressing that anger in a way that either hurts us, others, or things. Though we cannot eliminate the feeling of anger from our psyche, we can develop better control over how we give vent to it.

Past anger regression
How does your child express his anger? Does he:
Explode?
Stew?
Sulk?

Plot to take revenge?
Deny the emotion?
Repress anger?
Nurture it for a later bigger and more powerful expression?
Get pain somewhere or get ill?
Make someone else the punching bag?
Withdraw into a shell?

Ask your child about the normal course of action he adopts in response to anger. If possible make him write down the ways he usually deals with the sizzling anger within.

Negative consequences

Make the child analyse the ramifications of those reactions.

Ask your child whether he can identify with:

Problems in relationships – Under the influence of anger one usually becomes cruel, rash and unjust. Anger prompts one to over react. It causes problems in relationships with friends, family and even teachers and mentors. An example could be peer rejection—Every time Ketan had a conflict of opinion with his friends he would just storm out of the game and the game would get disrupted. After a few such incidents his friends decided to shun him from the game altogether. They got together and decided, 'We will not play with Ketan. We do not like him.'

Loss of control over self – In the long run self-efficacy suffers. The angry person may feel better for a short time after raging but underneath he often feels worse for losing his cool. Every time Tarana was mad she would say hurtful things which she would regret later. She told her mother, "I don't know, but when I am angry it is as if I don't know what I am saying'.

Loss of fun and enjoyment – Anger has the power to consume happiness. Anger causes stress and unhappiness. Games get disrupted, negative feelings override peace and harmony and the situation generally turns taut and strained. When Karen's mother blew up on her for not picking up her stuff, Karen screamed back too and then burst into tears. It took both of them an hour to regain their composure.

Decline in performance – Performance suffers because one can't concentrate well on the work in the state of arousal. Anger short-circuits the reasoning powers as well. Whether one 'flies off the handle' or represses the rage, anger can compound an already unstable situation. Pratik was angry with his friend and so could not give his best in the class test.

Loss of energy – Every outburst of anger arouses, misdirects and depletes much of the vital energy. Kanchan was angry with her younger sister and not one to take it out on her she shut herself in her room and seethed and boiled within. She felt exhausted for a long time after.

Damage to people and property – Before Tarang and Prarit could be disentangled from their fist fight they had already given each other a black eye. Their self esteem took longer to heal.

Ask your children if they could rewind the situation and play it all over again would they have liked happier results to their anger retaliations? More importantly do they think that there is a better way to handle their anger responses? Suppose the two of you could strategise and come up with ways to be anger-smart, would your child be game for it?

Be anger-smart

What you can control. <u>Your anger is your responsibility</u>

Pushkar screamed, 'But he drove me to hit him'.

Anandi declared, 'When I see red I lose all control over myself. I can't help it'.

Children should be made to realise that though they can't control feelings of anger they surely can control how they react to that anger. They can make healthy choices. All they need is to chalk out their choice, options and strategies beforehand and work on them. Like one goes through training sessions to acquire a particular skill in any field, similarly one can train oneself to internalise suitable ways to deal with his/her anger. Others may tease, provoke or invite him to be angry, but in the end his response is his choice and he is responsible for the choice he makes and its consequences. During my conversation with my daughters I said, 'We all can help each other to make better choices. We can learn ways to deal with those "mads" in safe ways, so that no one gets hurt and we feel better'.

9.7 Triggers! What makes your child see RED?

Track down the cues about the kinds of things, situation, people and events that trigger your child's anger. What makes your child mad? Children should learn to see what is making them feel the way they do, and this will help them know what they need to change. Some of the common anger triggers are:

Being teased – Girija's elder sister was teasing her with a repeated, 'You are a fatso'. Girija went up to her and gave her a whack. All Saket's friend said, 'You are a sissy'. It always brought the worst out of him.

Improper handling of their stuff (When their things, possessions are disturbed or taken) – Talat said, 'It makes me mad when other people borrow my things and return them in a damaged condition.' Prerna was irritated when the book she leant her friend had folds. 'Couldn't the friend have used book marks,' she said angrily.

Personal assault – Sohana was pushed over and she now wanted to go and slap the perpetrator right on the face. When someone shouts, hits, nags and criticises; children get angry in retaliation.

Frustrations over failures – Paremeshwar said, 'I planned my strategy in chess but somehow got disoriented and lost the match. I am so angry with myself.' Sneha said, 'I completely forgot about my oral spelling test and made a fool of myself in class. I am mad with myself.'

Helplessness – Juhi was trying to get her mother on the cell phone and her mother was not answering. Juhi got angry and started crying. Kahan could not get the relevant information from the net and he was beginning to get very angry.

Unmet desires – Kangana wanted the new Barbie and her mother said a categorical 'no'. Kangana was now expressing her anger through a sulk. She even refused to have her lunch. When children do not get what they want—a chocolate, a toy, an outing with their friend—they usually respond with anger.

Misplaced and misdirected anger – Prashant said, 'I got a scolding when it was not my fault, I spit my anger out on my younger brother.' When children feel that they have unwittingly been a victim in a situation, it angers them.

Children should list down their triggers in black and white. Once they do this they will know exactly when the anger-torque presents itself. I remember the time I had written down on paper about how teaching mathematics to my children especially in the afternoon hours usually led to my short fuse and the ones electrocuted with my high voltage power would be my children. When I wrote down my triggers I automatically even came up with solutions for them. To tackle this particular trigger I decided to shift the mathematics lessons to the mornings. That definitely reduced the anger outbursts, but even then there were times when we took up the subject in the afternoons. But during these times if I were flying into a rage along with the increasing temperature was also the increased awareness of, 'here I go again' and this awareness was enough to snap me out of it. Most of the times I could manage to do something to cool myself down. At all times my children escaped my afternoon wrath of the earlier voltage.

If children were to write down their anger-torques every time a situation arises, they would know, 'here they go again'. That is enough to begin with.

Give your child his options—To explode or not to explode

To explode or not to explode

Go behind the feeling and understand it

Anger is usually a secondary emotion. Anger often is so intense that it hides the underlying feeling which is a clue to the real problem.

Getting in touch with that feeling may be the beginning to finding a solution. Help your child understand what he feels before he feels angry. Does he feel scared, helpless, frustrated, disappointed, exhausted, threatened or insulted? Studies show that the ability to identify and label emotions correctly, and talk about them straightforwardly to the point of feeling understood, makes negative feelings dissipate. And the physiological arousal that accompanies those feelings also diminishes dramatically.

Communicate openly and articulately

Encourage your child to communicate his feelings behind the anger to the person concerned. He should talk about his anger or hurt. Tell the person how he feels before he loses control. Sometimes this is enough to make the 'other' (children) act differently. Given below are a few examples on how feelings of anger are expressed without getting volatile.

Girija told her sister, 'Whenever you call me 'fatso' it embarrasses me and makes me feel ugly. I feel I am not good enough. It hurts me and then I feel like hurting you.'

Ankit told his society friends, 'When you leave me out of the game I feel rejected. And then I want to somehow disrupt your game so that even you can't have fun. But inside I want to play and have a good time too.'

Tarang told his mother, 'Do not scream at me, especially in front of my friends. It hurts my sense of self worth and then I want to either get back by being worse or just scream back at you. I even make faces once you are out, to show my friends that you-are-no-big-deal, but inside I seethe and hurt.'

Ketan told John, 'Please do not snatch the car. You can have it once I finish playing, which will be in a short while.'

Lalit said to his friend, 'Do not hit me. I feel threatened and then in the anxiety I want to hit you back even worse.'

Children can often explode in anger, yet not be able to tell what their anger is all about. By expressing their feelings behind the anger, children have a chance to change the situation. Telling someone we are angry brings feelings of relief, especially when we also express why we are angry. Psychologists believe that the relief we feel under those circumstances results not from venting the anger but from identifying the anger-arousing circumstances and working towards a solution. Encourage your child to vent his feelings but in measured tone and words. Tell your child to be assertive but not aggressive in expressing himself. Assertiveness requires speaking in an effective, nonviolent way. You can even help him rehearse his response before delivering it.

Alternatively, you can also encourage your child to speak to you about every 'xyz' person or event that angers him. Lend your child a sympathetic, interested and loving ear for him to vent out his woes, whether it is about a friend in school or a neigbour in the society. Listen to his feelings.

Shilpa mouthed the words, 'Looks like you are really upset with...' That was enough to open the door of communication. She helped him drain off his intense emotions by acknowledging feelings. She also helped him find suitable words to speak to the friend about his emotion.

Seven year old Ansh said, 'When I talk about my problems with someone who really listens to me, I feel that my anger has dissipated.'

Prakash told his nine year old daughter, 'Looks like you are really angry. Want to speak about it?' As she opened her Pandora's box she felt lighter and her anger with herself dissipated.

Sometimes, just stating, 'I can see that you're really mad,' can diffuse the angry situation, says Stacy Kaiser, a mother of two school-age children and a Van Nuys marriage and family therapist.

Tell your child it is a challenge to go behind the anger and see what has perpetrated it and then talk to the person concerned without blowing up. But it is important to remember that the child must not be compelled to share. Provide the ambience only, the opening up will happen.

Did your child somehow start the entire anger-hurt cycle

Make the child question his behaviour. Ask your child on whether he did something to cause hostility and anger in the 'other'. Some children can irk others with their bossiness, while some can be fickle-minded and still, some can be sore losers, thus inviting the wrath of their friends. In fact my younger daughter would storm out of the game at the slightest difference of opinion. This would disrupt the game. Her friends decided to keep her out of the game, which in turn escalated her anger even more. But the root cause of it all was her getting angry at small differences to begin with.

Children see things primarily from their own perspective. They may be completely unaware of how their behaviour affects other people, except when another person interferes with their needs. To negotiate solutions that are fair to everyone, children need to know how others feel. Ask the child, 'How do you think he must have felt? What would you have done if you were in their shoes?'

In situations where we know that somewhere it is our child who is at fault, we should try to work with 'put-yourself-in-his-shoes-and-see-what-you-would-have-done' mode. Karen told her daughter, 'It's natural to get defensive when you're criticised, but don't fight back. She might be feeling neglected and unloved'.

Children at times are quick to think that the other person was mean on purpose. Joanne was completing her picture when due to an accident shove by her younger brother the picture got spoilt. She immediately started her barrage of accusations, 'You always do it. You are mean on purpose'. Help children stop and ask themselves if the other child was being mean on purpose. Go over the situation and all the reasons why it might have been an accident.

Let go when the 'other' would not let go

Often times expressing one's feelings might not be enough to change the situation. There will be times when 'others' would still be mean and thoughtless. Some would provoke and cause fights on purpose. Even in such cases, getting angry and blowing one's fuse doesn't fix the situation but makes it worse. What options do our children have then? We can tell them to 'Let go of what is beyond their control. Work on what is...your reaction to the anger'.

Ignore the troublemaker.

Stay away from the menace.

Try to keep calm and not take it personally. Staphna reasoned, 'Freya must be having a bad day'. Arnav said, 'Too bad for that person, being so mean all the time.'

Teach yourself positive self-talk

Children can develop a repertoire of calming statements in the face of anger. Aggressive thoughts intensify anger, calming statements help equalise emotions. Teach your child to substitute aggressive thoughts with calming ones like. A few examples:

I can handle this

I am in charge of how I react

I know he is being unfair but getting angry is not going to fix anything

Take away their power

Radhika was tired of being called a slob by her class bully Tanya. Her repeated requests to stop failed. Eventually Radhika and her mother decided on a course of action where Radhika acted completely indifferent to Tanya's consistent name calling. After a week she went off to Tanya and said, 'You can call me any number of names you want. They do not bother me anymore. You have no power to hurt me now'. Tanya stopped wasting her energy on Radhika and went off to find a new victim.

Sort out the important from the unimportant

Make your child question whether, what you are angry about is really worth getting angry at. What do you believe is at stake here? Separate the Big Deals from the Little Deals. Solve big deals. Let go of little deals.

Saarang's friend Sohail was waiting in Saarang's room for his return and in the meantime amused himself with Saarang's Pokemon collection. He messed up his friend's settings and placed the Pokemons in different boxes. When Saarang came home he was extremely upset with his friend. Yes, Sohail was his very good friend but he had no business touching his Pokemons and that too without asking his permission first! Saarang flew into a rage and both friends ended up with a 'please-do-not-come-to-my-house-again'. The rage subsided in a few days from both their fronts. They started missing their playtime together. But who was going to wave the white flag first?

It is then that Saarang's mother taught Saarang about the 'big deal' and the 'small deal'. She said, 'Yes. Your collection was precious to you but Sohail did not lose, break or damage any. As for him messing up your set, you took just about 15 minutes to put everything the way you wanted to. Nothing awful really happened. Let go of small deals.'

In our experience with our children too, many a time we find them sulking, fighting and getting angry over nothing. It is then that we should train them to see the bigger picture. Saarang's mother said, 'I am not asking you to let people "walk all over you." However, let grudges go; life is really too short to keep a feud going.'

Lengthen your fuse. Pause before you blow off

LENGTHEN YOUR FUSE...

Teach children acceptable ways to blow off steam.

They can calm themselves by:

- Writing down their feelings (journaling)
- Drawing a picture about the situation that made them angry
- Making big, mad noises – They can yell in a paper bag, in an enclosed room, scream in a vacant field or park
- Let out their 'mads' by hammering nails in a board, ripping newspapers and old magazines, pounding on a pillow or a mattress, beating drums.
- Deep breathing – Breathing deeply will ease the tension and help lower their internal anger—meter
- Splashing water on the face
- Listening to music
- Counting backwards
- Using their energies – They can get involved in their favourite hobby or sport like riding a bike, dancing, hitting the ball on the wall and catching it on the rebound, running around the house, jump a skipping rope, cutting wood, walking their dog.
- Walking away from the situation – Sometimes in an angry situation it is best to walk away until everyone can cool off. We can tell our children that it can be hard to walk away, but it is the only responsible thing to do when they realise that their anger has overcome their reason.

When to walk away:

- If they cannot think straight, no matter how hard they try
- Their point is just not getting across to the other person
- If they find themselves crying, yelling or hitting
- If they are being abused, physically or verbally
- They need to realise that things will only get worse before they get better. By withdrawing in a positive manner, before it all begins, they can prevent further pain and anger from worsening the situation.

Ask your child, 'What could you have done differently?'

Make your child go through any anger-causing situation of the past which has left an unpleasant memory and ask, 'Let us suppose the situation presents itself again, what then would you do differently? If you could step into any of the phases and redirect your responses what would you have done? Not all anger is misplaced. Given that your anger was justified, what else or how differently could you have handled the expression better?' Ask your child what else could he have done besides yelling and hitting? How could he have problem solved in an amiable way?

Here is a case in point:

Tanmay wanted to go to Pizza Hut with his older sister Parul, for the birthday party of her school friend.

Parul, 'You are not invited. How can I take you?'

Tanmay, 'Can you bring me a pizza when you come home?'

Parul, 'You think of food all the time. No wonder mum says that you are adding fat everywhere.'

Tanmay, 'And you keep standing in front of the mirror for hours admiring yourself. How do you think mom feels about that?'

Parul, 'Just because you are envious that I am going to have a good time....'

It was then that their mother intervened.

Mother, 'Parul, tell me one thing in the recent past that Tanmay has done for you.'

Parul, 'Tanmay is mean. I do not like him.'

Mother, 'You are upset with him right now, I can understand, but try and say one good thing about him please.'

Parul reluctantly, 'Hmmm.....okay. The other day I had forgotten my I-pod in the theater and Tanmay reminded me of it.'

Tanmay, 'How could I have not reminded you, I know how much you love your I-pod.'

Mother to Tanmay, 'Now you say something which Parul has done for you?'

Tanmay, 'She helped me with my spellings and I scored well in the spelling bee.'

With their mom's positive intervention they could get out of a cycle where they would have probably used hurtful words for each other but instead, got into a positive mode.

9.8 Miscellaneous tips

Be with your children during their 'mads'

Patty Wipfler of the Parenting Leadership Institute advises parents to stay with their children when they're angry. 'Don't get involved in arguing with them,' she says, 'just be there'. Once when her son got angry over ice cream in a store, 'he burst into tears and was thrashing around in the cart. He kept telling me that I was a bad mommy,' she says. Wipfler left the store and sat with her son. When he told her she didn't love him, she replied quietly, 'I'm sorry you feel that way, but I'm not going to get the big ice cream today.' Eventually, she says, he 'got around to being a reasonable person again. I know that it was really important for me to stay with him and listen to him during that time.'

As parents, we know that we can't always do what our children want, but we can explain to them when we can't do some things.

Set and enforce ground rules

You have to set certain ground rules. Aggression as a means of expression of anger should not be permitted under any circumstances. Small everyday conflicts in my house, between my two children do lead to verbal volleys and name calling, but it stops short of getting converted into a full-bodied fight because I always put the dreaded question, 'Who hit first'? Set clear rules. Tell your children, YOU CANNOT:

- Break something
- Hit, push, pinch or bite someone
- Hurt yourself

Use pre-agreed punitive methods in case the ground rules are broken. It is important however to convey to them, although they are accepted and loved unconditionally, that their current behaviours are unacceptable. Time Out is probably the most widely researched technique for dealing with unwanted behaviour in young children. Time Out means removing the child from all rewarding activities for a short period.

9.9 Keep children away from harmful effects of media

Encounters, bomb blasts, gun violence, mob rage, riots...violence is everywhere, be it in movies, T.V., newspapers, magazines or video games, play stations and rap songs. Though the sheer quantity of violence affects these young tender minds, worse still is the false message that media violence sends. The message flashed today is that:

'Violence is cool' – Conflicts are resolved with fists and weapons

'Violence is funny' – 'Hagar the horrible' is angry with his wife and so pours the entire dinner over her head.

Repeated exposure to violent television, movies, and music, desensitises children to violence and encourages aggression and unhealthy behaviour. Felton Earls, professor of social medicine at Harvard Medical School and professor of human behaviour and development at Harvard School of Public Health says, 'Violence may be viewed as an infectious disease'.

Researched facts

Dr Michele Borba, author of the book, *Building Moral Intelligence: The Seven Essential Virtues that Teach Kids to Do the Right Thing* says, 'The single greatest trend I've seen as a consultant to hundreds of schools over the past ten years is the marked increase in anxiety and anger in our children. We shouldn't kid ourselves: the steady onslaught of stress and violent images is taking a major toll on our children's emotional and moral well-being.'

The American Psychological Association says there are three major effects of watching violence in the media (i.e. video games/television) children may become less sensitive to the pain and suffering of others, children may be more fearful of the world around them, and children may be more likely to behave in aggressive or hurtful ways toward others.

Violence-prevention expert Deborah Prothrow-Stith of the Harvard School of Public Health, says media violence both reflects and contributes to a growing 'culture of meanness', a fertile ground for real-life violence

One key study that showed the connection between media violence and real violence was the one by Dr Leonard D. Eron. He followed a group of young people for twenty-two years and found that those who watched more television at age eight were more likely, at age thirty, to have committed more serious crimes, to be more aggressive when drinking, and to punish their children more harshly than others. Others have repeated Eron's study and found similar results throughout the United States and other countries as well.

According to the report of Bushman, 2001, children are affected at any age, but young children are most vulnerable to the effects of media violence. Young children

¤ are more easily impressionable.
¤ have a harder time distinguishing between fantasy and reality.
¤ cannot easily discern motives for violence.
¤ learn by observing and imitating.

The average child sees 8,000 murders and 100,000 other violence acts by the end of elementary school. Children's T.V. programmes have five times as many acts of violence per hour as an adult's T.V.

The message from all quarters is unequivocal-once people have been exposed to violent behaviour, they are more likely to react that way themselves. I am sure the researched fact given above is not something you did not already know. But what have you done personally and consciously to filter the effects of media violence on your child? Are you one of those who blame the media for its irresponsibility and then abdicate your own sense of accountability and allow the child unhindered and unfiltered screen hours?

☑ *Reality check*

Do your children jog their blood circulation through watching WWF?

Do they get their 'violence of the day' share in flashes from the 'C' grade movies which are telecasted liberally in more than ten Hindi and English movie channels?

Do you monitor your child's screen time?

Yes, it is convenient to get them off our hands for the assigned one hour everyday with the electronic babysitter but it may cause irreparable damage to their tender psyches. Take control. Minimise the harmful effects of media and reshape the media environment that your child is growing up in.

Ways to combat the hazards of Media violence

Filter the content to which your children are exposed. Discuss and work out which shows are okay and which are not. Familiarise yourself with the content of a movie before your child sees it. Use a filter or a screening program on your home computer to block entry to certain websites, visit the site http://www.familysafemedia.com/parental_control. html to know of the latest equipment to help you monitor and regulate what your child watches.

Help children develop thoughtful and responsible media viewing habits. Teach your children what the rating systems mean. If a programme offers the warning that the content is not suitable for children or young people, believe it. These warnings offer good advice as to the intensity or level of violence contained in programmes and help you gauge whether your child should tune in. Says Glenn Sparks, Ph.D, Professor, Dept. of Communication, College of Liberal Arts, Purdue University 'Children are not too naïve nor too young to begin learning what we call critical viewing skills. Just as we would talk about a food diet and about what's healthy and what's unhealthy, we should begin to talk to them about their media diet.'

Watch T.V. with your child. Talk to them of your concerns about media violence. Point out when you disapprove of a character's violent acts and when you think there are better ways to resolve problems. Ask your child, 'What do you think about how xyz solved his problem? If you had a problem like that what could you do/say? Can you think of a way to solve that problem where no one gets hurt?' Explore with your child nonviolent strategies for solving problems.

Help children understand that T.V., video games, and cartoons are not real. Help sort out fantasy from reality. Help clarify confusion by saying things such as, 'In real life, things don't get sorted out with a bullet'. Help your child understand that T.V. violence lasts for the flickering second that it is on the screen, but real-life violence has long-term consequences.

Talk with your children about what they see. This is vital. Be sure they know what you think. Be sure you know what they think.

To minimise peer pressure to watch violent shows, you can even talk to the parents of your child' s friends and agree to similar rules.

Reward even a miniscule success in handling anger

We as adults are far more likely to attend to annoying behaviour than desirable behaviour. Glenn Latham, Ed.D, a family and educational consultant, has found that adults typically ignore ninety% or more of the good things children do. Instead, they pay attention to children when they behave badly. Be on the alert for behaviour that indicates growing maturity: Praise them every time they handle their anger positively. Children need acknowledgement and praise when they solve problems without being aggressive. This is just as important as stopping the hitting.

9.10 We are our children's role models! What are we exhibiting?

Tanmay screamed at his son to stop screaming.

Sapna hit her son because she was angry at him as he hit his younger sister.

States ten-year-old Raaghav, 'I had a fight with my younger brother and we were both screaming at each other at the top of our lungs. Mom came into the room, took on a volume higher than both of us, tone ruder and started yelling at us with how many times we have been told not to shout and use bad tones with each other. Her face got redder and she came very close to hitting us'. We can imagine what the children picked up.

Children who see adults handle their feelings by being aggressive all the time will assume that it's okay for them too. Whatever rules, advices and conduct we set for our children, if they are not in tandem with our own behaviour, chances are that they will not have much influence on our children. The way we deal with our anger is instinctively teaching them what to do with theirs. If it is not okay for our children to lash out in a temper why should it be okay for us? Find acceptable ways to deal with your anger not just with your children but with others who trigger off a spark.

Handling our anger better

Give your child the facts straight and simple. Sharmila told her son, 'I had a bad day today and can't take so much noise from you right now. Can you please either go to your room or do something quietly in the living room'. Tarang told his son, 'You will not be able to bully me into getting you the new toy gun. So do not throw a tantrum for the same. We can use the time in getting an ice-cream instead.'

Change your thoughts when angry. Anger is directly related to our thoughts. If we have angry thoughts we will become angry. I had barely managed to eke out that miniscule teeny weenie half hour for an afternoon nap. I instructed my children not to disturb me, sank into the inviting comfy mattress and shut my eyes. One kid was trying out her drum skills, the other took to the whistle, clatter of the utensils rose from the kitchen sink, but since none of the noise was directed towards me, I felt at peace even with the clamour around.

I was slowly moving towards the famous half sleep alfa stage when my children rudely pulled me out of my much-deserved nap with an inconsequential, could-have-been-easily-avoided brawl. The two were trying to settle a difference of opinion and in the process tuned their vocal chords to the maximum volume they could. Determined to finish the promised half hour, my body stayed in bed but my mind was in complete attention. My ears pricked up as I tried to piece the fragments of what was decipherable in order to know who began the clamorous saga and that too during this precise half hour. Five more minutes in bed and I knew that it was the older child who was at fault here. I thought how wonderful it would be to get up, go straight to the children's room and give her a slap on the bum. I got up, walked straight to the children's room and gave the elder one a hard pat on the bum.

I had never hit them before and we were all shocked! My kids, mother-in-law, domestic help and most of all me! What had I done? How could I have done it? Though my child ought to have behaved better, my reaction could not be justified at all. More importantly, how could I give vent to my anger in this irresponsible aggressive manner?

The answer was clear. It was because I visualised myself doing it, got into an emotional state and did exactly that.

How many times do we visualise ourselves screaming and we scream, see ourselves hitting and we hit, think of...and it happens. Though we later always, always do regret and console ourselves with, 'it was not in my control'. But it always is. All we have to do is to put a stop right there...for me when the tape of hitting her began playing, I should have just switched it off.

What we can do when we lose control as we sometimes will, is apologise to our children. Besides the fact that it is only fair that we do so, it will also serve as a good example for our children to follow when they lose their cool.

Aparna Sen

Aparna Sen and her younger sister went on a 'not-talking-to-papa' phase in response to an anger outburst of his at the maid, which they thought was unfair and exaggerated. Two days later, their father, confused and a little irked, asked them the reason for their behaviour. Aparnaji said, 'We told him that he was very rude to the maid and we thought that was unfair. We even said why we thought it was unfair. He kept quiet for a while and then said, "I am sorry". Both of us immediately burst into tears and hugged papa. But this has left a profound impact on the way I deal with my anger outbursts. I knew then that I too must own up to my unreasonableness, for I will behave so at times, even though if the understanding comes through someone much younger and I should even apologise if need be. I hope that I can pass this in turn to my children too.'

It's difficult but not impossible to help our children change their response to anger. A cycle of anger can be changed with awareness, persistence and support. Each time they look for a better way to express their anger instead of hitting, they will grow in their ability to be in control of their anger. It is hard work, but the

> 'I am too busy with my cause to hate – too absorbed in something bigger than myself. I have no time to quarrel, no time for regrets, and no man can force me to stoop low enough to hate him.'
>
> – LAWRENCE JAMES

rewards return three-fold in an environment rich in mutual respect, peace, harmony and love. The process of managing anger requires structured teaching, a lot of practice, and frequent feedback that's both positive and corrective. Managing anger can take months, even years, to achieve, and slip-ups are inevitable, so it's important for parents to focus on children's successes and encourage them to view the rough spots not as failures, but as opportunities to learn and grow.

9.11 Fear in children

Mummy, do not switch off the lights. Ants will crawl into my bed!

It is raining heavily. I can hear creepy noises too. Please do not go out of the house!

That watchman outside with the big moustache has red eyes. I am scared of him, mommy!

I am not going to remember anything in the examination tomorrow. I am sure to fail!

I do not want to go to the doctor? He will give me an injection!

A child's world is full of dangers, real and imaginary, as was ours when we were young. But now that we have grown up we know that ants (cockroach, lizards) can't hurt us, rains can't melt us and the burly watchman out there is for our protection and not vice versa. A deep breath is all that is required for those dates, formulae and answers to flow in and we know that the vaccine that we have to take is a two second pain but a safeguard against much more suffering and disease. Fortunately we have outgrown our fears, but it is simply intolerable when our children refuse to enter the bathroom because they have spotted a minuscule, harmless and probably even more mortified cockroach trying to make itself invisible, by crouching further and further in. We throw up our hands and utter, 'Don't be silly. There is no way that the tiny thing could cause you any harm.' Inside we are saying, 'Why is my child such a wimp', forgetting that we were probably worse off at that age.

Fear is a basic emotion that we all experience. It is a normal part of life and a basic survival instinct. Because our natural inclination is towards growth and development, we would not survive as a species if it were not for our ability to hold back and appraise and avoid danger. It is a protective mechanism and a normal part of development. We as adults too have fears though they are radically different from those of our children. Our fears are solid, grounded in reality with larger consequences. When we think of our issue of, 'what if I am sacked for that error' and compare it to 'Daddy, there are monsters in my cupboard' or 'what if my spouse finds someone better' and compare it with 'what if I forget all my lessons', we can't help but shrug and dismiss the trivial and unreasonable.

But if our fears are real to us, so are theirs to them. Childhood is a journey through unknown territory. A child's world is constantly expanding and they try to make sense of what's going on around them without understanding the rules and the cause and effects. Fears often arise as they find themselves unable to cope with a situation and so feel threatened. Dr. Robert Schacter, director of the Phobia Centre for Children in New York and co-author of, *Why Your Child Is Afraid* (Simon and Schuster) says, 'As kids go through different developmental stages, which means they develop capabilities to do more things, they get into new situations, and because of that develop fears.' Throughout the growing-up years, perhaps even into adulthood, a new fear usually pops up just as an old fear is conquered. Child psychiatrist Benjamin Wolman estimates that 90% of normal children develop fears appropriate to their age.

Typical childhood fears include fear of strangers, heights, darkness, animals, blood, insects, and being left alone. Children often fear a specific object or situation after having an unpleasant experience, for example getting lost in a public place, or an accident (slipping into the swimming pool can cause the fear of water), hospitalisation or an illness. They need extra support and help to work through such fears which result due to specific experiences. Children going to school normally have fears of separation from mother, new faces and surroundings (especially starting school) and bullying children.

Whether a child's fear is considered normal generally depends on his or her age, background, and most importantly by how much it interferes with his or her normal daily activities. The first step is to assess whether the fear is age-normal. Following are some normal fears and their approximate age of occurrence.

Age Common fears

Infants and toddlers – loud noises
 – separation, strangers

Preschoolers – animals – especially dogs
 – the dark
 – ghosts and monsters

School-going – social rejection
- fear of failure
- the news and T.V. shows
- blood, injury, and sickness
- being home alone
- death

Fears appear and disappear in an ordered, patterned fashion that is similar from child to child.

We must act:

- if they persist for too long
- if the child is overly preoccupied with the subject that is feared, severely inhibiting the child's day-to-day functioning
- if the child cannot be distracted away from the fear or reassured

A 1986 survey by Kaoru Yamamoto, Ph.D., an educational psychologist at the University of Colorado, found the 'top 20' troubles of children. The list, with their greatest fear first and in descending order, may surprise you.

1 Losing a parent
2. Going blind
3. Academic retainment
4. Failing in class
5. Parental fights
6. Caught in theft
7. Suspected of lying
8. Poor report card
9. Sent to principal
10. Having an operation
11. Getting lost
12. Ridiculed in class
13. Moving to a new school
14. Scary dream
15. Not making 100 on a test

16. Picked last on a team
17. Losing in a game
18. Giving a class report
19. Going to a dentist
20. New baby

Fluid and Fixed Fears

Researchers distinguish between fluid and fixed fears. A fluid fear is one that comes and goes. If the fear changes from week to week or remains for a limited period and begins to fade away, it can be considered normal. A fixed fear is one that remains or may even intensify. Fixed fears may require a lot of patience to work through, and may even require special attention from a professional.

Rudy Giuliani once said: 'Courage is not the absence of fear; rather it is the management of fear.'

Let us help our children control and manage their fears effectively.

9.12 Helping children deal with fear

The golden mean! Do not invalidate. Do not escalate. Acknowledge!

Do not laugh, dismiss, ridicule or belittle their fears.
You don't? Have you used statements like:-
Stop acting like a baby.
You are being silly.
That doesn't happen in real life.
I have no time for your stupid and unreasonable fears.
How many times do I have to tell you that there is no one is under the bed?

Acknowledge and respect the child's feelings. Accept them. Researchers say that since the minds and logical abilities of children have not yet fully developed, the lines between reality and fantasy are

thin and often blurred. They cannot formulate for example, that the bombs which are tearing Iraq away that they have just witnessed on T.V. cannot drop onto their homes. To them their fears are very real.

When they choose to confide in us regarding them we must respect and acknowledge their apprehensions. Sapna told her daughter, 'It's okay to feel scared of lightening and thunder. But they are not so bad. They happen as night and day happens.' Shrena validated her child's feelings with 'I'm sure it must have been very frightening for you to....'

Once we acknowledge our child's fear they feel that they can trust us with the specific details of the fear. The more articulate they are the better will be the understanding 'why, how and to what extent is the fear affecting them. If we don't empathise, we lose our audience. They won't stick around for the lesson, because they think we don't understand the problem in the first place.

We too, probably have our own fears and anxieties. We can talk about them to our children in an honest way, (taking care that we do not put our anxieties onto them). We can reminisce about the fears that we felt as a child and how we eventually conquered or moved past them. This will show them that everyone has fears and with the passage of time one outgrows them. We can even share some specific fear that we were haunted by when young.

My elder daughter, Aishwarya, had a nightmare in which she was surrounded by insects trying to gobble her up! She woke up screaming, sweaty and terribly disturbed. We linked the nightmare to the movie *The Matrix* which we had seen the day before. The movie carried a scene wherein an icky insect makes its way inside the hero, Keanu Reeve's, stomach and disappears. All my arguments to convince my child of the unreality of it happening in real life fell flat. What worked was when I shared the story of my own Gabbar phobia. I told her that Gabbar Singh terrified me even in my dreams, with his famous laugh and the dialogue, '*Kitne aadmi the*'. With a wink I said that I capitalised on my fear and shifted base to my parent's room and slept safely cocooned between mom and dad long after my fears had dispelled. I could sense my daughter's body language changing. Her shoulders relaxed, her mind unknotted itself and I could literally see the feeling 'oh, it happens to everyone' ease out the anxiety from her brows. I gave her an instance to identify with. Though the image of the movie still left her trembling, her mind could now understand the episode through my experience and perspective and that was a great source of relief to my then nine year old.

Perhaps she will be telling the famous *Matrix* story to her children or grandchildren and easing them out of their fears.

Encourage expression of concerns, worries, or fears

The most significant factor in overcoming a fear is first identifying that fear. Often enough children are unable to pinpoint exactly what they're afraid of until they start discussing it. Encourage children to talk about their fears. Allow expression of apprehension. Let me cite an instance from my daughter's life. Whenever my husband and I had the slightest difference of opinion or even a small argument, my eldest daughter would be visibly distressed. She would either beg us to stop arguing or run away from the scenario. Our conflicts were like normal conflicts which any couple would have. I did find her reaction strange; attributed it to an oversensitive personality; but never thought that there was a fear behind her exaggerated reaction to our fights. One day, we were reading a story together in which the ten-year-old narrator's parents separated after a major showdown. With the most solemn expression my child shot out, 'Can one of your fights lead to your separation too?' I was SHOCKED!!! My daughter's best friend lived with her mom as her mother had separated after a major fight. It was then that I understood the fear behind her behaviour...what if her parents separated too!!! We sat and discussed the issue.

Me: 'Do you have disagreement, fights, complaints with your younger sister?'

She: 'Yes, mommy!'

Me: 'With your friends?' I tried and recalled as many names as I could and asked her individually if she had had fights with them.

She: 'Yes mommy. Though more with some and perhaps less with others.'

Me: 'Have you had complaints and disagreements with me too?'

She: 'Yes'.

Me: 'With your dad (he did not get you those crackers that he promised), grandmom (She nags too much about washing up).

I then said, 'Your father and I too, do have differences of opinion which at times take on a louder, ruder tone; but we work around each other as you do with your friends, cousins and sisters.' We chatted honestly for over an hour and I could put her imagined phobia to complete rest.

This was a chance understanding. But there could be fears lurking in our child's psyche which they never get enough confidence to spill out. They need a safe place to voice their fears. Let us as parents provide them with this haven. Children may repress and never work out their fears unless they talk about them. No matter what's causing a childhood fear, experts agree it should never be ignored or it could turn into permanent insecurities in adults.

Encourage questions.

Help the children learn about what scares them.

Ask:

What do you fear? You will be amazed at their answers. Ashiana went to a personality development class where she was asked to note down her fears. One of her fears were, 'When my mom compares me with my friend and tells how good her handwriting is'.

Why do you fear it? 'Pratik said that he felt someone would come and kidnap him in the dark. I have seen it happening in many movies.'

What is the worst that you think could happen? Aishwarya thought that the end result of our fights would be a separation.

When we talk to them about their fears we get an idea of exactly what our children are afraid of and how serious the fear is. This information is useful when coming up with ways to help children confront their fears. Talking about their fears often helps children feel better. Many a times just sharing their deepest anxieties can make them feel better, because they know that someone who cares also knows. Words have a way of taking some of the power out of negative emotions and making them more manageable for young children.

Help children face their fear and move past them

Offer exposure. Gradually expose them to their fears in unthreatening ways, so that they feel safe and more secure over time. Build on their knowledge. Knowing how things work and what to expect can make things less scary.

Aditi was horrified of lizards. Her father explained to her that lizards are a part of the natural world just as we are and that we all have our own place. Yes, they can be dangerous, but so long as we're careful and take a responsible attitude, they do not go out of their way to make our lives tough. In fact they fear us as much as we fear them.

To make Tarangini overcome her fear of lightening and thunderstorm, her mother involved her society children in 'The dynamic sky' project. They read about it in books, built models, had power point presentations and quiz sessions. Before long Tarangini was awaiting the monsoon to record the sound of thunder which was to be a part of her 'thunder project'.

Kartik encouraged his son to draw the monsters that he was afraid of. He found them less terrifying in the picture.

Sanjeev explained to his son, who had a fire-phobia, about the presence of smoke sirens which make a fatal fire unlikely.

Premal read to his son from Child Craft about how dentists help children fight against decay and rotting teeth. The section had interesting caricatures where soda pops, ice-creams were guised as devils. This helped mitigate his son's fear of the dentist's chair.

We can look for information on the net, read from books, organise group discussions, dramas and role plays(they may pretend to be growling dogs, one-eyed monsters, gruff doctors, or roaring lions, and meet their fears vicariously) and use play-way methods to help children face their fear and see them in realistic light. We can even have them write out their fears in a journal: If they are too young to write we can have them dictate words to us and we can write it for them.

It is, however, important to help them cope with fear at a pace they are comfortable with. The pace could be a slow one, but we must not rush it. The mind, like the body, takes time to overcome fears and injuries. No child should be forced into dealing with something she is afraid of before she is ready. Forcing him to do something makes him more anxious. He'll fear you and doubt himself.

Give your child the reassurance she needs. She may want you to listen to her account of the fearful happening more than once, and she may ask you to explain it over and over again. It's okay to crawl under the bed or go into the closet to prove to your child that there is nothing dangerous in the room. If the child wants a light left on, leave it on. If he wants the bedroom door open, leave it open.

Reassure your children that you are there for them always and do your best to see no harm comes their way.

Help the child construct her own understanding of fear

A personal example

This was during the outbreak of dengue in Gujarat when my younger child Sanaya recorded a temperature of 104 degree Fahrenheit. Her paediatrician prescribed a blood test. Of course the pandemonium which is expected of a small child who has just realised that she will be pricked did happen but we got her tested and the results were normal. But the fever persisted and on the 4th day the doctor recommended another test fearing a secondary infection. The fear heightened her sixth sense and even before I had dropped the receiver she sensed what was to come. To say that she was uncooperative would be an understatement. Outraged and terrified, she howled and screamed for the full forty-five minutes that the pathology clinic man took to reach our place. By then we were both exhausted. The sight of him, however, gave her fresh energy and I had to seek my neighbour's help to hold her down to extract the blood.

I was miserable, she was exhausted and we had nothing to say to each other. Not the end of the story though. Unfortunately she had contracted a seven day viral and on the 6th day the doctor prescribed another blood test. I shuddered at the thought and knew that there was no way that I could put her and myself through the same scene once again. I turned to the only tool I had, reason and logic. Before calling the path-lab I spoke to my child. Here is the conversation which I still remember word to word.

Me: 'You know that had it not been absolutely essential I wouldn't have done it?'

Sanaya: 'Yes'

Me: 'You also know that if I could have taken the pain for you I would have gladly taken it?'

Sanaya: 'Yes.'

Me: 'Sanaya, tell me what was worse, the fear that you went through between the time you came to know of the injection, or the three-second prick itself?'

Sanaya: 'The needle was painful but not as much as I had thought. I was so scared of it that I do not even remember the needle's pain but I do remember the cries before it.'

Me: 'So, the pain and anxiety which you suffered due to the anticipation of the needle could be robbed of its power if you chose to do so. And the actual pain anyways has little power because it is for such a short while.'

Sanaya: 'Yes.'

Me: 'Suppose I were to tell you that we need another test, what would you do?'

Sanaya: 'Mom, we need another test???'

Tears welled up in her eyes and I just held her for some time without speaking a word. Once her sobs subsided, she looked into my eyes and saw my helplessness and pain. She said, 'Mommy, I will be brave this time.'

Me: 'I promise we will hold hands and think of wonderful things for those three seconds. What do you say, my lioness?'

Sanaya: 'Yes.'

Yes, we eliminated the ugly scene before the dreaded needle but even more important, she understood that she could control her fear and overcome it...it was a choice that she could make. Sanaya was then seven years old.

We assume that it is beyond a child's ability to understand or behave with maturity especially when issues like physical pain are concerned. But when I actually gave my child the power and time to understand and handle her own fear she did so with amazing prudence. I am not saying that she has completely overcome her fear and pain of the needle (we do go for her regular vaccines and it is not as if she laughs her way to the doctors' chamber) but now she knows what she can tell herself to keep the pain to a minimum and she does that every time unfailingly!!!

We can go over the fear with our children and encourage them to let them come up with what can be done about it on their own.

9.13 Are you unconsciously/consciously making your kid fearful?

Children learn about the world by and large part through their parents' eyes and actions. Parents who are anxious and tend to see the world as dangerous and unsafe will instill, intentionally or not, similar attitudes in their children. Ask yourself, am I, through my actions, making my child more fearful? There are many ways parents can do this.

Some parents spin into a panic after reading or listening to news filled with horrors of child pornography and child abduction. Determined to protect children at any cost, such parents may actually put them to greater risk. Desperate to keep them safe, they seek to instill fear in their children. 'Don't talk to strangers; Stay inside where it's "safe"; Stay off the internet chat lines. Look out! Be careful.' Such imposed fear may shut down the greatest chance of survival our child has in any situation—his connection to his own instincts which have the ability to keep him safe. Yes, it is important for children to know that there are real threats in life. Parents need to monitor, especially younger children, to make sure they remain safe at all times. However, as children grow, it is also important to gradually allow them opportunities to successfully respond to age and skill appropriate challenges, so that they can increase their ability to cope with these challenges. Children must be taught about safety skills such as stranger danger, internet safety, bicycle rules, fire and disaster readiness, traffic regulations, seat belts, etc. These issues are dealt with in the chapter trial and error.

At times, parents pass down their fears onto their children unknowingly. A mother who has perhaps escaped drowning as a child or witnessed someone have a close brush in a similar incident, does not just become pool-averse herself but unconsciously/consciously passes her fears onto her children too. A superstitious father will unwittingly make his children fearful of black cats, walking under ladders. Tuhin, illustrator of this book says, 'My mother was always extremely fearful of heights and warned me to avoid it. As a result, I never learnt kite flying. Even today I am uncomfortable with altitudes.' Unwittingly, we pass on our fears of even creatures who are weak, fragile and small enough to be stamped on but that are icky. These fears (lizard, cockroach, spiders, mice etc.) run across at times, through generations.

At other times parents unintentionally reinforce or promote the very fear that we want them to overcome. In their bid to make them feel secure they may overreact, be extra protective or simply shower them with a dose of our attention that the children begin to enjoy. Param thought, 'Every time thunder crashes my family rushes to check in on me! Wow, It is so exciting!' He was enjoying a sense of power and was working on extending the data base of his fears.

While his friend Kiran concluded, 'Thunder must be something very horrid to create such a furore in the home. What will happen to me?'

At times parents use fear as means to an end-to keep children safe, out of mischief, to make them finish up the healthy but unsavoury dishes in the plate. Classic examples of these are:

Finish your milk otherwise 'Gabbar' will come.

You are being very naughty. I will ask that burly haired watchman to take you away.

Now, go off to sleep or the night demons will come and take you away.

Do not:

- Try not to tell your child that they will be a 'big boy' or a 'big girl' when they overcome their fear. This puts too much pressure on the child.

- Do not use fear to scare the child into good behaviour. Some examples could be: Eat your veggies or the uncle there will come and take you away. 'Phantom' you must come tonight

Shashank is really misbehaving. I will call the doctor if you do not listen to me. Come 'bhow' take Harshita away.

• Don't transmit personal fears to children. Children readily adopt the fears and frightened attitudes of those around them. Even fear and distrust of people who are different can be passed from parent to child, from generation to generation.

• Do not overprotect your child. Children who are overly cautioned and protected can be made to feel anxious and fearful of their environment.

IT IS THE VISUAL THAT COUNTS. SUPERVISE THE LEVEL OF YOUR CHILD'S EXPOSURE TO T.V. AND MOVIES

One in three Australian children attribute their night-time fears to frightening images on television and film, a Monash study has found. Dr Gordon, from the Faculty of Education, interviewed more than 500 Victorian children aged eight to sixteen years about their night-time fears. Nearly thirty per cent of the children said their fears stemmed from frightening images on television, videos and movies.

Joanne Cantor, Ph.D., professor of communication at the University of Wisconsin in Madison, and author of *Mommy, I'm Scared: How T.V. and Movies Frighten Children and What We Can Do to Protect Them* says: 'Certainly kids have the ability to imagine monsters on their own. But the mass media provides an intense dose of things children would not have imagined.'

'The average kid, from kindergarten through 12th grade, will have seen 2,00,000 acts of violence on the tube. That's got to impact somewhere down the line,' says Hyman C. Tolmas, MD, a pediatrician for the last fifty years in the New Orleans.

Stephen Garber, PhD, co-author of *Monsters Under the Bed and Other Childhood Fears*, says it's no wonder more kids are seriously scared these days, given what they're exposed to through the media.

Prevention is better than cure. Try and ensure that the child is not exposed to situations of unfounded fears. Watching films on the subject of crime and punishment, watching and listening to horror stories on television, reading and listening to murder and mystery stories and even reading accounts of fearsome events in the papers and journals can be harmful for children. In many cases, T.V. and radio provide live reports and graphic details of terror attacks and other disasters. These reports, meant for adults and suited to them, may be too distressing to children.

> One hundred years from now it will not matter what my bank account was, the sort of house I lived in, or the kind of car I drove...but the world may be different because I was important in the life of a CHILD.
>
> — ANONYMOUS

Bibliography

Hall, J. (2001). Children Playing with Fire. National Fire Protection Association:
Ibid
Rochester Fire Department data, 1985-1993
Cole, R.E., Crandall, R., Bills, J. (1999). *Firefighter's Complete Juvenile Firesetter Handbook*. Fireproof Children Company. 1999
Grolnick, W.S., Cole, R.E., Laurentis, L. & Schwartzman, P., *Playing With Fire: A Developmental Assessment of Children's Fire Understanding and Experience*, Journal of Clinical Child Psychology. 1990
Grolnick, W.S., Cole, R.E., Laurentis, L. & Schwartzman, P., Playing With Fire: A Developmental Assessment of Children's Fire Understanding and Experience, Journal of Clinical Child Psychology 19 1990
American Academy of Paediatrics, *Committee on Sports Medicine and Fitness. Organised athletics for preadolescent children. Paediatrics* 1989
American Academy of Paediatrics, *Committee on Sports Medicine and Fitness. Fitness, activity, and sports participation in the preschool child. Paediatrics* 1992
American Academy of Paediatrics. *Some things you should know about media violence and media literacy.*
Accessed at: www.aap.org/advocacy/childhealthmonth/media.htm
American Academy of Paediatrics, *Committee on Sports Medicine and Fitness Risk of injury from baseball and softball in children.* Paediatrics. 2000
[Abstract/Free Full Text]
American Academy of Paediatrics, *Committee on Sports Medicine and Fitness Safety in youth ice hockey: the effects of body checking.* Paediatrics. 2000
[Abstract/Free Full Text]

American Academy of Paediatrics, *Committee on Sports Medicine and Fitness Climatic heat stress and the exercising child.* Paediatrics. 2000 [Abstract/Free Full Text]

American Academy of Paediatrics, *Committee on Sports Medicine and Fitness Physical fitness and the schools.* Paediatrics. *2000* [Abstract/Free Full Text]

American Sport Education Program. *SportParent.* Human Kinetics Publishers Inc., 1994

Amato, Paul R., *Children in Australian Families: The Growth of Competence.* Prentice Hall, 1987.

Amato, P.R., *Parental absence during childhood and depression in later life.* Sociological Quarterly. 1991.

Amato, P.R., & Keith, B., *Separation from a parent during childhood and adult socioeconomic attainment.* Social Forces. 1991

Amato, Paul R. & Rivera, Fernando. *Paternal Involvement and Children's Behaviour Problems,* Journal of Marriage and the Family. 1999

Anand, Dr. Y.P., *Mahatma Gandhi & The Railways.* Navjivan Publishing House

Anderson, C.A. *An update on the effects of violent video games.* Journal of Adolescence. 2004

Anderson, Craig A. and Bushman, Brad J., *Effects of violent video games on aggressive behaviour, aggressive cognition, aggressive affect, physiological arousal, and prosocial behaviour: A meta-analytic review of the scientific literature.* Psychological Science. 2001

Alvirez, D., & Bean, F.D., & Williams, D., *The Mexican American Family.* In C. Mindel & R.W. Habenstein (Eds.), *Ethnic families in America.* Elsevier. 1981

Angel, Ronald J. and Angel, Jacqueline L., *Painful Inheritance: Health and the New Generation of Fatherless Families.* University of Wisconsin Press. 1993

Angel, R. & Worobey, J.L., *Single motherhood and children's health.* Journal of Health and Social Behaviour. 1988

Apfel, N. H., & Seitz, V., *Four models of adolescent mother-grandmother relationships in Black inner-city families.* Family Relations. 1991

Atkinson, B., & Ogston, D.G., *The effects of father absence on male children in the home and school.* Journal of School Psychology. 1974

Badaines, J., *Identification, imitation, and sex-role preference in father-present and father-absent Black and Chicano boys.* Journal of Psychology. 1976

Bane, M.J., *Blacks, welfare, and family structure: The War on Poverty did not cause the disintegration of the Black family.* Governance. 1986

Bannon, J.A. & Southern, M.L., *Father-absent women's self-concept and modes of relating to men. Sex Roles.* 1980.

Barclay, A., & Cusumano, D.R., *Father absence, cross-sex identity, and field-dependent behaviour in male adolescents.* Child Development. 1967

Barnett, R.C., & Baruch, G.K., *Determinants of fathers' participation in family work.* Journal of Marriage and the Family. 1987

Baruch, G.K., & Barnett, R.C., *Consequences of fathers' participation in family work: Parents' role strain and well-being.* Journal of Personality and Social Psychology. 1986

Batstone, David. *Why Kids Hate Sports.* Sojourners. 2001

Baydar, N., *Effects of parental separation and reentry into union on the emotional well-being of children.* Journal of Marriage and the Family. 1988

Bee, H.L., *Overview: On the importance of fathers.* In H.L. Bee (Ed.), *Social issues in developmental psychology*, Harper & Row. 1974

Belsky, J., *The determinants of parenting: A process model.* Child Development. 1984

Belsky, J., Youngblade, L., Rovine, M., & Volling, B., *Patterns of marital change and parent-child interaction.* Journal of Marriage and the Family. 1991

Bergen, D., *Play as a Medium for Learning and Development.* Heinemann. 1988

Berger, E.H. & M.J. Pollman. *Multiple intelligences: Enabling diverse learning.* Early Childhood Education Journal. 1996

Bestor, Arthur E., *Thomas Jefferson and the Freedom of Books: Three Presidents and Their Books.* Urbana: University of Illinois Press, 1955

Biller, Henry B., *Father and Families: Paternal Factors in Child Development.* Auburn House. 1993

Biller, Henry B., *The Father and Personality Development: Paternal Deprivation and Sex-Role Development,* in Michael E. Lamb, ed., *The Role of the Father in Child Development.* Wiley & Sons. 1981

Biller, H.B., *Fatherhood: Implications for child and adult development.* In B.B. Wolman (Ed.), Handbook of developmental psychology. Wiley & Sons. 1982

Biller, H.B., *A note on father absence and masculine development in lower-class Negro and White boys.* Child Development. 1968

Biller, H.B., *Father absence, maternal encouragement, and sex role development in kindergarten-age boys.* Child Development. 1969

Biller, H.B., *Father dominance and sex-role development in kindergarten-age boys.* Developmental Psychology. 1969

Biller, H.B., *The mother-child relationship and the father-absent boy's personality development.* Merrill-Palmer Quarterly. 1971

Biller, H.B., *Paternal deprivation: Family, school, sexuality, and society.* Lexington Books. 1974

Biller, H.B., *Father absence and the personality development of the male child.* Developmental Psychology. 1970.

Biller, H.B., *Father, child, and sex role: Paternal determinants of personality development.* D.C. Health. 1971

Biller, H.B., & Weiss, S.D., *The father-daughter relationship and the personality development of the female.* Journal of Genetic Psychology. 1970

Bing, Ellen. The Effect of Child-Rearing Practices on the Development of Differential Cognitive Abilities. Child Development. 1963

Blankenhorn, David. *Fatherless America: Confronting Our Most Urgent Social Problem.* Basic Books. 1994

Boone, S.L., *Effects of fathers' absence and birth order on aggressive behaviour of young male children.* Psychological Reports. 1979.

Boss, P., *A clarification of the concept of psychological father presence in families experiencing ambiguity of boundary.* Journal of Marriage and the Family. 1977

Brady, Frank. *Children's Organised Sports: A Developmental Perspective.* Journal of Physical Education, Recreation & Dance. 2004

Brenes, M.E., Eisenberg, N. & Helmstadter, G.C., *Sex-role development of preschoolers from two-parent and one-parent families.* Merrill-Palmer Quarterly. 1985

Brook, J.S., Whiteman, M., Brook, D.W., & Gordon, S., *Depressive mood in female college students: Father-daughter interactional patterns.* Journal of Genetic Psychology. 1983

Broude, G.J., *Protest masculinity: A further look at the causes and the concept.* Ethos. 1990

Buchanan, A.M., Gentile, D.A., Nelson, D.A., Walsh, D.A. & Hensel, J., *What goes in must come out: Children's media violence consumption at home and aggressive behaviours at school.* Paper presented at the International Society for the Study of Behavioural Development Conference, Ottawa, Ontario, Canada. 2002 Available online at: www.mediafamily.org/research/report_issbd_2002.shtml

Caldwell, B., *Aggression and Hostility in Young Children*. Young Children. 1977

Carson, Rachel. *The Sense of Wonder*. HarperCollins. 1998.

Cazenave, N.A., *Middle-income Black fathers: An analysis of the provider role*. The Family Coordinator. 1979

Chan, S., *International context of Asian emigration. Asian American: An Interpretive History*. 1991

Chawla, Louise. *In the first country of places: Nature, poetry, and childhood memory*. SUNY Press. 1994

Chawla, Louise. *Significant Life Experiences: A New Research Area in Environmental Education*. Journal of Environmental Education. 1980

Chenfield, M.B., *The whole truth about hole language-Whoops! I mean the hole truth about whole language-Can you dig it?*, Early Childhood Education Journal. 1996

Cherlin, A.J., *Marriage divorce and remarriage: Changing patterns in postwar United States*. Urban Institute Press. 1981

Clarke-Stewart, K. A., *And Daddy makes three: The father's impact on mother and young child*. Child Development. 1978

Clinton, W.J., *Supporting the Role of Fathers in Families*. Memorandum for the heads of executive departments and agencies. Washington, D.C., 1995

Cobb, E., *The ecology of imagination in childhood*. Columbia University Press. 1977

Cohen, D.H., V. Stern & N. Balaban. *Observing and recording the behaviour of young children*. Teachers College, Columbia University. 1983

Coltrane, Scott. *Father-Child Relationships and the Status of Women: A Cross-Cultural Study*. American Journal of Sociology, 93. 1988

Comstock, G.A. & Paik, H., *The effects of television violence on antisocial behaviour: A meta-analysis*. Communication Research. 1994

Congressional Public Health Summit, *Joint statement on the impact of entertainment violence on children*. 2006
Accessed at: www.aap.org/advocacy/releases/jstmtevc.htm

Cooksey, E.C., & Fondell, M.M., *Spending time with his kids: Effects of family structure on fathers' and children's lives*. Journal of Marriage and the Family. 1996

Courtney, D., & Schell, L.M., *The effect of male teachers on the academic achievement of father-absent sixth grade boys*. Reading Improvement. 1979

Deacon, James. *Chasing the Dream: Never Mind the NHL Playoffs. The Real Drama Is At Neighbourhood Rinks*. Maclean's. 2002

Diaz, Jaime. *Measuring Up? The First Tee Is Banking On Juniors for the Long Haul. Here's What's Happening.* Golf Digest. 2004.

Dowell, William, et al., *Inside the Crazy Culture of Kids Sports: Competitive athletics can help keep children happy and out of trouble – but it takes over some families' lives.* Time. 1999

Duncan, G.J., Brooks-Gunn, J., & Klebanov, P., *Economic deprivation and early childhood development.* Child Development. 1994

Dupree, Allen & Primus, Wendell. *Declining Share of Children Living With Single Mothers in the Late 1990s.* Center on Budget and Policy Priorities. 2001

Eberhardt, C.A., & Schill, T., *Differences in sexual attitudes and likeliness of sexual behaviours of Black lower-socioeconomic father-present versus father-absent female adolescents.* Adolescence. 1984

Edelman, M.W., *Families in peril: An agenda for social change.* Harvard University Press. 1987

Elder Jr, G.H., *Children of the Great Depression.* University of Chicago Press.

Ewing, Marty. *Promoting social and moral development through sports.* 1997 Available: http://ed-web3.educ.msu.edu/ysi/Spotlight1997/social.html

Fein, G., *Pretend Play in Childhood: An Integrative Review.* Child Development. 1981

Fields, Jason. *The Living Arrangements of Children: Fall 1996 Current Population Reports,* U.S. Census Bureau. 2001.

Finn, K., Johannsen, N., & Specker, B., *Factors Associated with Physical Activity in Preschool Children.* The Journal of Paediatrics. 2002

Fish, K.D., & Biller, H.B., Perceived childhood paternal relationships and college females' personal adjustment. Adolescence. 1973

Furstenberg, F.F., Jr., & Harris, K.M., *When and why fathers matter: Impacts of father involvement on the children of adolescent mothers.* In R. Lerman & T. Ooms (Eds.), *Young unwed fathers: Changing roles and emerging policies.* Temple University Press. 1993

Furstenberg, F.F., Jr., Morgan, S.P., & Allison, P.D., *Paternal participation and children's well-being after marital dissolution.* American Sociological Review. 1987

Furstenberg, F.F., Jr., & Nord, C.W., *Parenting apart: Patterns of childrearing after marital disruption.* Journal of Marriage and the Family.1985

Gallup, George. *Report on the Status of Fatherhood in the United States,* Emerging Trends 20. 1998

Gardner, H., *Frames of mind: The theory of multiple intelligences.* Basic Books. 1983

Gardner, H., *Reflections on multiple intelligences: Myths and messages.* Phi Delta Kappan. 1995

Garvey, C., *PLAY.* Harvard University Press. 1977

Generation M: Media in the lives of eight to eighteen year olds. Kaiser Family Foundation. 2005

Available online at: http://www.kff.org/entmedia/entmedia030905pkg.cfm

Gentile, D.A. & Anderson, C.A., *Violent video games: The newest media violence hazard.* Praeger Publishing. 2003

Glik, D.C., Greaves, P., Kronenfeld, J.J. & Jackson, K.L., *Safety Hazards in Households with Young Children.* Journal of Pediatric Psychology. 1993

Gottman, J. & J. DeClaire., *The heart of parenting.* Simon and Schuster. 1997

Greenberg, E.F., & Nay, W.R., *The intergenerational transmission of marital instability reconsidered.* Journal of Marriage and the Family. 1982

Green, R.G., & Crooks, P.D., *Family member adjustment and family dynamics in established single-parent and two-parent families.* Social Science Review. 1988

Greif, J.B., *Fathers, children, and joint custody.* American Journal of Orthopsychiatry. 1979

Grossman, F.K., Pollack, W.S., & Golding, E., *Fathers and children: Predicting the quality and quantity of fathering.* Developmental Psychology, Cradles of Eminence. 1988

Hainline, L., & Feig, E., *The correlates of childhood father absence in college-aged women.* Child Development. 1978

Harris, K.M., & Morgan, S.P., *Fathers, sons, and daughters: Differential paternal involvement in parenting.* Journal of Marriage and the Family. 1991

Hart and Teeter Research Companies for NBC News, *The Rise of Single-Parent Households.* Wall Street Journal. 1999

Henderson, A.T., & Berla, N. (Eds.), *A New Generation of Evidence: The Family is Critical to Student Achievement.* National Committee for Citizens in Education. 1994

Herzog, E., & Sudia, C., *Children in fatherless families.* In B. Caldwell & H. Ricciuti (Eds.), *Review of child development research Vol. 3.*, University of Chicago Press. 1973

Hetherington, E.M., *Effects of father absence on personality development in adolescent daughters.* Developmental Psychology. 1972

Hetherington, E.M., & Camara, K.A., *The effects of family dissolution and reconstitution on children.* In N.D. Glenn & M.T. Coleman (Eds.), *Family relations: A reader.* Dorsey Press. 1988

Hetherington, E.M., Camara, K.A., & Featherman, D.L., *Achievement and intellectual functioning of children from one-parent households.* In J. Spence (Ed.), *Achievement and achievement motives.* W. H. Freeman. 1983

Hetherington, E.M., Cox, M., & Cox, R., *The aftermath of divorce.* In J.J.H. Stevens & M. Matthews (Eds.), *Mother-child, father-child relations.* National Association for the Education of Young Children. 1978

Hill, Anne & O'Neil, June. *Underclass Behaviours in the United States: Measurements and Analysis or Determinants.* City University of New York. 1993

Hill, M. S., *The role of economic resources and remarriage in financial assistance for children of divorce.* Journal of Family Issues. 1992

Horn, Wade F. & Sylvester, Tom. *Father Facts, Fourth Edition.* National Fatherhood Initiative. 2002

Hossain, Z., & Roopnarine, J.L., *Division of household labor and child care in dual-earner African-American families with infants.* Sex Roles. 1993

Huesmann, Rowell. The psychology of media violence: Why it has a lasting impact on children: The impact of entertainment media and violence on children and families. Iowa State University. 2001
Accessed at: www.extension.iastate.edu/families/media/program.huesmann.html

Hunt, J.G., & Hunt, L.L., *Race, daughters and father loss: Does absence make the girl grow stronger?* Social Problems. 1977

Hunt, L.L., & Hunt, J.G., *Race and the father-son connection.* Social Problems. 1975

Huston, A.C. et al., *Big world, small screen: The role of television in American society.* University of Nebraska Press. 1992

Ihinger-Tallman, M., Pasley, K., & Buehler, C., *Developing a middle-range theory of father involvement post divorce.* Journal of Family Issues. 1993

Ishii-Kuntz, M., *Are Japanese families "fatherless"? Sociological and Social Research.* 1992

Jarrett, R.L., *Living poor: Family life among single parent, African-American women.* Social Problems. 1994

Johnson, D., *Disentangling race and poverty.* Paper presented at the Child and Family Advocacy Institute, University of Wisconsin-Madison. July 1995

Johnston, Shawn. Forensic Psychologist, quoted in *The Pittsburgh Tribune Review*, March 29, 1998, from Wade and Sylvester, 2002

Kamii, C., *Young Children Invent Arithmetic: Implications of Piaget's Theory.* Teachers College Press. 1985

Kamii, C., & DeVries, R., *Group Games in Early Education: Implications of Piaget's Theory.* National Association for the Education of Young Children. 1980

Kamm, R.L., *A developmental and psychoeducational approach to reducing conflict and abuse in Little League and youth sports.* Child Adolescent Psychiatry Clinic North America. 1998 [Medline]

Kantrowitz, Barbara. *Don't Just Do It For Daddy: Parents Can Push. But Real Success Awaits the Kids Who Want to Achieve For Themselves.* Newsweek. 1996

Kaplan, R. & Kaplan, S., *The experience of nature: A psychological perspective.* Cambridge University Press. 1989

Kellert, S., Introduction. In S.R. Kellert & E.O. Wilson (Eds.) *The Biophilia Hypothesis.* Island Press/Shearwater. 1993

King, N., *Play and the Culture of Childhood.* In G. Fein & M. Rivkin (Eds.), *The Young Child at Play.* National Association for the Education of Young Children. 1986

Koestner, Richard et al., *The Family Origins of Empathic Concern: A Twenty-Six Year Longitudinal Study.* Journal of Personality and Social Psychology. 1990

Krampe, E.M., & Fairweather, P.D., *Father presence and family formation: A theoretical reformulation.* Journal of Family Issues. 1993

Lamb, Michael. E. (Ed.), *The role of the father in child development.* John Wiley. 1976

Lamb, Michael E., *Fathers: The Forgotten Contributors to Child Development.* Human Development. 1975

Lee, T.R., *The Role of Fathers.* Utah State University Cooperative Extension Service. 1990

Lempers, J., Clark-Lempers, D., & Simons, R., *Economic hardship, parenting, and distress in adolescence.* Child Development. 1989

Lessing, E.E., Zagorin, S.W., & Nelson, D., *WISC subtest and IQ score correlates of father absence.* Journal of Genetic Psychology. 1970

Lord, Mary. *Dangerous Games.* U.S. News & World Report. 2002

Lord, Mary. *Too Much, Too Soon?* U.S. News & World Report. 2000

Lord, Mary. When Cheers Turn Into Jeers (and Tears). U.S. News & World Report. 2000

Lynn, David B., *The Father: His Role in Child Development.* Brooks/Cole. 1974

Maccoby, Eleanor E., *The Two Sexes: Growing Up Apart; Coming Together.* Harvard University Press. 1999

Malina, R.M., *Physical growth and biological maturation of young athletes.* 1994

Marino, C.D., & McCowan, R., *The effects of parent absence on children.* Child Study Journal. 1976

Marsiglio, W., *Paternal engagement activities with minor children.* Journal of Marriage and the Family. 1991

Martens R, Seefeldt V, eds. *Guidelines for Children's Sports.* National Association for Sport and Physical Education. 1979

Martin, E.P., & Martin, J.M., *The Black extended family.* University of Chicago Press. 1978

McAdoo, J.L., *Father-child interaction patterns and self-esteem in Black preschool children.* Young Children. 1979

McAdoo, J.L., *Changing perspectives on the role of the Black father.* In P. Bronstein & C.P. Cowan (Eds.), *Fatherhood today: Men's changing role in the family.* New York: Wiley. 1988

McAdoo, J.L., *The roles of African American fathers: An ecological perspective.* Journal of Contemporary Human Services. 1993

McBride, B.A. & McBride, R.J., *The Changing Roles of Fathers; Some Implications for Educators.* Journal of Home Economics. 1990

McLanahan, S., *Family structure and stress: A longitudinal comparison of two-parent and female-headed families.* Journal of Marriage and the Family. 1983

McLanahan, S., & Sandefur, G., *Growing up with a single parent: What hurts, what helps.* Harvard University Press. 1994

McLanahan, S., & Booth, K., *Mother-only families: Problems, prospects, and politics.* Journal of Marriage and the Family. 1989

McLanahan, S., & Bumpass, L., *Intergenerational consequences of family disruption.* American Journal of Sociology. 1988

McLanahan, S., Wedemeyer, N.V., & Adelberg, *Network structure, social support, and psychological well-being in the single-parent family.* Journal of Marriage and the Family. 1981

McLindon, J.B., *Separate but unequal: The economic disaster of divorce for women and children.* Family Law Quarterly. 1987

McLoyd, V.C., *The impact of economic hardship on Black families and children: Psychological distress, parenting, and socioemotional development*. Child Development. 1990

McLoyd, V.C., Jayaratne, T.E., Ceballo, R., & Borquez, J., *Unemployment and work interruption among African American single mothers: Effects on parenting and adolescent socioemotional functioning*. Child Development. 1994

Mitchell, D., & Wilson, W., *Relationship of father-absence to masculinity and popularity of delinquent boys*. Psychological Reports. 1967

Montare, A., & Bonne, S.L., *Aggression and paternal absence: Racial-ethnic differences among inner-city boys*. The Journal of Genetic Psychology. 1980

Moore, L., Di Gao, A., Bradlee, L., Cupples, A., Sundarajan-Ramamurti, Proctor, M., Hood, M., Singer, M., Ellison, C., *Does Early Physical Activity Predict Body Fat Change throughout Childhood?* Preventive Medicine. 2003

Moore, R., *Playgrounds at the Crossroads: Policy and Action Research Needed to Ensure a Viable Future for Public Playgrounds in the US*. Altman, I. and Zube, E. (Eds). *Public Spaces and Places*. Plenum Press. 1989

Moore, R., *The Need for Nature: A Childhood Right*. Social Justice. 1997

Moore, R., *Streets as Playgrounds. Public Streets for Public Use*. Van Nostrand Reinhold.1987

Moore, R. & Young, D., *Childhood Outdoors: Toward a Social Ecology of the Landscape*. Children and the Environment. In Altman, I. & Wohlwill, J (Eds.). Plenum Press. 1978

Moore, R. & Wong, H., *Natural Learning: Rediscovering Nature's Way of Teaching*. MIG Communications. 1997

Moore, R.C., *Childhood's domain*. Croon Helm. 1986 (Reprint, MIG Communications, 1990).

Moore, R.C., *Plants for play: A plant selection guide for children's outdoor environments*. MIG Communications. 1993

Moore, R.C. & Wong, H., *A natural way of learning: The experience of the Washington environmental yard*. MIG Communications. 1997Mott, F.L., *Sons, daughters and fathers' absence: Differentials in father-leaving probabilities and in-home environments*. Journal of Family Issues. 1994

Moynihan, D.P., *The Negro family: The case for national action*. U.S. Department of Labor, Office of Policy, Planning, and Research. 1965

Nabhan, G.P. & St. Antoine, S., *The loss of floral and faunal story: The Extinction of Experience. The Biophilia Hypothesis* S.R. Kellert & E.O. Wilson (Eds.), Island Press/Shearwater. 1993

Nabhan, G.P. & Trimble, S., *The geography of childhood: Why children need wild places*. Beacon Press. 1994

National Association for Sport and Physical Education. *National Standards for Athletic Coaches: Quality Coaches, Quality Sports*. Kendall/Hunt Publishing Co., 1995

Nord, Christine Winquist, Brimhall, DeeAnn, & West, Jerry. *Fathers' Involvement in their Children's Schools*. U.S. Department of Education, National Center for Education Statistics. 1997

Nugent, J.K., *Cultural and Psychological Influences of the Father's Role in Infant Development*. Journal of Marriage and the Family. 1991

O'Connell, Kathleen. M., *Rabindranath Tagore on education. The Encyclopedia of Informal Education*. 2002

Ogden, C., Flegal, K., Carroll, M., & Johnson, C., *Prevalence and Trends in Overweight among US Children and Adolescents, 1999-2000*. Journal of the American Medical Association. 2002

Parke, Ross D., *Fatherhood*. Harvard University Press. 1996

Pearson, J.L., Hunter, A.G., Ensminger, M.E., & Kellam, S.G., *Black grandmothers in multigenerational households: Diversity in family structure and parenting involvement in the Woodlawn Community*. Child Development. 1990

Pederson, F.A., *Does research on children in father-absent families yield information on father influence?* Family Coordinator. 1976

Peterson, L., Ewigman, B. & Kivlahan, C., *Judgements Regarding Appropriate Child Supervision to Prevent Injury: The Role of Environmental Risk and Child Age*. Child Development. 1993

Piaget, J., *Play, Dreams and Imitation in Childhood*. Norton. 1962

Plomin, R., *Nature and nurture: An introduction to human behavioural genetics*. Brooks/Cole. 1990

Poinsett, Alex., *The role of sports in youth development*. 1996 Available: http://www.carnegie.org/reports/poinst1.htm [1998, May 13].

Popenoe, David. *Life Without Father: Compelling New Evidence That Fatherhood and Marriage Are Indispensable for the Good of Children and Society*. The Free Press, 1996

Portz-Shovlin, Eileen. *Golden Shoe Award*. Runner's World. 2000

Preboth, Monica. *Sport Specialisation in Young Athletes*. American Family Physician. 2000

Pruett, Kyle D., *Fatherneed: Why Father Care is as Essential as Mother Care for Your Child*. The Free Press. 2000

Radin, Norma. *Father-Child Interaction and the Intellectual Functioning of Four-Year-Old Boys.* Developmental Psychology. 1972.

Radin, N., *Childrearing fathers in intact families, I: Some antecedents and consequences.* Merrill-Palmer Quarterly. 1981

Rivkin, M., *Outdoor Experiences for Young Children.* ERIC/CRESS. 2000 http://www.ael.org/eric/page.cfm?&scope=oe&id=237&pub=x

Roemmich, J.N. & Rogol A., *Physiology of growth and development: its relationship to performance in the young athlete.* Clin Sports Med. 1995.

Rohner, Ronald and Veneziano, Robert. *The Importance of Father Love: History and Contemporary Evidence.* Review of General Psychology. 2001

Rowland, T.W., *Clinical approaches to the sedentary child.* In: *Exercise and Children's Health.* Human Kinetics Books. 1990

Sachs, Michael L., *Lighten Up, Parents!* USA Today. 2000

Sallis. J., McKenzie, T., Conway, T., Elder, J., Prochaska, J., Brown, M., Zive, M., Marshall, S. & Alcaraz, J., *Environmental Interventions for Eating and Physical Activity: A Randomized Controlled Trial in Middle Schools.* American Journal of Preventive Medicines. 2003

Santrock, J., *Relation of type and onset of father absence to cognitive development.* Child Development. 1972

Santrock, J.W., *Effects of father absence on sex-typed behaviours in male children: Reason for the absence and age of onset of the absence.* The Journal of Genetic Psychology. 1977

Schell, L.M., & Courtney, D., *The effect of male teachers on the academic achievement of father-absent sixth grade boys.* The Journal of Education. 1979

Schutz, William. *Profound Simplicity.* Bantam Books. 1979

Seltzer, J.A., *Relationships between fathers and children who live apart: The father's role after separation.* Journal of Marriage and the Family. 1991

Seltzer, J.A., & Bianchi, S.M., *Children's contact with absent parents.* Journal of Marriage and the Family. 1988

Seltzer, J.A., & Brandreth, Y., *What fathers say about involvement with children after separation.* Journal of Family Issues. 1994.

Senate Committee on the Judiciary. *Children, violence, and the media: A report for parents and policy makers.*1999 Available at: http://judiciary.senate.gov/mediavio.htm

Shinn, M., *Father absence and children's cognitive development.* Psychological Bulletin. 1978

Sitz, Rick. *Sportsmanship: Encouraging our kids to be good sports.* Winnetka Alliance for Early Childhood Newsletter. 1998

Slaughter, D.T. (Ed.). *Black children in poverty: A developmental perspective. New directions for child development series (No. 42).* San Francisco: Jossey-Bass. 1988

Smith, Charles A., *Effective Discipline.* Cooperative Extension Service, 1979/1980.

Snarey, John. *How Fathers Care for the Next Generation: A Four Decade Study* Harvard University Press. 1993

Snipp, M., *The changing political and economic status of the American Indians from captive nations to internal colonies.* The American Journal of Economics and Sociology. 1986.

Snipp, M., *Demography of Native American populations* [Lecture]. University of Wisconsin. 1995.

Sobel, David. *Beyond Ecophobia: Reclaiming the Heart in Nature Education.* Orion Society. 1996

Stanton, Glenn T., *Why Marriage Matters: Reasons to Believe in Marriage in Postmodern Society.* Pinon Press. 1997

Stephen, Andrew. *How Lacrosse Became a Blood Sport.* New Statesman. 1996

Stewart, Mark. *Good Sports? Insight on the News.* 2000

Stevenson, M.R. & Black, K.N., *Paternal absence and sex-role development: A meta-analysis.* Child Development. 1988.

Stop the Insanity: Parents in Minnesota Are Starting a Small Rebellion Against the Tyranny of Overscheduled Kids. Will Their Revolt Spread?, Newsweek. 2000

Stryer B, Toffler I.R., Lapchick R., *A developmental overview of child and youth sports in society.* Child Adolescent Psychiatric Clinic North America. 1998

Thomson, E., McLanahan, S.S., & Curtin, R.B., *Family structure, gender, and parental socialization.* Journal of Marriage and the Family. 1992

US Department of Health and Human Services. *Physical Activity and Health: A Report of the Surgeon General.* Centers for Disease Control and Prevention. 1996

Video Games and Children, Child Development Institute, 2003 http://www.childdevelopmentinfo.com/healthsafety/videogamesandchildrens.htmlVillani, Susan. *Media Violence: More than Just Child's Play?,* Facts of Life: Issue Briefings for Health Reporters. 2003

Waite, Linda & Gallagher, Maggie. *The Case for Marriage.* Doubleday. 2000

Waite, L.J., & Lilliard, L.A., *Children and marital disruption*. American Journal of Sociology. 1991.

Wallerstein, J.S., *Children of divorce: Report of a ten-year follow-up of early latency-age children*. American Journal of Orthopsychiatry. 1987

Wallerstein, J.S., Children of divorce: Stress and developmental tasks. In N. Garmezy & M. Rutter (Eds.), *Stress, coping, and development in children* Johns Hopkins University Press. 1988

Wallerstein, J.S., & Kelly, J.B., *Effects of divorce on the visiting father-child relationship*. American Journal of Psychiatry, 1980.

Weinraub, M., *Fatherhood: The Myth of the Second Class Parent*, in J.H. Stevens and M. Matthews, eds., *Mother/child and Father/child Relationships*. National Association for the Education of Young Children. 1978.

Wells, N., *At Home with Nature: Effects of "Greenness" on Children's Cognitive Functioning. Environment and Behaviour.* 2000

Whitehead, Barbara Dafoe. *Facing the Challenge of Fragmented Families*, The Philanthropy Roundtable. 1995

Wilson, M., *Mothers' and grandmothers' perceptions of parental behaviour in three generation Black families. Child Development.* 1984

Wilson, M., *The Black extended family: An analytical consideration*. Developmental Psychology. 1986.

Wilson, M., *Perceived parental activity of mothers, fathers, and grandmothers in a three generational Black family*. Journal of Black Psychology, 1986.

Wilson, W.J., *The truly disadvantaged*. University of Chicago Press. 1987

Wolff, Alexander. *Baseball or Bust: With Big League Dreams, Cooper Moseley Played 127 Games in 10-and-under Ball*. Sports Illustrated. 2003

Wolff, Alexander. *The American Athlete, Age 10. Sports Illustrated.* 2003

Yablonsky, Lewis. *Fathers and Sons*. Simon and Schuster. 1982

Yogman, Michael **et al.**, *Father Involvement and Cognitive/Behavioural Outcomes of Preterm Infants*. Journal of the American Academy of Child and Adolescent Psychiatry.1995.

Young, E.R., & Parrish, T.E., *Impact of father absence during childhood on the psychological adjustment of college females*. Sex Roles. 1977

http://www.missingkids.com/en_US/publications/NC122.pdf#search='teaching%20 children%20safety'

on-line: http://www.pta.org Project SAFE, National Child Advocacy Center on-line at http://www.ncachsv.org

Prevent Child Abuse America, 1-800-CHILDREN and on-line at: http:// www.preventchildabuse.org

http://www.jrf.org.uk/knowledge/findings/socialpolicy/n71.asp
http://www.evancarmichael.com/Famous-Entrepreneurs/626/Lesson-4-Try-
   Something-New.html
http://www.lovelibraries.co.uk/quotes.php
http://www.cfah.org/factsoflife/vol8no10.cfm